CONQUEST

CONQUEST
THE ROMAN INVASION
OF BRITAIN

John Peddie

Bramley
Books

A Sutton Publishing Book

This edition published in 1998 by Bramley Books
An imprint of Quadrillion Publishing Limited
Godalming Business Centre, Woolsack Way,
Godalming, Surrey GU7 1XW

ISBN 1 85833 830 1

This book was designed and produced by
Alan Sutton Publishing Limited, an imprint of
Sutton Publishing Limited
Phoenix Mill · Thrupp · Stroud · Gloucestershire GL5 2BU

Typesetting and origination by
Sutton Publishing Limited.
Printed in Great Britain by
WBC Limited, Bridgend, Mid-Glamorgan.

'Cities and Thrones and Powers,
Stand in Time's eye,
Almost as long as flowers,
Which daily die.
But, as new buds put forth
To glad new men,
Out of the spent and unconsidered Earth
The Cities rise again'

Rudyard Kipling

'The same principles of war which were employed in the past, appear again and again throughout history . . .'

FM Viscount Montgomery of Alamein

CONTENTS

ILLUSTRATIONS

PREFACE

Dio Cassius, a Greek historian whose life spanned the 2nd and 3rd centuries AD, described, in his *Narratives*, the Roman landings in Britain in AD 43. He ambiguously stated that the invasion fleet sailed from Boulogne 'in three divisions'. Inevitably, his wording has caused much discussion, with some historians propounding that the task force came ashore at one place only, in the sheltered waters offered by the Wantsum Channel, and others suggesting a variety of landing places, ranging from Deal to Dorset.

I personally encountered the debate more than ten years ago now, when, having agreed to write part of a local history of the Deverill valley in Wiltshire, I was introduced to a Roman road, traces of which can be clearly seen as it crosses the downs above the river Wylye. It had been constructed during the Roman conquest of southern Britain and was named Vespasian's tactical road: it ran from Hamworthy, near Poole, in Dorset, to Bath. I wondered both at its name and purpose, but it quickly became clear that, to seek further enlightment, I would have to discover more about Vespasian's operational task. Since this, in its turn, was more than probably linked to the overall invasion plan, I referred back to where it all began, Gaul. I turned my eyes, in the first instance, to the marshalling of the Roman invasion army and to the political circumstances which caused Claudius to invade Britain.

It is an age-old principle for military success that the objective of a war should be clearly defined and that its conduct should be meticulously detailed, both strategically and logistically. The plan of any war, so wrote the Prussian military expert, General Carl von Clausewitz,

> comprehends the whole Military Act; through it that Act becomes a whole, which must have one final determinate objective, in which all particular objects must become absorbed. No War is commenced, or, at least, no War should be commenced, if people act wisely, without first seeking a reply to the question, What is to be attained by and in the same? The first is the final object: the other is the intermediate aim.

xiii

There are, of course, examples of wars being commenced without their purpose being clearly defined. The Second Punic War was one of these and Carthage, the instigators in that instance, were the losers. But we may be certain that, in AD 43, the Romans, reaching the height of their military power and with the military experience of three centuries of conquest and expansion, knew precisely where they were heading. Moreover, having secured a successful landing, their intermediate aim, to use the Clausewitz phrase, their next task would have been to push speedily forward to their main objective, for time was limited. The emperor, Claudius, had expressed a firm desire to lead his army in the final stage of the conquest but could not afford to spend more than sixteen days in Britain before returning triumphantly to Rome.

The target they had noted for immediate conquest, and there were good political reasons for it, was the territory of the Trinovantes, the capital of which was *Camulodunum*, present day Colchester. We may say with certainty that, at this stage of the programme for the conquest of Britain, Rome would have had no desire to extend the war beyond the limited bounds she had set out to achieve. This fact, combined with the need for speed desired by Claudius and the inevitable uncertainty of the situation which confronted the commanding Roman general, Aulus Plautius, suggests that the latter would have opted for a policy of concentration of force. His prime task would have been to keep his army so deployed that, at any critical moment, and these were times of poor communications, it could be brought together without an unnecessary expenditure of effort. There is also the point that, unless the military situation demanded it, and there is no proof that it did, a widely deployed force would have posed wasteful logistical problems, not only in Britain but in the departure ports of Gaul.

Embarkation ports are places of organised confusion and Boulogne, on this occasion, nearly 2,000 years ago, would have been no different. The scene would have been recognisable to any soldier, of whatever generation, who had ever sailed away to war. The task force to be embarked was to be self contained upon arrival, for Julius Caesar had learnt the lesson of planning to live off the land. It numbered, in total, some 45,000 men, including 5,000 cavalry, artillery weapons and a potential of 10,000 baggage animals, depending upon how much reliance was to be placed upon waterborne transport. Its administration needs would have been vast. We may imagine that its shipping requirement, an estimated total of more than 900 vessels, either accumulated, constructed for the purpose or requisitioned, stood ready, earmarked for allocation to formations and units. The soldiery were encamped, waiting to be called forward and detailed to vessels for embarkation. Supplies of grain, sown a year or more ago, would already have been gathered in granaries, some of it having been issued to formations and units, but the bulk being retained as a reserve for later despatch. Arrangements for the loading of the animals, cavalry, light and heavy artillery, and baggage animals would have been well discussed.

Amidst all this bustle, Narcissus, the private secretary of the emperor Claudius arrived at Boulogne. He was a former slave who had risen to being a clerk in the civil service and was later to be appointed secretary-general and head of the state department. I conjecture (see page 35) that he had doubtless been sent, before the departure of the army to Britain, to make arrangements for the arrival of his master, in a few weeks time. In a later work, I go further than this and suggest that he arrived as a personal representative of his master, authorised to sort out last minute problems, acting almost in the role of chief of staff, and perhaps bringing with him a staff team from the secretariat in Rome, if, indeed, it were not already present. It is a suggestion which has brought criticism on the grounds that I am inventing a staff corps, but I am unrepentant. I am convinced that, for an operation of this scale, with such a great administrative and financial commitment, some staff organisation must have existed.

I recall, during the Burma campaign of the Second World War, I was adjutant of an Indian infantry battalion. It was due to entrain early next morning, for operations in the Lushai and Chin hills. It had been a busy day and I was resting in our makeshift mess, after supper, when my commanding officer came to me and suggested that we should both go down to the railway siding to 'load the mules'. He was a delightful man and I dutifully followed in his wake. It was after midnight before I got back to bed and, as I struggled into my bedding roll, tired and sore, with reveille at 4 a.m., I recall thinking – commanding officers should not load mules! Nor, metaphorically speaking, should Roman generals, and I do not believe they did.

John Peddie, 1997

ACKNOWLEDGEMENTS

I am greatly indebted to a number of eminent and busy people for the help and advice with which I was provided when producing my manuscript. Not least of these was Brigadier B.G. Fawcus, RE MA, then Commandant of the Royal School of Military Engineering at Chatham. When I approached him he willingly undertook a study of the time taken to construct the Roman road between Richborough and London (see Appendix C). Major D.A.S. Davies, RE BSc MICE, undertook the detailed work. I am also grateful to Dr Paul Robinson, Curator of the Wiltshire Archaeological and Natural History Society at Devizes for his many helpful suggestions; to Professor Malcolm Todd of the University of Exeter for his advice on archaeological developments in the West Country; and to the late Mr G.C. Boon, at that time Keeper of Archaeology and Numismatics at the National Museum of Wales, who read and commented most helpfully on my completed draft.

The photographs of Roman Army activities in the field I obtained through the good-natured enthusiasm of the Ermine Street Guard, led by their Centurion and Commandant, Mr Chris Haines, who I found at Butser Hill Iron Age Camp, near Petersfield, on an unforgettably cold Easter morning. My appreciation of their kindness has not been dimmed by passing years. I am indebted also to my brother-in-law, Wing Commander H.C. Randall, for his work with the camera.

Finally, I must express my gratitude to Mrs Joan Lilly, for the maps illustrating the Medway battle; to Mr Michael Marshman and the staff of the Wiltshire County Council Library and Museum Service for their unfailing help; and to my dear wife, Doreen, for her extraordinary patience and her ever-present logistical support.

CHAPTER ONE

CAESAR'S BRITISH LEGACY

These far flung isles are rich in tin and lead,
Their people proud of heart and vigorous,
Able and shrewd, with trade always in mind;
In woven craft they sail afar,
Through the rough waters of their narrow seas
And the wide ocean's monster-haunted waters.
They have no art of building ships
With pine or maple, or the tall fir,
As most men do. Instead they curve the frame . . .
And sail the high seas in a shell of hide.

Avienus, after *Periplus Massiliensis* (60 BC)

Seven hundred years before the birth of Christ, a small farming community in Central Europe, in the beautiful Halstatt area of Upper Austria, discovered the technique of making iron. The community was already comparatively prosperous, for their habitation adjoined an extensive salt mine, active until a century or so of the present day. They soon learnt to fashion the iron they were producing into agricultural equipment and the improved standard of living created by this means brought about a rapid expansion in the population. A class-orientated society soon evolved, the upper echelons of which, since they had now learnt to make swords as well as ploughshares, contained a considerable warrior element.

By the 4th century BC the Celts had raided into the Carpathians and the Balkans and had achieved such a reputation for soldiering that they were readily able to sell their services as mercenaries. In some areas to which they penetrated they drove out the original inhabitants; in others they were absorbed by them. Whichever way, by mid 4th century BC Celtic culture had reached the height of its influence, cutting a swathe across Europe from northern Spain to southern Germany; and extend-

1

ing from the western frontiers of Turkey to the western shores of
Britain. However, despite this expansion, the Celtic outlook was dictated by loyalty to the tribe and to the chieftain; inevitably, this destroyed
any ambitions of nationhood, if indeed these were possible with the
admixture arising from such a wide geographical spread. And through
the long years of their wars with Rome, it was this weakness, more than
any other, which was to bring about their ultimate destruction.

By 5th century BC the Celts had crossed the Alps and had established
trade routes with the Etruscans in northern Italy, whose territory they
were soon to occupy; and in the year 387 BC they thrust south towards
Rome on a raid which was to mark the zenith of their power. They
sacked the city and their leader, Brennus, demanded tribute equivalent
to his weight in gold. When the senators protested at what they
considered to be the excessively punitive level of the tribute, Brennus
called for his sword and caused it to be weighed upon the scales with
him, uttering the famous words: 'Vae victis' – woe to the conquered!
But they were words which, in due course, were to rebound upon the
Celtic people with accumulated interest for, by the year 190 BC, the
Romans had regained the conquered northern territory of Cisalpine
Gaul; and seventy years later had crossed the Alps into Gaul itself, the
home of many powerful Celtic tribes, to occupy the area of the lower
Rhone known as Transalpine Gaul. The province of Transalpine Gaul
was assigned to Caesar in 59 BC and from there he launched the
campaign which was to place the whole country under Roman control.
The area which he seized included the lands of the Armorican tribes,
living in Normandy and Brittany, who succumbed without resistance;
and the territory of the Belgae, one of the main divisions of the Gallic
peoples, which included northern France, Belgium, southern Holland
and that part of Germany west of the Rhine. Caesar achieved this
success in a short but bloody war which lasted little more than a year;
but it took a further six years of fighting, a period which included two
expeditions to Britain, to crush a series of rebellions before his conquest
could be considered complete.

The first of these rebellions erupted in 56 BC in Armorica, when
Caesar might have had every reason to believe that Gaul had been
pacified. He had deployed his legions to their winter stations and had
then departed for the eastern Adriatic, an area for which, he is careful
to record, he had command responsibility. The legions at once looked
to their administration and Publius Crassus, the legate commanding VII
Legion, sent staff officers to the tribes in Armorica requisitioning corn
and other foodstuffs. Perhaps they were too heavy-handed or over-
zealous in their demands, for the Veneti rose in revolt. They were the
most powerful tribe on the Atlantic coast, with a large fleet capable of

1. Julius Caesar, from a bust in the Palazzo di Conservatori, Campidoglio, Rome.

navigating the tempestuous seas frequently encountered in that area. They seized the visiting Roman officers and demanded of Crassus that he should return to them the hostages which they had been compelled to yield as a surety of their good behaviour. They were at once joined by neighbouring tribes, who made similar demands, and Crassus wasted no time in notifying Caesar of what was happening. Caesar was still homeward bound when news of the uprising reached him: his response was immediate and unerringly accurate in his appreciation of what was to be done. He instructed his staff that the remainder of the winter was to be employed in the construction of warships on the river Loire, which were to be of a quality at least equal to those of the Veneti; and sailors were to be enlisted and trained in the handling of them. It was a wise decision, for the type of coastal stronghold favoured by this Gallic tribe proved difficult to overcome and produced a military stalemate, which forced a confrontation at sea: and it was a remarkable decision, for it at once underlines Caesar's extraordinary grasp of military matters and his capacity for anticipating problems which yet lay ahead. There could only be one outcome to the uprising and the Veneti[1]

> surrendered themselves to Caesar, with all their possessions. He resolved to make an example of them in order to teach the natives to be more careful in future about respecting the rights of ambassadors; he had all their councillors executed and the rest of the population sold as slaves.

Julius Caesar was more than just a brilliant general, abounding in energy in mind and body; he was a born leader, with considerable personal courage. His biographer, Suetonius, relates that once he had routed enemy troops, it was his rule never to allow them time to rally. It was this determination to maintain the momentum of the attack which gained him many of his victories and which contributed to the high morale of his soldiery, to whose welfare he was dedicated but whom he commanded with an iron discipline. He was probably seeking to emphasise his philosophy of maintaining the military momentum and not to stress his many victories, when he decorated one of the display wagons participating in his Pontic triumphal procession with the words – I came, I saw, I conquered.

The Armorican tribes, and particularly the Veneti with their sea-going experience, had close trading links with their neighbours across the Gallic Sea, in south-west Britain; these were the Dumnonii, mainly of Devon and Cornwall, and the Durotriges, whose territory extended east to the Hampshire Avon and westwards to the river Exe. Both of these peoples almost certainly provided their continental cousins with

2. A hoard of slingstones uncovered at Maiden Castle: they probably came from Chesil beach, near Weymouth.

support and encouragement in their resistance to their Roman invader and it would be natural to expect that those Venetians who had managed to escape Caesar's wrath after their rebellion, would have fled for succour across the Channel. It would thus be surprising if the Durotriges did not share with them a dislike of their common enemy. There is evidence that some Wessex hillforts about this time were strengthened with the newly imported art of slingstone warfare, a skill at which the Veneti were already particularly adept. Archaeological excavation has identified two hoards of slingstones with this period and with Chesil Beach, near Weymouth. One of these at Maiden Castle[2] contained some 38,000 stones and a further cartload was unearthed by Colt Hoare at Bratton Castle at the beginning of the 19th century.[3]

The excavation of the main gate at Danebury hillfort, dated to 1st century BC and revealed in 1970 by the site work of Professor Cunliffe, has shown with great clarity the tactical thinking introduced by the advent of slingstone warfare. The single ramparts of the main fort, protected by a deep ditch were extended on each side of the gate and at right angles to it. This created a narrow corridor, flanked by high ramparts, along which the attacking force was compelled to fight its way, running the gauntlet for more than fifty yards. The occupants of the hillfort concentrated their defence on the right hand spur, as one looked at the gate, which was constructed in such a manner as to give them an external view of their own main gate but to conceal it from their enemy. The command post of the defending force was probably located at the end of this spur, which provided the key to the whole defensive plan. From this high vantage point, protected by breastworks, they were enabled to shower their enemy with slingshot, directing their fire at his exposed right side, which was left unguarded by the shield habitually carried on the left arm. The task confronting an assault was, however, further complicated by the fact that the main gate with its flanking spurs was additionally safeguarded by an outer gate and ramparts. Once this outer position had been breached, attackers were cunningly confronted with three routes, to left or right along deep, flanking ditches leading nowhere but around the perimeter of the hillfort: or up a blind alley in the centre, straight into the defensive trap.

Roman soldiers were trained in the use of the slingshot, although it seems to have been a weapon which was used by the auxiliary forces rather than the legionaries.[4] Vegetius records that, during young soldier training, archers and slingers used to set out bundles of twigs and straw as targets and that they could hit these with regularity from a range of six hundred feet. Every soldier was required to practice throwing stones of up to one pound in weight by hand and to be able to discharge his slingstone with accuracy after only one turn of the sling around his head. Slingers who were exceptionally proficient marksmen were frequently 'brigaded' within their units and were sometimes provided with lead shot, particularly during the Republican period. In later years the sling fell out of favour and came to be regarded as a barbarian weapon. The account of its uses, handed down to us by Vegetius, does, however, give us an idea of the standards of marksmanship obtainable by the British Iron Age tribesmen.

The flight of the Veneti, and the help which they received from their brethren in the mysterious and apparently prosperous island across the Channel, attracted Caesar's attention. He determined to reconnoitre it because, although he had no intention of remaining there, Britain had rendered assistance to his enemy in all his Gallic campaigns and he felt that

> it would be a great advantage merely to have visited the island, to have seen what kind of people the inhabitants were, and to have learned something about the country with its harbours and landing places.

It was a snap decision, made in the late summer of 55BC and, since he was aware that autumn weather in north-west Europe can frequently be unpredictable, Caesar hastened forward his preparations for his expedition. He despatched an officer, Gaius Volusenus, in a warship to search the British coastline for a suitable landing place and with instructions to report back as soon as possible: he moved a task force of two legions, with a regiment of cavalry, into Artois, where the mainland of Gaul was closest to the coast of Britain: and he assembled a fleet of about eighty ships at Boulogne for the transportation of men, animals and stores across the Channel. Intelligence of these military movements, some of which were beginning to wear the uncharacteristic appearance of inadequate preparation, soon reached Britain, from whence a number of tribes sent envoys to the continent, promising hostages and offering submission. Caesar was quick to take advantage of this hopeful gesture and, upon their return to Britain, sent with them his friend and ally, Commius, ruler of the Atrebates, to announce his impending arrival and good intentions.

Caesar sailed from Boulogne at midnight on about 25th August. It was clearly his intention to travel light and, where possible, to live off the land: indeed, it is doubtful if the number of ships he had commissioned, albeit for a limited operation, would have permitted the carriage of much heavy baggage, or any large numbers of pack animals or quantities of food reserves. His initial aim had been to join up at sea with the cavalry contingent, which was planned to sail simultaneously from their more northern embarkation port but, to use his own barbed comment, they delayed carrying out their instructions and started too late. In the event, their departure was foiled by adverse weather conditions and they never caught up with the main body: his operations were consequently drastically handicapped by their absence.

Caesar arrived off the coast of Britain, probably at Dover, in the early morning: he at once noted[5]

> enemy forces standing under arms all along the heights. At this point of the coast, precipitous cliffs tower over the water, making it possible to fire from above directly on to the beaches. It was clearly no place to attempt a landing . . .

Caesar rode at anchor until about 3.30 pm, awaiting the arrival of the rest of the fleet. He used this interval to summon his staff and commanders for a conference,[6] to inform them of Volusenus' reconnaissance report, the details of which he does not recount, and of his intention to sail about eight miles up Channel, to seek a more suitable landing place, with a sloping beach. The British, making full use of their

3. The ancient castle and Roman *pharos* (lighthouse) at Dover probably stand on the cliffs from
which Julius Caesar was attacked by British tribesmen in 55 BC.

cavalry and war chariots, had little difficulty in keeping pace with his
change of direction. When he reached his chosen disembarkation point,
the possible whereabouts of which is discussed below, they were once
again ready to oppose his landing.

Caesar's assault force was immediately in trouble for, although the
beach was sloping and suitable for the grounding of ships, the deep
draught of the Roman vessels kept them some distance from the shore
line. The soldiers, weighed down with their armour and weaponry, and
uncertain of the depth of the water, were fast losing their zest for the

fight when the standard-bearer of X Legion flung himself into the sea and, holding aloft the eagle, thrust forward towards the beach, shouting for others to follow him. There was, as a result, a general advance and the ensuing action was bitterly contested. Caesar, keeping to seaward in a warship, watched for places where his men were being hard pressed and, using the small craft of the fleet, he transferred men from one danger area to another, until he had gained sufficient ground to allow the legions to be marshalled for a set-piece assault. When it was launched, it was irresistible. The British fled but Caesar was unable to exploit his success due to the absence of his cavalry: he was thus denied a decisive victory. The Britons called for terms and rendered hostages, bringing with them Commius who, upon his arrival from Gaul, had been arrested and thrown into prison.

Four days after these events, the cavalry transports were sighted by Caesar but almost immediately were again dispersed by a violent storm which drove them back to seek refuge across the Channel. The same storm, coupled with a very high tide, damaged much of the fleet in its anchorage and Caesar was compelled to recall his legions to the beachhead, in order to reorganise his scattered administration and repair his unseaworthy ships. The incident caused considerable consternation amongst the troops ashore: the campaigning season was drawing to a close and the season of equinoctial gales was approaching. Their morale was not improved when a sizeable party of VII Legion fell into a trap whilst out foraging for grain and allowed themselves to be ambushed. The outcome could have been more serious had Caesar himself not heard the noise of the fighting and moved promptly to their support. He remarked[7]

> the Legion recovered its morale. The moment, however, was clearly inopportune to precipitate a general engagement so I . . . led the troops back to camp.

In view of Caesar's normal reaction of rapid response to this sort of situation, this is a very telling comment and, although fate had dealt him a cruel blow by leaving him bereft of cavalry, it does appear that the position in which he found himself stemmed from his original, hasty and inadequate preparation for the campaign arising, perhaps, from early over confidence. Even so, one is left to wonder why he risked so much, at such an inopportune time of the year, for apparently so little purpose or gain.

The instructions which Caesar gave to his staff for his second expedition to Britain are worthy of comment because, to a degree, they reflect the problems and weaknesses which emerged in the campaign he had just concluded. Immediately upon his return to the continent he issued orders for the construction of as many ships as possible during the coming winter months, and the repair and alteration of others. He stipulated their shape, dimension and load-carrying role and plainly wished them to be so designed as to make the task of disembarkation much easier:[8]

> To simplify loading and beaching they were to be constructed with a somewhat lower freeboard than that commonly used ... To allow for heavy cargoes, including numerous pack animals, they were to be rather wider in the beam than those used in other waters ...

On this occasion his fleet was to consist of more than 800 vessels and it was to transport an army of five legions and some four regiments of cavalry. He originally planned to embark in early summer but was compelled to alter this date to July because of tribal troubles in Gaul. Local grain stocks in Britain would have been low in early summer, especially after the previous year's fighting, and on this occasion he was apparently determined to travel independent of local resources. He was concerned that there might be trouble in Gaul during his absence. For this reason he left his deputy commander, Labienus, with three legions and 2,000 cavalry to guard his base ports, arrange food resupply and to keep secure his rear communications.

Caesar sailed from Boulogne on his second expedition to Britain, probably on 6th July 54 BC; it was his intention to cross the sea by night and arrive off the British coast at dawn on the following day. In order to achieve this timing, he left harbour shortly before sunset, hoping by this means to correct his previous late arrival when, it will be recalled, he sailed at midnight but the main body failed to arrive until mid-afternoon; but once again the unforeseen occurred. Strong tides carried them off course and it was only by strenuous efforts, with plentiful use of their oars, that they reached their assault beaches by noon. By this time the British, who had assembled a large force on the beach to oppose their landing, had withdrawn inland to high ground, possibly to Bigbury Woods;[9] they were doubtless overawed by the very size of the assault fleet. Caesar commenced disembarkation immediately and at midnight, with his customary urgency and leaving the unloading of stores and heavy baggage together with the construction of beachhead defences in the hands of Quintus Atrius, set out on an approach march of about twelve miles to the British defensive position. His enterprise and skill are to be admired. As events were to prove, it must have been a cloudy and dark night and it could not have been easy to move this distance, over unfamiliar ground and with a large force, even assuming he made use of local guides.

VII Legion had little difficulty in storming the British position and, after a short pursuit, Caesar employed the rest of the day in consolidating his gain. Next morning he had just despatched a follow-up party of three light columns to re-establish contact with the enemy, when he received disastrous news from the beachhead. An overnight storm had wrecked nearly all his ships or driven them ashore: about forty were a total loss and the operational and administrative consequences were daunting. He sent an urgent message to Labienus to commence the building of replacement ships and withdrew all craftsmen from the legions to tackle the huge repair task which now had to be undertaken. All vessels were ordered to be drawn up on the beach and the soldiers worked night and day for ten days to enclose the area with a single line of fortifications. It seemed, in Caesar's words, the best thing to do in spite of the labour involved: he was not guilty of exaggeration when he referred to the size of the project for even assuming tight packing and double banking of the ships involved, the task of protecting the fleet in this' manner must have required a defensive line of some four or five miles.

4. British War Chariot.

Upon completion of the beachhead, Caesar returned inland to discover there had been a new and important development. The tribes with whom his legions had been engaged had sunk their local differences and, banding together, had placed themselves under the supreme command of Cassivellaunus, a powerful chieftain, who had considerable influence with another federation of tribes, north of the Thames, and whose territory adjoined that of the Trinovantes, of modern-day Essex, to their east. Caesar moved forward to meet him and in the immediate actions which then ensued both sides learnt some useful lessons. Caesar recognised the mobility and resilience of the British tribal warrior. Cassivellaunus was taught the futility of taking on the professional Roman army in any form of set-piece action and he absorbed his lesson with considerable success, for he now disbanded most of his force and was content to harry Caesar's increasingly long lines of communication. He constantly threatened the flanks of the Roman column, cutting off isolated parties, inevitably affecting the forward movement of supplies to the advancing legions; even more seriously, he haunted their axis of advance, driving cattle and inhabitants from it and destroying reserves of food. It was under these trying circumstances that Caesar reached the banks of the Thames and, undeterred, he thrust across it, brushing aside the opposition on the far bank by the aggressive use of his cavalry. The infantry followed, wading head high through the waters of the ford.[10]

At this stage, the reader of Caesar's *Gallic Wars* begins to wonder at these apparently foolhardy acts of generalship by their author, as he plunges deeper into hostile territory and separates himself still further from his main supply base; but Caesar now reveals an important fact which, until this moment, he has been careful to conceal from us. At some time in the past, possibly when the tribal envoys crossed the Channel in 55 BC to pay homage to him in Gaul, a young British prince, Mandubracius, had fled to Caesar for protection, upon the murder of his father, the king of the Trinovantes, by Cassivellaunus. Caesar claims that the elders of the tribe now sought him out, promising submission and obedience to his orders and seeking his continuing protection of the prince, whom they wished to be returned to them as their chieftain. This could not have been an unexpected happening but Caesar chose to treat it as such in his written account of the incident, thus adding to the many questions which surround his version of the expedition: nor could it have been pure coincidence that Mandubracius chanced to be travelling with the Roman task force. Caesar relates that he at once demanded from them forty hostages and a plentiful supply of grain for the troops: these were promptly delivered and he allowed Mandubracius to go. He then commenced his march

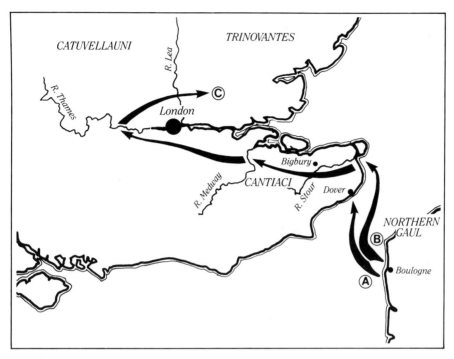

5. Julius Caesar's landings in Britain. Arrow A points to Caesar's possible landing place in 55 BC. In the following year (B) he landed to attack the British hillfort at Bigbury and then thrust inland to cross the Thames and meet with Trinovantian elders east of the river Lea (C). See also Appendix A.

back to the coast, diverting from his path to storm Cassivellaunus' stronghold, concealed in woods and marshland, probably near Wheathampstead.

Whilst these operations which detained Caesar on the north bank of the Thames were in progress, Cassivellaunus, who was not occupying his base, again revealed his shrewd military sense by sending messages to the Kentish tribes, instructing them to attack the Roman beach-head. According to Caesar, the garrison sallied forth and repulsed the Britons with heavy loss, to a degree that Cassivellaunus, acting through Commius, sent a delegation to negotiate terms of surrender: but he virtually negates this statement in his next sentence and one is left with the impression that it must have been a mutually agreed cessation of hostilities, a possibility emphasised by the fact that the valuable Commius again emerged to be used as go-between[11] (author's italics)

> I had decided to winter on the continent for fear of sudden risings in Gaul; besides summer was nearly over *and it was clear the enemy*

> *could easily hold out for the rest of the campaigning season*; so I
> demanded hostages, fixed the annual tribute payable from Britain
> into the Roman treasury, and strictly forbade Cassivellaunus to
> interfere with Mandubracius and the Trinovantes.

Upon receiving the hostages, Caesar returned to the coast and found the
fleet had now been repaired and was launched awaiting his arrival. The
replacement ships he had ordered from Labienus had not arrived so,
after awaiting for them in vain for some days, he crowded his army on
to the available transports and sailed for home.

Caesar carefully spelt out his intention before launching his first
expedition to Britain in 55 BC: it was a justifiable reconnaissance to
discover something about the country, its inhabitants, its harbours and
its landing places. It was, however, hastily organised and strangely
ill-prepared. He gave no reason for his return in the following year and
we are left to make our own assessment. His single minded march to the
Thames crossing-place and from thence to Essex, with his obviously
pre-arranged meeting with the envoys of the Trinovantes, leaves little
doubt that his main purpose was the return of Mandubracius to his
people. He is unlikely to have done this without expecting some
profitable return for his effort and it is of interest that archaeological
studies of the distribution of Italian wine amphorae imported during
1st century BC[12] have shewn beyond reasonable doubt that the bulk of
pre-Caesarian trade passed over the Dorset coast into central southern
Britain, whilst most of the post-Caesarian trade was conducted with the
tribes located in the Essex and Hertfordshire regions. According to
Cunliffe this drastic change in a well-established trading pattern could
only have resulted from Caesar's activities. In his view, the bald
summary which the Roman general gave of his British achievements
conceals a complex series of trading agreements which could well have
been negotiated by him at that time, with not just the Trinovantes but
the Catuvellauni as well. Tacitus' comment that Caesar revealed rather
than bequeathed Britain to Rome may not have been entirely accurate.
However these arrangements may have materialised, whether by treaty
or as a result of private initiative, there can be no doubt of the impact
which his two, seemingly inconclusive expeditions were ultimately to
have upon the history and development of our islands.

Examining the campaign of 54 BC from this range in time, at the
moment when Cassivellaunus disappears from our historical vision, it is
hard to believe that his military performance against Caesar had in any
way diminished his personal standing amongst his countrymen or his
ability politically to influence future events. Indeed, there is every
reason to suspect, from the circumstances described by Caesar sur-

rounding his opponent's final surrender, whom he said had 'employed Commius as an intermediary', that the Roman himself had initiated the negotiations, else Commius could not have been made available. Caesar at this moment would have been almost more concerned than his enemy to bring fighting to an honourable end, for any hint of disaster could surely have been politically damaging for him in Rome. Consequently, it is not impossible to imagine that Cassivellaunus and his people, even if they agreed to pay tribute for a period of years, were able to extract some benefit for themselves, albeit to a minor degree, from the trade arrangements which followed in the wake of Caesar's expeditions.

In the absence of any proper record, and despite the many successes enjoyed by archaeological research, it is not easy to piece together the happenings which culminated in the emergence of Cassivellaunus' apparent successor, Tasciovanus, although it is more likely that there was some intervening hiatus before he reached this position.

Tasciovanus almost certainly was the product of a tribal regrouping, to the north and east of Cassivellaunus' area, possibly stimulated by the improved economic conditions created by Caesar's treaties with the Trinovantes. His tribal origins are obscure but numismatic evidence shows him to be a contemporary of Addedomaros, ruler of the Trinovantes circa 25–5 BC, with whom it is suggested he may have shared a common ancestor;[13] but he might equally have been a descendant of Cassivellaunus or an aristocrat of one of the tribes comprising the newly formed federation, who saw an opportunity to assume its leadership. Tasciovanus' first appearance on the political scene is apparently in the heart of the area with which Cassivellaunus was identified by Caesar. He seems to have been an ambitious and dynamic man, who wasted little time in acquiring an additional slice of territory, located within the western frontier of the Trinovantian kingdom, and in expanding his influence south of the Thames; but there is no indication in either case of how these gains were achieved. Significantly, his arrival in power appears to have coincided with a general shift in the settlement pattern of the population for, by the time of his coming to the throne, their capital had been established at *Verulamium* (St Albans).[14] It has been suggested that the Catuvellauni

6.   A Gold coin of Tasciovanus, ruler of the Catuvellauni tribe, *c.* 20 BC–AD 5.

may have originated about this time, the name either being adopted by the leaders of the tribes from whom it was created or by Tasciovanus himself.[15] It is equally possible, and perhaps more likely in the circumstances, that this happening occurred some few years beforehand. If, as seems possible, Cassivellaunus' people formed part of this new grouping, it is interesting to speculate how much influence they were able to exert on its political outlook, for much will have changed in the decades since Caesar's departure.

Addedomaros' seat of government, in the early part of his reign, appears to have been located in the vicinity of Braughing, in Hertfordshire, to which there was vigorous flow of trade from Italy and Gaul in the post-Caesarian era. This was borne from the continent, along the Wantsum Channel, which separated the Isle of Thanet from mainland Kent, to the Thames: thence it was carried up the river Lea to Ware, where it was transferred into smaller, shallow draught vessels for the final lap of its journey up the river Rib to Braughing. The benefits of this trade appear to have extended north-westwards beyond the Trinovantian frontiers and there is evidence to support the view that at least part of the pre-conquest community around Braughing included literate Romans or Romanised Gauls,[16] presumably attracted by the commercial potential of the area. The military implications of this interesting fact are considerable for it means that, even assuming these people had been expelled to the continent as British relationships with Rome deteriorated prior to the landings of AD 43, the Roman army must have come ashore provided with an invaluable knowledge of the terrain and riverways over which it was to operate including, importantly, its landing zone in the Wantsum Channel.

Shortly after acceding to his throne, circa 25 BC, Addedomaros moved his centre of government eastwards to establish a new tribal capital, the original *Camulodunum* (Colchester), on a sacred site at Gosbeck's Farm, south west of Sheepen. The reasons for this move are not hard to find. Addedomaros must have felt increasingly under threat from the growing strength of the Catuvellauni, whose tribal base adjoined his frontier and was situated only a few miles from the river Lea. The river trading route was long, complicated and vulnerable; and any threat to it was a threat to the prosperity of the Trinovantian people. The time had undoubtedly come to find an alternative supply line, shorten his line of communication with the continent and secure his position by establishing a new capital in a position easy to defend, within reach of the harbours and estuaries of the east coast and readily accessible to the riverways communicating with the hinterland. His new capital fulfilled all these requirements and rapidly expanded to become a thriving commercial port, open to trade with shipping crossing the

Channel from northern Gaul and sailing from the waters of the Rhine. A rare bronze coin of Cunobelin, soon to inherit the Trinovantian throne, depicts a tall-sided sailing ship of commercial design which was doubtless used for this purpose. It is notable that, despite this switch in the pattern of trade flowing from the continent, which might have been expected to diminish the volume being carried along the Lea, a prosperous business appears still to have been conducted within the Braughing area until early 1st century AD.[17]

Opinion is divided as to who directly succeeded Addedomaros to the throne of the Trinovantes. The popular choice appears to be one Dubnovellaunus, a chieftain who is thought to have ruled over an area of north-east Kent before being ousted by Eppillus, a son of Commius, some time about AD 1.[18] There is, however, evidence that Tasciovanus was there before him; the latter minted coins at *Camulodunum* and occupied that capital for some period of his reign, which spanned circa 20 BC–AD 7. These coins have been rarely found and it is therefore speculated that his stay cannot have been of long duration before he, in his turn, gave way for Dubnovellaunus and returned to *Verulamium*. The circumstances of Tasciovanus' arrival on the throne of the Trinovantes, and his sudden move back to his old tribal capital, are clouded with uncertainty and may only be conjectured. Those were disturbed days, with many ambitious men jostling for power and land; it is not impossible that Tasciovanus was responsible for the removal of Addedomaros or that, upon the death of the latter, he moved swiftly to seize the throne. Equally, if the two men shared a common ancestor, as Rodwell suggests, he may have come to it by right of succession, until the emergence of Dubnovellaunus who appears, in one form or another, to have produced a more persuasive argument to be its occupant. Whatever this may have been, the rule of Dubnovellaunus was also shortlived; he was removed within a decade by Cunobelin, a self-declared son of Tasciovanus, and fled to the continent by the year AD 7 to join the growing community of refugee British princes living in Rome.

The origins of Cunobelin, as seems almost inevitable in this era of British history, are also unclear. As a son of Tasciovanus, he might have been expected to have made an early political appearance at *Verulamium* or in Catuvellaunian territory but this does not appear to have happened. He first comes to our notice upon his acquisition of the territory of the Trinovantes. Later, upon the death of Tasciovanus, he combined the two tribal domains into one, fast expanding Catuvellaunian empire, which he governed from *Camulodunum* for rather more than thirty years. During this period he issued a series of coins in gold, silver and bronze and achieved such a position of power that the

7. Gold *staters* of Cunobelin, *c.* AD 25.

Romans came to regard him as *Britannorum Rex*, the king of the
Britons. Amongst these coins were an estimated one million gold
staters, the equivalent of 3,000 Roman pounds weight of gold,[19] a great
accumulation of wealth which, it must be presumed, represented the
profits of trade conducted by the Catuvellaunian peoples with the
Roman continent. The bulk of this trade, which probably included,
amongst other commodities, the export of grain, precious metals,
cattle, hides and slaves, passed through *Camulodunum* and attracted a
lively community of merchants and craftsmen.

In Cunobelin's declining years, it is not difficult to imagine that the
political uncertainties created by an ageing prince, who had been long
in power, persuaded Rome that the time was fast arriving when this
valuable commercial asset would have to be secured, either by renewed
treaties or by military force. In view of the city's rapid development as a
commercial centre and the enhanced value of trade since Cunobelin's
accession to the throne, they may have noticed an increasing confidence
amongst their British allies, raising doubts that any new trading

8. '. . . a rare coin of Cunobelin depicts a tall sided sailing ship . . .'

arrangements could be negotiated to their advantage. The military option therefore had its attractions to Rome: indeed, the occupation of the island seems to have been a possibility never far from Roman thought in the second part of 1st century BC[20] but they were aware it would be expensive in terms of military resources which were, at that time, heavily committed elsewhere. Augustus (31BC – AD14) sought to re-establish the balance of power in Britain in the Roman favour by giving his support to the Atrebates, where Commius, having fled Gaul after a quarrel with Caesar, had developed a vigorous kingdom centred on the Thames, north of Silchester (*Calleva*) Their original *oppidum* may have been situated at Dyke Hills,[81] near Dorchester-on-Thames until an extension of their influence brought about a move which established a new tribal centre of gravity south of the river. It is difficult to determine with accuracy when this may have happened but there is evidence to show that, after about 35 BC, COMMIOS gold staters were in use in the areas of present day Odiham, Guildford, Reading and Basingstoke.[22]

Augustus' intervention in support of the Atrebates appears to have been directed towards gaining their territorial expansion into north-east Kent and thus establishing a friendly face on that coast line. It is significant that Cunobelin crossed the river Thames in about AD 11, ejected the Atrebates and seized this area for himself. Some fifteen years later, his brother, Epaticcus, seized the whole of the northern part of their territory, including *Calleva*, bringing it into the expanding Catuvellaunian empire.

Cunobelin had several sons of whom three, Togodumnus, Caratacus and Adminius, were to feature in the events about to unfold. They probably shared administrative responsibilities for various parts of their father's kingdom during his lifetime and lived in their respective provinces. It is uncertain where Adminius had his headquarters but the extremity of north-east Kent has been suggested.[23] The fact that he held pro-Roman sympathies, taken with the Roman propensity to make alliances with rulers holding coastal domains, suggests that this area of Kent may well have been his territory, particularly because of the presence within it of the Wantsum Channel and the Richborough Harbour site, which was soon to provide a bridgehead for the disembarkation of the Roman invasion force. The loyalties of Togodumnus and Caratacus, however, were diametrically opposed to those of their brother. Without doubt, they would have wished to extract the best possible trading terms from the Romans for the benefit of their people: but they would have been naive beyond belief if they had not appreciated that the Romans would take by force anything they could not negotiate by treaty.

It was conceivably because of this that a quarrel arose which resulted in the expulsion of Adminius by Cunobelin. He fled to Gaius Caligula, taking with him a wealth of local knowledge and valuable military intelligence, and is said to have persuaded that unstable Roman emperor that Britain was ripe for his intervention and to have diverted his attention from the operations he was then conducting in lower Germany against the Canninefates.[24] In reality, it is more probable that Gaius had already been secretly planning with Adminius an assault across the Channel, for it would surely have been a matter of great logistical difficulty to switch from an essentially land campaign across the Rhine to a major seaborne operation across the Gallic Sea, unless the planning for it was already well advanced.

In the event, the troops refused to embark and then, either in a fit of extreme rage, of which he was more than capable, or as a gesture of contempt for their behaviour, he is said to have paraded them in battle array on the shore and commanded them to collect sea shells. The mutiny by the legions resulted in the abandonment of his invasion plans, if indeed they existed, but this did not prevent Gaius from erecting a great lighthouse at Boulogne, where it stood as a memorial to the event until it was pulled down in AD 1544. Two years later, Gaius was cut down by the hands of assassins outside the theatre in Rome and was succeeded by Claudius.

Upon the death of their father, Togodumnus and Caratacus, now well alerted to the possibility of Roman landings, began a calculated expansion of their tribal sphere of influence, the former basing himself

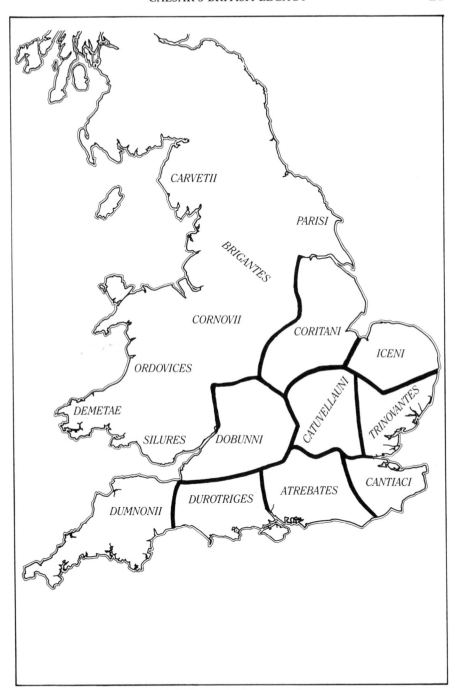

9. British Tribes in the Pre-Roman Iron Age.

upon *Camulodunum* and Caratacus continuing to be located at *Calleva*, which he had occupied from about AD 40. Caratacus was strategically well placed at Silchester, where there is known to have been a flourishing settlement of some 325 hectares at the time of the invasion. From this position he was able to thrust westwards to consolidate his grasp on the lands of the northern Dobunni and south-westwards into the realm of the Atrebates to seize West Sussex, ruled by the elderly Verica. Verica fled, taking the well trodden path to Rome, to seek the help of Claudius; and the two brothers, exhilarated by their apparent successes, and perhaps encouraged by the failure of the strange expedition initiated by Gaius Caligula, now demanded that Claudius should return Adminius and Verica to Britain. If they were aware that by this action they were triggering an explosive response, it did not appear to occur to them that they might fail to contain it.

At the hour of the Claudian invasion of AD 43, the sympathies of the tribes in the southern half of Britain were, as ever, widely at variance. To the north and east of the Catuvellauni lay the Coritani and the Iceni, two important kingdoms which had almost certainly felt the expansionist weight of their southern neighbour; if they had no cause to welcome a Roman intervention, there was little reason for them to resist it and they were to remain firmly neutral during the opening phases of the landings. Some, such as the Catuvellauni and the Trinovantes, recognised the threat it posed to their ambitions and prosperity and were prepared to resist with all the resources at their disposal. Other subjugated tribes, such as for example, the Cantii of Kent and possibly some of the Dobunni, appear to have been willing to resist the invaders so long as victory remained a possibility: yet others, such as the Atrebates, recognised the advancing legions as saviours, freeing them from the subjection of the Catuvellauni. Even so, it must be doubtful that there was tribal unanimity in these postures, for the northern Atrebates, as one example, had been ruled from *Calleva*, firstly by Epaticcus and then by Caratacus, for nearly twenty years and it would be surprising if the latter, a flamboyant and personable leader, had not in his time gathered a strong following.

It was from these sources that the British battle line was to be provided.

CHAPTER TWO

THE ROMAN ARMY AND ITS LOGISTICS

Administration is the servant of operations; but it is a servant
which is indispensable to its master . . .
A Principle of War

Famine makes greater havoc in an army than the enemy, and it is
more terrible than the sword.
Vegetius, III 3

Claudius, who was seeking a triumph to demonstrate his power to the
Senate and the people of Rome, and who had selected Britain as the
target for his venture, probably set about assembling an army for the
purpose immediately upon coming to the throne in AD 41. He did not
have far to look for his commander-in-chief, for his glance fell upon
Aulus Plautius, a kinsman of his first wife and a campaign-hardened
veteran who at the moment of his selection was Governor of Pannonia,
a province in the area of the Danube. Significantly, when moving to
take up his appointment, Plautius took with him to Gaul IX Legion
Hispana, then probably on garrison duties at Sisak in Pannonia; its
qualities may be assumed to have particularly suited the invasion plans
which were being prepared. The remaining three legions which were to
make up the Task Force were all drawn from the two Rhine Com-
mands, II Legion *Augusta* being transferred from Strasbourg, XIV
Legion *Gemina* from Mainz and XX Legion *Valeria* from Neuss. It has
occasionally been suggested that VIII Legion *Augusta* was also moved
from Pannonia at the same time to be used in part to provide
administrative back-up for the operation; but Keppie[1] considers its
presence as a formation to have been improbable and its presence in
part to be an open question, since this would be 'quietly to ignore the
numbers of *auxilia* involved'. There were many of these, probably
drafted from the army in lower Germany, as well as the Batavi tribe,
which specialised in river crossing techniques. When formed the total

10. The tombstone of an *aquilifer* of XIV Legion *Gemina*, at Mainz.

force numbered between 40,000 to 50,000 men, not including the additional manpower required for its naval transports and local administration. Its movement into the closely populated area of northern Gaul must have created a number of logistical problems and Caesar demonstrated some of these at an earlier time, when describing the emigration of the Helvetti[2] who, he wrote

> bought up all the draught cattle and wagons they could, sowing as much land as possible in order to secure an adequate supply of corn for the journey . . . they thought two years would suffice for the preparations . . .

His mention of the length of time taken to prepare for the emigration provides an interesting yardstick for the time which may similarly have been needed to make the necessary provision for rations for the men and animals involved in the Claudian invasion of Britain.

Auxiliary units were recruited from almost every peripheral province in the Roman Empire and enlistment was encouraged by the expectation of the grant of Roman Citizenship upon retirement or, in the case of tribal groups such as the Batavi, by remitting taxation. There were three types of auxiliary unit: the cavalry *ala*, the part mounted infantry unit and the infantry cohort. Details of all units which may have participated in the invasion are given at Appendix C. The total number of cavalry regiments taking part is not known but comparison elsewhere can provide us with some guidance. Agricola, at Mons Graupius, had under command a force of about 21,000 men, made up of two legions, 8,000 auxiliary infantry and 5,000 cavalry.[3] It would not therefore be unreasonable to assume that Plautius landed with at least a similar number of cavalry to support his four legions: indeed the total may have been greater but in the initial stages of the landings, the strength would probably have been restricted for logistical reasons. This figure would have meant that the task force came ashore with ten regiments of cavalry. Additionally, each legion held 120 cavalry horses upon its established strength and the total of riding horses to be embarked could thus have numbered at least 5,500, exclusive of transport animals. It should be noted that the horses upon which the *alae* were mounted were not the robust chargers to be seen in later history but were much lighter, very hardy animals, probably of 13 to 14 hands.[4]

The quality and training of the cavalry contingent was equally as important as a factor for a successful campaign as that of the infantry, particularly in view of the known British skill in chariot warfare. It would have been essential, therefore, that considerable care be given to

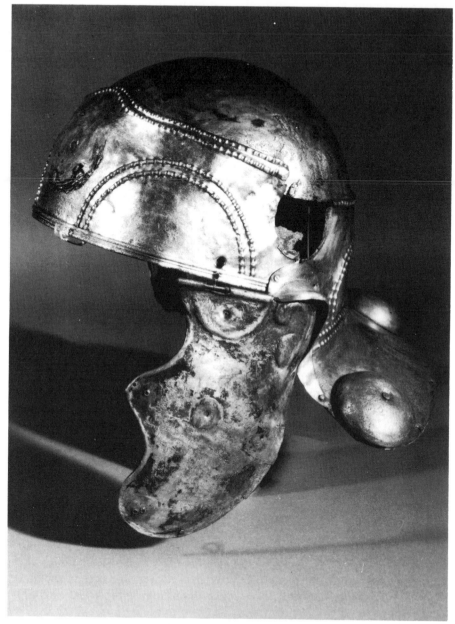

11. A cavalryman's bronze and iron helmet, 1st century AD, found at Witcham, near Ely, Cambridgeshire.

the appointment of the cavalry commander to fill the rank of *praefectus equitatum*. If Didius Gallus was selected to fill this post, as is sometimes suggested then his subsequent career as proconsul of Africa and one of the most successful Governors of Britain (AD 52–57) is testament to how worthily he would have filled it.

A legion was commanded by a legate, usually a senator appointed by the Emperor; he was provided with six tribunes, the senior of whom acted as his second-in-command, the others holding administrative or operational positions on his staff. It comprised ten cohorts, each of six centuries: each century, with the exception of the first cohort in every legion, having a fighting strength of eighty men and being commanded by a centurion, himself probably promoted to that rank for disting-uished military service or gallantry in the field. The first cohort was special: as opposed to the others within a legion, it consisted of five centuries of double strength, commanded by the five most senior of the centurionate, the senior one of these receiving the title of *primus pilus*. He was an officer of considerable experience and influence, authorised to attend staff briefings, where his advice must have been widely sought and greatly valued. He generally held this appointment for one year and then either retired or could be appointed to higher rank, for example, *praefectus castrorum*. In this appointment he would have been third in command to the legate and would have been responsible for the administrative staff such as clerks, as well as armourers, medics, carpenters, blacksmiths and technicians of all categories held on establishment. There can be little doubt that the remarkably high standards of the Roman Army, both in peace and in war, stemmed from the experience and leadership qualities of the battle-hardened centu-rions by whom it was led.[5]

A century was further sub-divided into ten sections of eight men each, *contubernia*, the equivalent of a present day rifle section within an infantry company, and each of these, when in the field, was provided with a tent and a mule with which to transport it and some of the other heavy equipment issued to the junior ranks.[6] This, according to Josephus,[7] consisted of saw, axe, sickle, chain, rope, spade and basket. Many of these items were required for the constructional work, and the forest clearance, which they were frequently required to undertake when on operations and may well have fitted into a satchel with which they were also issued. On the other hand, the relief on Trajan's Column, depicting an army parading for a review, shows the men marching with a stake over their left shoulder carrying five objects: a string bag for forage, a metal cook-pot and a metal skillet for cooking and eating, a sack containing rations or clothing, and the satchel which has already been mentioned above, for the retention of tools. It has

12. A detachment of XX Legion.

been suggested that this device was introduced by Marius in order to economise in baggage animals but it is improbable that it would have been carried on to the battlefield, where the movements of the fighting soldier would have been inhibited by it. It was thus conceivably only used for inspection parades to obviate the need for bringing mules on to the ground on those occasions and for this reason the operational necessity of a pack mule for each eight men may be considered unchanged. When calculating the total number of pack animals required for this purpose, it must also be assumed that the cavalry and other 'teeth' arm units had a similar need for tentage and transport to carry it, thus posing a total requirement of between 5,000 to 6,250

13. Horses used by the Roman Army were probably descended from *Equus przewalskii* and related to the Tarpan of South Russia.

mules. Over and above this figure there would have been an additional demand to lift other heavy baggage, and the final figure would proportionately have been much the same as that estimated by Breeze[8] when discussing the logistics of Agricola's final campaign in Scotland. He calculated this to be 3,050 baggage mules for a force of 21,000 men. As daunting as these totals may at first sight appear, there was a still further transport requirement to be satisfied.

A fourth century historian, Ammianus Marcellinus,[9] records that when on operations each soldier was accompanied by 17 days rations, his load being lightened by the use of transport animals moving with the supply train. The normal diet of the Roman soldier consisted of a basic element of corn, bacon and rough wine, supplemented by beer, venison, fish, poultry and vegetables. Archaeological research has revealed[10] that the largest percentage of his normal meat consumption was provided by the domesticated ox, although sheep and pork was also eaten in large quantities. However, the general outlook appears to have been 'if it moves it can be eaten', for such miscellaneous animals as fox, vole, badger, beaver and mole are shown frequently to have found their way to his camp fire. The iron rations which a soldier carried on active service are confirmed by several sources[11] to have consisted of the basic element of his normal diet, which has been mentioned above. In 2nd century AD, for example, Avidius Cassius forbade soldiers in the field[12] to carry anything for this purpose except bacon, hard tack and sour wine: this was the drink of the ordinary soldier and was similar to that which was proffered to Christ upon the Cross. The hard tack may be identified as *bucellatum*, biscuit baked from part of the corn ration which, according to Polybius, was issued to each man on a scale of 3lbs a day.

On this basis alone, there would have been a daily requirement to provide the army with between 53 to 70 tons of grain, dependent upon its size and assuming, as seems likely from the timing of the invasion, that a decision had been taken by the commander to operate independently of local supplies. Not all of this tonnage would have needed to be transported to the front line soldier, for many would have been engaged in garrison duties and administrative duties at base; but it would not be wrong to assume that a force of approximately 35,000, comprising four legions, the bulk of the cavalry and many auxiliary contingents, would have been required in the events leading up to, and following the Medway battle (see Chapter IV). To have provided grain alone to this army would have involved a daily lift by 650 mules which, according to the number of days march it had advanced inland, would have had to be multiplied by double that number in order to allow for the return journey. Thus an army at Rochester being supplied overland from Richborough would, on the basis of these calculations, have required a supply column involving 2,600 mules, without allowance yet having been made for rest days and reserves. The load carrying capacity of various types of animal, together with their comparative performances, is given in Table I and, as will be seen, is based on the experience of the Imperial British Army in India and South Africa.

The Roman commander would have been mainly dependent upon pack animals for transport; mule carts or ox wagons might have provided him with an improved performance, in terms of weight shifted per animal, but an essential requirement would have been reasonable track communications and he would have lost the important cross-country mobility offered by pack animals. It may be assumed he would have surrendered this with great reluctance and this may be why the four-wheeled wagons, featured on Trajan's Column, are so infrequently pictured. Indeed, the baggage train in the episode showing the army on the march[13] is made up of pack mules and two-wheeled carts and the latter, in a variety of scenes, are shown carrying weapons, shields, helmets, tentage and water barrels and are pulled, in different scenes,

TABLE I
Animal Transport – Comparisons

Serial	Item	Mules second class	Donkeys second class	Oxen	Pack horse
		(a) Daily Rations, War Scale (wt in lbs)			
1.	Grain	5	4	4 (pack) 6 (draught) 7 (siege train)	
2.	Fodder (Note B) a. Green b. Dry	25 13	20 10	30 14	(Note A)
3.	Salt	½ oz	–	½ oz	
		(b) Performance			
4.	Loads (lbs)	160	160	160	
5.	Speed (mph)	3 to 4	2½ (Note C)	2½ (draught) 2 (pack) (Note D)	
6.	Distance – miles per day	20–25	15	15–20	

Source: *Animal Management, 1901*, prepared in the Veterinary Department for the General Staff, War Office (reprinted 1914).

Notes: A. The same scale for rations and performance of pack horses applies as for mules.
B. Green and Dry are alternative feeds. If one considers green fodder alone and accepts a yield of half a ton per acre, then a contingent of 5,000 mules or horses would consume 112 acres of grass daily on this scale.
C. Pace slow compared with the mule but the donkey demands little attention and does well on poor forage.
D. Pack bullocks were driven in droves and tended to straggle: draught animals were easier to control but were normally worked in pairs and harnessed in teams of four. Estimated cart load, 1,500 lbs and wagon load, 3,000 lbs.

either by two mules or two oxen. Due to the limited performance of oxen as draught animals, it is probable that mules were used in preference to them on the occasion of active service (Table II). Richmond suggests[14] that carts were allocated one to each century, a scale identical to the Roman distribution of artillery (*carroballistae*). Artillery carts were purpose-made for their task and provided a platform from which the weapon was fired, the main structure of the cart being strikingly similar to the gun limber of the Royal Horse Artillery, with a box constructed for the storage of ammunition. Even the distribution of carts in this seemingly modest manner produces a requirement of 236 supply carts, 236 artillery carts and an additional 944 animals, probably mules, without taking to account the needs of the double centuries of the 1st Cohort in each legion.

Although the animal transport requirement already discussed is considerable, it is not difficult to visualise other needs which would impose further substantial demands upon it. There must have been, for example, a continuous forward flow of supplies to replace weapons, clothing and equipment damaged or destroyed in battle: and there was the, as yet, unconsidered problem of feeding all animals marching with the task force. According to a papyrus from Egypt,[15] 625 tons of barley were needed each year for the horses of a cavalry regiment (*ala*), a daily feed of 7 pounds. The ration scale for transport animals, prepared in 1908 for the General Staff of the War Office, recognises the need of all transport animals (Table II) for grain to boost their supplies of fodder and, although it is unlikely that they were over cossetted by their Roman handlers, even limited quantities fed to them would once again have added considerably to Plautius' transport and supply problems, because of the very large numbers of animals concerned. If it had been his intention to make use of British reserve stocks of grain, assuming these had been left available to him by his opponents, then much would have depended upon the timing of his landings. In fact, circumstances allowed Plautius a very limited range of options when selecting his invasion date and it is necessary here to pause for a moment to examine these.

*   *   *

Caesar sailed on his first campaign at the end of August, 55 BC, planning to stay only a few weeks and to take full advantage of the harvest about to be garnered in Britain. This vital factor would have been an important consideration when drafting his final plans. In the following year he sailed in early July, having decided to travel self-sufficient in foodstuffs and thus had no need to arrive in time to profit from the harvest. His departure had been delayed for three weeks by contrary north-west winds and then for a further few days because he felt it necessary to arrest a local Gallic leader, Dumnorix, who had been under confinement in the Roman camp and who had taken the opportunity to escape, presumably judging that Caesar was fully committed to embarkation. It was a mistake he was to pay for with his life.[16] It would thus appear that, although Caesar set forth in early July, he must originally have selected a date in early June for his expedition, just as the Allied Forces did some two thousand years later in 1944, when embarking for Normandy. Even that great event, despite the time of the year and the many resources made available to it, was nearly aborted due to bad weather. Finally, Caesar gave a clear indication of the timing of his return to the continent when he related that the approach of the equinoctial gales had threatened to prevent him from sailing for home unless he immediately embarked. It is significant that Polybius, writing more than a century earlier than these events, remarked

> It is the choice of the right moment which controls all human action, and above all the operations of war. This means that a general must have an exact knowledge of the dates of the summer and winter solstices and of the equinoxes . . .

The equinoxes occur bi-annually, in Spring and Autumn, approximately on 20th March and 22nd September respectively. It would thus seem likely that Caesar returned to Gaul from Britain during the third week of September in 54 BC.

The planning task confronting Aulus Plautius was more complex for, apart from the necessity to allow a margin of time for possible adverse weather conditions, he had also received instructions to send for Claudius 'if anything untoward should happen.' It seems probable that his emperor, whose British campaign up to that moment, according to Suetonius, had been his only one of importance, had made it clear to his commanding general that he wished to be present for the final and decisive phase and was to be summoned when that moment arrived. Plautius had therefore to allow time, in his initial planning, for a message to be despatched to Rome for this purpose from his headquarters on the Thames, a present day distance by road of some 1,200 miles; and for Claudius, with his entourage of staff and courtiers, with a detachment of his Praetorian Guard, to set forth by sea to Marseilles and thence northwards by road and river to Boulogne. Bearing in mind the size of the party which accompanied the emperor (amongst others, his sons-in-law travelled with him) it is difficult to see how the whole journey could have been completed in much less than ten or eleven weeks, even assuming the message which summoned him had been passed by code-word along a chain of Roman signal stations. This timing is broadly confirmed by Suetonius, who records that Claudius was back in Rome, six months after his departure from that city. He spent only sixteen days in Britain but it may be thought likely that he also spent some time resting and visiting the garrison in Boulogne, on

either the outward or return journey. It must also be certain that the
reinforcing troops and elephants with which he was to arrive in Britain
had already been positioned at Boulogne, if they were not already
awaiting his arrival on British soil.

In the face of these facts, Plautius will have had little room for choice
when selecting a month for embarking his invasion force. He must have
had to allow a period of at least three months to allow for the emperor's
journey to Britain and to guard against the possibility of unfavourable
weather; equally, he will have wished to ensure Claudius' return to the
continental mainland before mid-September so that the latter was not
trapped, and his absence from Rome prolonged, by the coming of the
autumn equinoctial gales. If, in addition to these allocations of time,
Plautius had budgeted for a campaign in Britain of a reasonable eight
weeks duration before sending for Claudius, then he would have had
little option but to settle for a sailing date in mid-April, however
unwilling he may have been to accept such an early start. With tight
timing of this nature, there was a further major complication, which
must have come close to putting the whole enterprise at risk, when the
legions refused to embark upon being ordered to do so by their officers.
The effects of this mutiny are discussed below (Chapter IV) but since its

14. A section (*contubernum*) of eight men with its tent and some equipment settling down for
the night outside an Iron Age village. Note the *cornu*, a type of horn, leaning against the fence.

duration could have impinged upon the timing of the operation, it is necessary to consider that aspect here. Dio's account of it is, as ever, brief and ambiguous:[17]

> The soldiers grumbled at having to serve outside the inhabited world, as they put it, and they refused to listen to (Aulus Plautius) until Narcissus, who had been sent by Claudius, mounted the commander's platform and began to address them.

At first sight this statement reads as though Claudius, informed of unrest amongst the army at Boulogne, had sent his private secretary, Narcissus, as his emissary, to speak to the legions. It is apparent, however, that the timetable we have been examining would not have permitted a delay of this dimension: moreover, it must be doubtful that the emperor would have been so tactless as to choose someone with the background of a former slave and clerk for a task of such delicacy. The cry of '*Io Saturnalia*' with which the soldiers greeted the appearance of Narcissus tends to confirm this, if Dio's interpretation of it is correct:

> ... they were still more annoyed with Aulus Plautius and disinclined to let Narcissus utter a word; but all of a sudden they shouted out loud the well-known cry '*Io Saturnalia*' (this because at the festival of Saturn the slaves dress up in their masters' clothes to keep holiday).

The probability is that Narcissus was already in Boulogne, making arrangements with Plautius' staff, before the departure of the army to Britain, for the arrival of Claudius later in the year, with his reinforcing contingent of troops: and that, becoming increasingly aware of the possible failure of the mission, and the political repercussions this might set in train, not only for Claudius but also himself, for he was not a well loved man, he took it upon himself to address the legions on behalf of his master. Hence the mocking, perhaps grudgingly admiring, shout with which they accused him of donning the emperor's robes. However it came about, he achieved the outcome he was seeking and what might have been a serious and lengthy setback lasted only a few days and could not noticeably have affected the timetable of the operation.

*   *   *

The whole subject of the logistics and composition of the Roman invading army in AD 43 is obscure: consequently any attempt to piece together the administrative difficulties which confronted them, and the manner in which these were resolved, is highly speculative. No figures have been handed down to confirm the numbers of men and animals taking part in the landings; nor is it known with any degree of certainty how these animals were fed or what quantities were regarded as adequate for them. The scale of the problem can only be assessed with a high percentage of possible error and its dimension has been forcefully demonstrated by Rivet, who has estimated[18] that, allowing for the production of seed corn and land lying fallow, an area roughly equivalent to the old county of Rutland would have been required to produce the 530,000 bushels of grain needed annually to feed the invading army. The numbers of animals estimated to have been required for the expedition if normal practice was observed – whilst admitting that it was always open to Plautius to reduce these, at least in the initial stages of the campaign, if he felt it prudent to do so – present a formidable problem by themselves. These could have totalled as many as 14,750, including, as has been shown above, an estimated 5,500 cavalry horses, 5,150 mules with tentage for the *contubernia*, 1,000 animals with carts and artillery for the centuries, and a further 2,750 mules to convey rations to forward troops, a possible two days' march inland from the coast. None of the figures is extravagant in itself but the final total is daunting, bearing in mind the restrictions of the cross channel lift which preceded the landings and the fact that they would be operating in hostile territory (Table II).

Those responsible for planning the operation will at this stage have felt considerable administrative pressures building up against them. British stocks of grain in mid-April would in any event be depleted, even if they had been left available to the invaders, which is uncertain. There is little doubt that the animals would have been grazed wherever possible but much would have depended upon the freedom of movement allowed to the Romans by their enemy, once they were ashore, and their ability to advance out of their landing area: and even when they had done this, much would then have depended upon the availability of grass, which would doubtless have been found in quantity on the Downs but would have been less plentiful in the forests of the Weald and the marshes of the Thames estuary, the natural battlegrounds for tribal armies. The Veterinary Handbook of 1908 (Table I) allows a 2nd class mule 25 lbs of grass a day, augmented by 5lbs of grain: either of these amounts, on their own, present huge supply problems, assuming the animals were concentrated within a small area. The grass consumption, based on half a ton per acre, a small growth in modern terms, would have posed a demand for 329 acres of grass daily: and the grain consumption would have required the daily produce of 56 acres.[19] For all these reasons and uncertainties, it may be expected that the Roman commissariat arrived with sufficient grain and fodder for the initial stages of the campaign: ultimately, since it was the Roman custom to stock their forts with a year's supply of foodstuffs, it is probable that they imported enough for this purpose, at least for the first twelve months of their occupation. With a requirement of this size, it is probable that plans for its production were made at least in AD 42, if not as early as AD 41, possibly under the regime of Gaius Caligula.

A logistical problem of this scale could only have been resolved by adapting the operational plan to make use of every available facility; and Plautius was fortunate to have under his command a Squadron of the Roman Imperial Navy, the *Classis Britannica*, which had been initially created and based at Boulogne by Gaius, for service in British waters, when planning his earlier abortive invasion.

Starr has suggested[20] that this Squadron disintegrated when Gaius abandoned his plans to conquer Britain and that it was later resuscitated by Claudius from the nucleus which then remained; but there seems to be little evidence of this. However, it encountered little opposition in north-west Europe in its traditional role at sea and it probably slipped easily into the task of providing logistical support for the army, without the need to be maintained at full strength. The Roman Navy had considerable experience in work of this nature, not only in the uncertain waters of the Gallic Straits and the North Sea, but in the Mediterranean and on the Danube, where it had developed great skill in the use of river boats. Tacitus[21] has provided a description of some of the ships with which the *Classis Britannica* would have been equipped

> . . . some were of shallow draught, pointed bow and stern, and broad beamed to withstand heavy seas. Others were flat bottomed to allow grounding. Most of them were equipped with steering oars on both sides to allow quick movement forward and backwards. Many had decks for the transport of artillery, horses and supplies. They were easy to sail . . .

The transportation of the legions, with their supporting arms and baggage, and the administrative problems which they will have encountered at every stage of their operation, is something which is often too lightly considered by those writing about this period. Each aspect of the embarkation of the task force, its movement and conduct at sea, and its ultimate disembarkation, must have been subject to meticulous control and planning. The infantry, for example, were allocated space on the scale of one century of 80 men to a ship. Starr[22] estimates that sixty galleys of the Imperial fleet would have transported a legion of 5,000 men.

A cavalry regiment of the size which embarked for Britain was, as has already been mentioned, composed of 500 horses and was divided into sixteen *turmae* of roughly 30 horses each: it is probable that, for ease of command and administration, one *turma* would have been allocated to one ship for embarkation purposes. This ship, as described by Tacitus, would have been broad in the beam to reduce sea movement and flat bottomed to enable it to approach the shore or to be grounded, so as to facilitate the embarkation or disembarkation of troops and animals across the beaches. The instructions for this purpose contained in the Handbook of Animal Management, mentioned in Table I, have interesting comparisons. They advise that, if it were possible to ground the boat, then animals should be off-loaded using ramps. Failing this, they were to be hoisted over the side by the use of belly-slings, then carefully released and led ashore by neck halters; if, on the other hand, the water was too deep to permit this technique, then picket boats should be put out in sufficient numbers to ensure that, when released from their slings, the animals were directed safely ashore. The vulnerability of the *alae* to attack at this stage is only too evident; it was therefore essential, in the event of an opposed landing, for the operation to be conducted within a securely held beach-head.

A suggestion of the scale of the shipping requirement for the embarkation of the task force is given in Table II. This has been calculated on the assumption that Plautius, irrespective of the demands of his administrative 'tail', would have wished to land in Britain with a strike force of 40,000 men, comprising four legions (20,000), ten regiments of cavalry (5,000) and auxiliary cohorts (15,000). These totals have been increased in Table II by a further 5,375 men, to allow for such men, so often forgotten when considering military operations, as cart drivers and mule handlers, marching with the baggage and supply columns. A shipping element has also been included for the transportation of a modest 14 days reserve of grain for men and animals, adding a further 1,700 tons and 1,000 tons respectively to the loading manifest. A small cargo boat, of a type which could have been adapted for a shipment of this nature, has been recovered from the river mud at Blackfriars in the City of London.[23] It was a small, shallow draughted, sailing ship, over 50 feet long, with a beam of 22 feet, a capacious cargo hold and a burthen of a little under 100 tons. It was built of massive beams, with caulked planking upon a ribbed skeleton and its constructions date, broadly estimated by the discovery of a coin dated late 1st century AD beneath the stepping of its mast, was in the area of early 2nd century AD.

The high percentage error in calculating such logistical detail without firm information about Roman custom in these matters has already

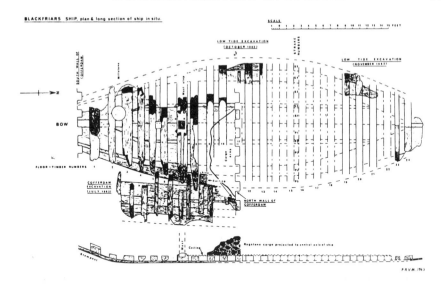

15. Roman river transport: this barge was preserved in the Thames mud for nearly 2,000 years. It once carried goods on the lower reaches of the river.

TABLE II
The Task Force: Estimated Shipping Requirement

Serial		Notes	Men	Animals	Shipping Requirement	Summary: Transport Animals	
1.	*Cavalry*						
	a. 10 regiments		5,000	5,000	167	*Baggage*	
	b. Transport					Cavalry	625
	(i) baggage	A	500	625		Legions	2856
	(ii) rations	B		375	33	Auxilia	1875
		C					———
							5156
2.	*Legions*					*Rations*	
	a. Cavalry		500	500	17	Cavalry	375
	b. Artillery/carts	D	750	1,000	34	Legions	1594
	c. Infantry		20,000	–	250	Auxilia	1125
	d. Transport	A					———
	(i) Baggage	B	2,125	2,656	142		3094
	(ii) Rations	C		1,594			
						Total	8250
3.	*Auxiliaries*						
	a. Infantry		15,000	–	188		
	b. Transport						
	(ii) baggage	A	1,500	1,875	100		
	(ii) rations	B		1,125			
		C					
4.	*Grain Reserves* *plus* other rations for one fortnight				2		
	TOTAL	E	———	———	———		
			45,375	14,750	933		

Notes:
A. Based upon a scale of eight men per tent: in administrative areas there was some sharing between night and day duties, thus allowing economies: these are not shown.
B. Based upon 3 lbs of grain per man per day: also sufficient transport has been allowed to reach units in forward positions, two days' march inland. Mule load, 160 lbs per animal.
C. Mules are unlikely to have been droved but would almost certainly have had handlers: these have been allocated on scale of one for two mules. Rations and bedding are assumed to be top-loaded, in the custom of the universal soldier.
D. Manpower allocated on the basis of one driver per cart, two gunners per *carroballistae*, doing the driver's duties.
E. Based upon a fighting strength of: Cavalry 5,000, Legions 20,000, Auxiliaries 15,000. *Total* 40,000.

been mentioned. The aim of Table II is to give some indication of the size of the bulk shipping requirement but much has been knowingly omitted from inclusion, such as the numbers travelling with the headquarters staff, including the units manning the heavy weapons supporting the army, remount animals, reserve supplies, technicians and a plethora of other things and people essential to the well-being of a military force in the field. Some of these have been discussed in Appendix C. Thus, although Table II shows a demand for 933 vessels, the final figure would probably have been nearer 1,000, providing roughly for: cavalry, 200 ships: infantry, 500 ships: headquarters staff, artillery and heavy baggage, 300 ships. In view of the fact that this army was sailing with conquest in mind, this number is fairly comparable with the size of the fleet which carried Caesar to Britain in BC 54: this, he recorded, numbered 'more than 800 ships, if one includes those which had survived last year's expedition and some privately owned vesels'.[24] Doubtless some privately owned vessels also sailed with Plautius.

In the above estimates of the numbers of transport animals needed for the invasion, sufficient animals have only been allowed to carry forward a daily grain ration to an army of 35,000 men, assuming them to be two days' march from the beach-head. Table III demonstrates the accelerating demand for transport which would have confronted the Roman commissariat as the task force penetrated further and further beyond this point. It should be emphasised that these figures represent only a daily lift of one day's rations, which replaces the one just consumed, and permit no margin for the necessary establishment of a forward supply dump, which would have been required not only for administrative but also tactical reasons. It is evident that the size of the increasing daily lift, with the transport needs required to set up forward depots, would have placed an intolerable burden on the supply system, which would quickly have become inoperable unless the Roman commander had been prepared to sacrifice his principle of total independence of supply during the opening stages of the campaign, or his mobility. As we will see in the ensuing chapters, he would appear to have done neither and one must assume that he found an alternative solution, namely the use of riverways and coastal waters. These had probably already been well reconnoitred by Roman traders, with their Gallic partners, as they conducted their business in Britain. A fleet of suitable rivercraft was thus an additional requirement which Plautius would have had to pre-arrange and bring with him for early use.

Transporting an army in such a large number of ships as we have considered in Table II would at any time have made great demand upon the organisational ability of the planning staff: in this instance, when

TABLE III
Mules for Ration Lift
(Note A)

Days march	Distance (miles)	Basic mule lift (NOTE B)	Muleteers required (NOTE C)	Ration mules for muleteers	Mule reserve (NOTE D)	Total Mule lift (NOTE E)
	10	656	219	5	33	694
day 1	20	1312	437	10	66	1388
	30	1968	656	15	100	2083
day 2	40	2624	875	20	134	2778
	50	3380	1127	25	170	3575
day 3	60	3936	1312	30	200	4166
etc						

Notes: A. One day's ration for 35,000 men at scale of 3 lbs per man per day or 105,000 lbs.
   B. Calculated at rate of 160 lbs per mule.
   C. Three mules per handler.
   D. 5 per cent of total, to allow for sickness etc.
   E. It should be noted that these totals only represent one day's ration lift and that allowance is made for mules returning to their start point unladen.

disembarkation was purposed upon a hostile shore, meticulous planning would have been required to ensure that units and formations sailed in fighting groups, that these were held together when at sea and that, upon nearing their objective, clear instructions had been issued so that disembarkation would take place in an orderly sequence. It was also essential that the soldiers of the legions, cavalry regiments and auxiliary cohorts, making their way ashore through the surf, should also understand the system which enabled them to sort themselves out with speed under their appropriate eagles and standards. This did not always happen, as Caesar recorded of his first expedition to Britain in BC 55, when the confusion was such that his soldiers[25]

> could not keep their ranks . . . or follow their proper standards, and men from different ships fell in under the first standard they came across and great confusion resulted.

It is possible to imagine from these words that, even in those early days, the Roman flair for military administration had already contrived the sort of beachmaster's organisation which played such an important part in the Normandy landings of 1944: but the standards of the legions provided more than just a rallying point in battle, for they could be handled in such a manner as to pass orders on the battlefield to formations and units, so that predetermined battle drills might be initiated. The attention of everybody concerned was attracted to the orders thus being passed by a series of calls upon the *cornu*, a musical instrument[26] with a distinctive note, which alerted commanders to look inwards towards the standard. This system of signalling and communicating, which was probably augmented at sea by the mast head display

16. The horn-blower (*cornicen*) played an important part on the battlefield, for a blast on it alerted soldiers to look to their standard for signalled orders.

of the appropriate formation emblem, could be adapted to most circumstances but, of course, depended upon a high state of training in its use. It must have proved most useful during a seaborne landing, to enable units to shake out into their operational groupings before hitting the beach or to reinforce success or lessen failure once they were ashore.

The Britons had none of the administrative or technical facilities of their opponents, nor did they possess the military knowledge or weaponry which enabled the Romans to achieve such high standards of proficiency on the battlefield. Indeed, the rank and file of their army generally fought without the protection of armour.[27] Tacitus commented that those defending Caratacus' final position against assault by Scapula[28] wore 'neither breastplates or helmets'. It is not easy to believe, however, that the southern tribes of Britain, the descendants of leaders like Commius, Caesar's famous ally and cavalryman, had not learnt the administrative and military benefits of being organised in companies and regiments.

Physically, the Britons were more than a match for their enemy – even Caesar had to admit that the Gauls were critical of the small stature of his men – and they possessed a natural, if reckless, zest for single combat. Diodorous Siculus, writing about their kinsmen across the Channel, described how, in the very midst of feasting, they would suddenly rise from the table and, with little provocation and without regard for their lives, would 'fall to with their swords'. Ammianus Marcellinus similarly left a vivid picture when he wrote[29] that they were

> of lofty nature, fair and of ruddy complexion: terrible from the sternness of their eyes, very quarrelsome and of great pride and insolence.

Dash and gallantry they possessed in abundance and logistically they had much in their favour, for they were operating from internal lines of communication and had few problems of supply: but they were sadly lacking in organisational ability and tenacity of purpose. In their defence, it must be said that many of their difficulties arose from the lack of a standing army, led by a professional officer cadre. Julius Caesar, always quick to appreciate a military weakness in his enemy, underlined some of the problems which bedevilled the assembly of a tribal host, when describing the manner in which the Gallic army assembled to oppose his conquest of Alesia in BC 51.[30] He commented

> ... they were afraid that, in such a mixed host, they would be unable to control their contingents or keep them separate, or to

organise an adequate supply of corn . . . (and when the host) had been gathered in the country of the Aedui, a start was made with the task of reviewing and counting them and choosing officers.

The army of Britons opposing Plautius must have experienced comparably the same difficulties of organisation; and, despite the firm leadership which may have been expected of Caratacus and Togodumnus, it is easy to imagine the jealousy and dissension amongst tribesmen of such natural arrogance and individuality, upon the appointment of field commanders. Nevertheless, the British had three dominant factors operating in their favour. They had, or should have had, control over locally produced stocks of food, although these were possibly at a low level: they had an intimate knowledge of the ground – the forests, the marshes and the hidden trackways – over which the campaign was about to be fought: and, although their use had been abandoned in Gaul long before Caesar's time, they possessed the mobility of a powerful force of chariots,[31] in addition to some cavalry, an arm which, although comparatively new to the British, had been generally adopted by their continental brethren for many years. These military assets, properly employed and combined with their native fighting skills, should have produced a guerrilla army of formidable quality: but, as

17. A reconstruction of a Welsh war chariot, 1st century AD.

will be seen, despite a gallant effort, circumstances and the highly professional quality of their Roman enemy did not allow this to happen.

There was one other matter of prime logistical importance which would have had to be determined by Plautius before the fleet set sail from Boulogne: this concerned the arrangements to be made for the reconstitution of friendly government as the various tribal territories occupied by the Catuvellauni were 'liberated' by his advancing troops. The sooner that friendly administrations could be established, the less need there would be to leave garrisons behind to police these areas, thus denuding the army of its valuable, superbly trained manpower; but perhaps of even greater consequence would have been the help thus given to the Romans by the release of local food resources. There were almost certainly many British refugees on the continent at this time who would have been only too eager to return home to help in this manner and re-establish themselves within their community, under Roman influence. One of these may have been Verica of the Atrebates, whose West Sussex kingdom was one of the last to fall to Caratacus. Another may have been the exiled brother of Togodumnus and Caratacus, Adminius, who had ruled over an area of north-east Kent before being banished abroad by his father and brothers. Yet another was Cogidubnus, about whom we shall hear much more, a young and ambitious man, possibly a *protégé* of Claudius, who emerged from the shadows at this moment to become one of the great characters of ancient British history. Tacitus[32] referred to him as an instrument of domination, and one could not wish for a clearer definition of the role he was destined to fill, in helping to establish Roman sovereignty.

There can be little doubt that the Roman military planners must have given careful thought to this latter aspect of their work for, without some previously planned form of civilian administration of this nature, the momentum of their campaign could not have been so vigorously sustained, as appears to have been the case, after the successful completion of its initial stage. The choice of civil administrators to fill these political posts would not have been haphazard: much would have depended upon their connections and influence in the territories behind the beaches about to be invaded. The beaches in their turn would have been selected because they were operationally and logistically the most suitable sites, which offered the greatest promise of success. The civil administrator appointed by the Romans thus had a dual task to perform; he had the responsibility of restoring stable government and easing the administrative difficulties of the Roman forces, which could so easily have crippled their operational plan.

CHAPTER THREE

THE LANDINGS IN KENT

'In the conduct of war as a whole, and in every military operation, it is essential to select and define the aim clearly . . . whatever the ultimate aim, each phase of the campaign and each separate operation, must be directed towards the achievement of the final result and must have a more limited aim of its own.'

A Principle of War.

The Britons had been kept well informed by their friends in Gaul of the assembly at Boulogne of the invasion force, and an army, raised from a confederation of tribes had been mustered in the neighbourhood of the Kent coast under the joint leadership of Togodumnus and Caratacus. At this stage news was received from the continent that the legions had mutinied; they had come to regard Britain as a mysterious island verging on the supernatural, and had refused to embark when ordered to do so by Aulus Plautius. The British tribesmen, encouraged by this intelligence, relaxed their vigilance and retired inland, many probably dispersing to their homes; as a result, a sudden change of heart by the Roman troops, brought about by the persuasive eloquence of Narcissus, found them totally unprepared and unable to reassemble in time to oppose the enemy landing on the beaches. Dio Cassius[1] relates that, their troubles overcome, Aulus Plautius' task force then set sail in three divisions

to avoid the delays in landing which might be occasioned by the ferrying over of a single force . . . they landed on the island without opposition, for the reports which reached the Britons had led them to suppose they would not come – consequently they had not mustered. Even at this stage they declined to meet them in the field, but took refuge in the swamps and forests, hoping in this way so to wear them down that they would sail away with nothing achieved – precisely as had happened in the case of Caesar. Aulus Plautius therefore had much trouble in making contact with them.

47

18.   A detachment of XX Legion prepare to attack.

This very slender description of the opening phase of the campaign is the only full historical account which has been handed down to us: it may be thought to provoke more questions than it provides answers but at least some of the answers are to be uncovered by considering the factors which would have influenced the decision-making of the respective generals. Others are to be revealed in the background of the years which led up to the landings.

Events in Britain in the decades immediately preceding the arrival of the Romans in AD 43, and the tactics employed at that time by their general staff, may both be linked to the wars waged in Germany by Augustus (31 BC–AD 14) and by Tiberius (AD 14–37), a generation later. The Emperor Augustus viewed with distrust the size and undoubted military ability of the Teutonic tribes inhabiting the northern bank of the river Rhine. The course of the river provided the north-western frontier of Imperial Rome and it was his opinion that it could only be properly secured from outside aggression by the occupation, and consequent control, of the tribal territories which stood upon its far bank. The Teutons both resented and resisted his intrusion and in 16 BC Augustus hastened to the border to set in hand preparations for a campaign which, despite considerable military exertions by the Romans, was to create a prolonged drain upon their resources and show very little success. Augustus' policy received a severe blow in AD 9 when Quinctilius Varus was disastrously defeated in a battle in the Teutoburg Forest[2] when according to Suetonius,[3] three legions with their commanders and all their auxiliaries were massacred. It is noteworthy that it was about this same time that the Catuvellauni finally abrogated the agreement which Cassivellaunus had made with Julius Caesar and struck against their neighbours, the Trinovantes, occupying their capital at *Camulodunum* (Colchester). It would be pure conjecture to suggest that Cunobelin of the Catuvellauni took advantage of this moment of Roman disarray in north-west Europe to attack their allies in south-east Britain, whom they had been assiduously cultivating for many years, or that Augustus' apparent acceptance of the fact could be accounted for by his heavy involvement in the Rhineland, with his consequent inability to commit himself elsewhere. It is, nevertheless, a thought which should not be lightly rejected.

These grinding wars of attrition north of the Rhine continued well into the reign of Tiberius until Germanicus, the father of Gaius Caligula, perceiving that successive expeditions were making little headway, resolved upon a change of tactics in AD 16 and, appreciating that the sea provided a better route into the German interior than the traditional one across the Rhine, he led a seaborne invasion of a thousand ships and defeated his enemy in two major battles. It was a bloody and merciless episode, when the Cheruscii were relentlessly slaughtered and the Angrivarii surrendered unconditionally and received an 'unqualified pardon'.[4] At the end of the campaigning season, Germanicus despatched a part of his victorious army overland to their winter quarters south of the Rhine and embarked with the remaining force on the fleet transports which were awaiting his arrival, anchored on the river Ems. When the fleet had set sail it was hit by a storm of extraordinary violence and, propelled by a tidal surge and gale force winds, it was swept out to sea, where it suffered great loss. The scene has been graphically described by Tacitus:[5]

> Horses, baggage, animals, even arms, were jettisoned to lighten the ships as they leaked at the joints and were deluged by waves. The North Sea is the roughest in the world, and the German climate is the worst. The disaster was proportionately terrible – indeed it was unprecedented. On one side were enemy coasts, on the other a sea so huge and deep, that it is held to be the uttermost, with no land beyond. Some ships went down. Others, more numerous, were cast on to remote islands . . . (some men) had been carried on to Britain and were sent back by its chieftains. Men coming from these remote regions told strange stories – of hurricanes, unknown birds, sea-monsters, and shapes half-human and half-animal, which they had seen or in their terror had imagined.

As a result of this calamity, and despite the optimism of Germanicus that he had found a winning solution for a problem which had existed for so long, Rome abandoned its plans of conquest beyond the Rhine for, as Tiberius explained, there had been enough successes and enough misfortune; it was an event not easily forgotten by the Roman soldiery who, for a generation, were to regard naval expeditions in northern waters with nervous suspicion.

Germanicus' final victories north of the Rhine were therefore dimmed by the culminating sea disaster, which had nothing to do with the campaign itself: he had found a means of penetrating deep into German territory and of shortening his always vulnerable lines of communication, which were greedy of manpower to guard them. This fact, together with the campaign experience of the Imperial Army gained whilst operating in small boats on the river Danube, will have impressed itself on the Roman general staff responsible for planning the later Claudian invasion of Britain. They could not fail to have observed that the river Thames, already noted by Julius Caesar as a major waterway providing access far into the interior of Britain, also penetrated the heart of the lands occupied by the Catuvellauni. The question for the military planners of the assault landing, therefore, was not so much whether they could use the river Thames for their purpose, but how it could be employed to gain maximum advantage. It may be simple coincidence that, when appointed to command the task force, Aulus Plautius was Governor of Illyricum in the Danube area, with considerable experience of water-borne operations and associated supply problems, and that IX Legion *Hispana* had been on continuous operations there since being transferred from Spain some time about AD 9. On the other hand, these facts could provide a clear indication of the direction in which the campaign was destined to move. Before we examine this possibility further it is necessary to consider the other factors which will have influenced the commanding general's decisions, not the least of these being the aim he was hoping to achieve.

It is remarkable that, despite the obviously careful planning of the three Roman landings in Britain, particularly Caesar's second expedition and the Claudian invasion of AD 43, their intentions should have been allowed to remain matters of so much conjecture. Especially is it surprising in Caesar's case, for he was a brilliant soldier, gifted with a flair for the written word, who might have been expected not to have left his actions to be a matter of speculation by future military generations. Claudius' biographer, Suetonius, provides very little guidance in his explanation[6] that the emperor's

> sole campaign was of no great importance. The Senate had already voted him triumphal regalia but he thought it beneath his dignity to accept these and decided that Britain was the country where a real

triumph could most rapidly be earned. Its conquest had not been
attempted since Julius Caesar's day . . .

In the absence of the missing chapters of the Annals of Tacitus, we are
compelled to turn once again to the Narrative of Dio Cassius[7] to
discover another reason. He tells us simply that

> Aulus Plautius, a very highly-considered senator, led an army into
> Britain. For a certain Bericus, chased out of the island by revolt,
> persuaded Claudius to despatch a force thither.

Today we have the benefit of hindsight, chiefly provided by the
considerable amount of information produced by twentieth century
archaeologists, together with what Dio tells, and we now know that the
main Roman assault came ashore in the broad vicinity of Richborough:
that the legions, after one or two brief skirmishes with the Britons led
by Togodumnus and Caratacus, defeated them in two major battles at
Rochester and at the crossing of the Thames: that the legions paused at
the Thames crossing to await the arrival of the emperor, Claudius, who
then led them to seize the enemy capital of *Camulodunum* (Colchester):
and that the legions then fanned out for a prolonged final phase – II
Legion under Vespasian to commence the conquest of the south-west,
XIV Legion to advance along the axis of what was to become Watling
Street and IX Legion to advance towards Lincoln and the Humber –
until by about AD 47 the Roman advance had stabilised along a
south-west to north-easterly line, which was to take physical shape as
the Fosse Way, the earliest Roman frontier road in Britain. AD 47 also
marked the end of the tour of duty of Aulus Plautius, with his
consequent return to Rome, where he was granted the honour of being
the last recipient to celebrate an ovation. It thus seems fair to suggest
that Plautius' arrival on the Fosse Way, and his transfer back to Rome
to be suitably honoured, signified that Claudius' immediate ambitions
in Britain had been achieved.

The accomplishment of the military aim, which presumably was
directed towards the prime intention of destroying the armed force of
the Catuvellauni, the subjection of the Durotriges and seizing for Rome
all territories under the influence of these two tribes, was not so
satisfactorily completed. The momentum of the Roman advance from
the Kentish coast must inevitably have been curtailed by the enforced
pause, it is estimated for a period of about six weeks, whilst awaiting
the arrival of Claudius. It is inconceivable that Plautius did not make
good use of this time but, nevertheless, it is possible that, because of this
period of waiting, the British were granted a respite which resulted in

19. A line of legionaries advance to attack with drawn sword. Note the shield boss which was also an effective weapon in a melee and the auxiliary soldiers deployed to protect their flank.

the escape of Caratacus from the Roman grasp, perhaps with a part of his army, to wage an energetic guerrilla war against them until his capture in AD 51. Worse still, if Claudius' presence during the ten days of his command of the army in Britain is judged a purely political gesture to enable his participation in the victorious entry into *Camulo-dunum*, then it may be that this preconceived, apparently inflexible plan for his arrival may well have affected the decision-making of his field commander at a vital moment in the progress of the campaign. The ultimate fate of Caratacus was already determined but his flight and subsequent actions enmeshed the Imperial Army in a costly continuation of the war beyond the planned bounds of its newly established frontier. If this did not impair the tidy victory sought by Claudius, it left a taste of unfinished business.

The ground, over which the initial stages of the invasion were fought, dictated the course of the battle: and the selection of Richborough as an important tactical feature and subsequent supply base is of special significance. It is arguable whether it was then a promontory connected to the mainland by a causewayed approach or whether it was an island: there is no doubt that at a later date the Romans constructed a causeway to it and the remains of this have been uncovered at the nearby Fleet Farm.[8] Richborough stands today, two miles inland, an impressive and weather-beaten ruin, surrounded by marshland which once formed the bed of a inland waterway known to the Romans as *Portus Rutupis*. The Saxons later gave it the name Wantsum to illustrate its decreasing size, for it was fast being filled with silt from the Thames estuary and from the Great and Little Stour rivers which flowed into it. The Wantsum Channel at the time of the Roman landings separated the Isle of Thanet from the mainland of Kent and provided the means by which a regular shipping trade was conducted, in one direction inland up the river Thames and, in the other, across the Straits of Gaul to Europe, thus sparing the small craft of the day the danger of venturing beyond the estuary, into the often turbulent waters of the North Sea. It had two entrances, one on the North Kent coast, known as Northmouth, whence it pursued a southerly course to a point level with the village of Sarre on the Thanet shore and with Chislet on the mainland. From there it turned easterly in a dog-leg fashion towards its second and major entrance, which allowed access to and from the narrow seas of the Gallic Straits (see map on page 62). The high ground of Richborough, with its sweeping view along the Wantsum valley to Sarre, dominated this approach from its position almost astride the channel. It also overlooked the wide, sheltered anchorage which lay between it and Stonar Beach, an eight-mile finger of land which jutted southwards from Thanet. On the southern extremity of this promontory, opposite Richborough, at one time stood the town of Stonar, finally destroyed by the French in 1385. It came into prominence during the late Roman period, when it replaced the island as a port, after the latter had silted up and become inoperable. It may thus be conjectured that the town had an earlier existence, perhaps traceable to AD 43.

It is not necessary to search far to demonstrate the importance of Richborough to the Roman administration for, outside its western gate, one of the great roads constructed by them to open up the British hinterland, Watling Street, began its journey towards the Thames crossing, possibly at Westminster, and thence north-westwards across the Midlands to Chester; and the island was used by them to the full to provide a variety of buildings and facilities, including an Amphitheatre. The harbour and the docks in its north-west corner were almost certainly used as a naval base by their fleet, the *Classis Britannica*, a force with a mainly logistical role due to the lack of naval opposition in northern Europe; and the large, first century granaries uncovered in recent times, also serve to underline the standing of the port as the heart of a vital road, river and sea network. The early military earthworks relating to the invasion which have been found on Richborough, on the other hand, are not extensive and are estimated to cover an area of some ten acres. Bushe-Fox[9] has calculated that this space would have accommodated some 2,500 men and has concluded, from the condition of the ditches, that the

> . . . earthwork was without doubt formed as a temporary defence
> to cover the disembarkation of the troops at the time of the

20. Aerial view of the Fort at Richborough, showing early features inside the walls of the later Saxon Shore Fort. The river in the left foreground is now all that remains of the Wantsum Channel.

invasion and to serve as a protection for the ships drawn up on the
shore during the initial stages of the campaign in AD 43. There is
no evidence of a heavy occupation at this period, and only a small
detachment may have been in garrison there: it may even have been
left derelict for many years.

The importance of these remarks lies in the fact that research has
revealed no evidence of a heavy military occupation at the time of the
invasion and that the defences erected upon the island during the initial
landings were of a purely temporary nature and were soon to be
abandoned. These thoughts are in line with the military fact that the
seizure of Richborough, and the occupation by the invasion fleet of the
Stonar anchorage and the waters of the Wantsum Channel, would be
sterile victories if either the island itself, or the southern part of Thanet,
or indeed both these areas, lay in hostile hands. We may be certain that
Aulus Plautius, who will have been well aware of the disastrous naval
losses inflicted upon Julius Caesar by the unpredictable weather of the
south coast, will have wished to get his fleet and transports into a safe
harbour at the earliest moment; he may thus be expected to have given
the highest priority to gaining possession of both these places. His first
troops ashore will have been given the task of taking hold of these vital
areas of ground and putting them into a defensive position, whilst
pushing forward on to the neighbouring mainland with mixed cavalry
and infantry fighting patrols to gain information of the whereabouts of
the Britons. He may be expected, almost simultaneously, to have
tightened his grip on the Wantsum Channel, which as a shipping route
was to play an important role in his future operations by taking
possession of the remaining, larger part of Thanet and establishing
military control of the northern mouth of the Wantsum, where it
entered the Thames estuary. This last possibility is becoming increasingly confirmed by archaeological research at *Regulbium* (Reculver), which is producing clear evidence of defensive pairs of ditches,
similar to those at Richborough, relating to this period and covering an
area of at least one acre;[10] that is to say, providing for a garrison of
about 250 men.

Whilst these preparatory moves were being conducted, Plautius will
have begun the task of setting up his supply organisation where space
existed to handle the large number of vessels involved, the quantities of
supplies brought by them and the inevitable redistribution of these once
the task force had disembarked and reformed. It is not impossible that
the organisation created for this purpose provided the much debated
origins of Stonar, where discoveries of 'coins, urns, swords, axes,
portions of armour and human remains' have testified to a considerable

21. The twin towers of the ancient church at Reculver mark the site of an early Roman fort dating from 1st century AD.

Roman presence.[11] In this locality, where vessels entered the calm waters of the Channel from the sea, an administrative base of this nature would have been ideally sited for the control of shipping, receiving and redirecting it according to need along the length of the Wantsum to Reculver, and thence to the Thames. It is conceivable that the importance of Richborough at this moment was not its value as the thriving port and supply base it was later to become, so much as the defensive features it had to offer and the access to the mainland which it could provide.

The mainland of Kent, at the time of the coming of the Romans, offered little choice of route to an invader thrusting inland. To the south-west of the county, where today the Romney Marshes and the

Isle of Oxney may be found, a large shallow bay swept inland, with its mouth reaching from Romney to Fairlight. This entrance was partially blocked by large sand bars and lengthy beds of shingle, through which the river Rother had carved for itself a passage. Two other rivers, the Tillingham and the Brede, also flowed into the bay, all of them carrying alluvial mud which in due course was to choke the inlet and create the flat, marshy land which now lies behind Dungeness. At high tides the creeks and mud flats were covered by sea water, the greatest depth, paradoxically, being nearest to the shore line. On the rising ground, behind these extensive, coastal marshes, stood the great oak forest of Andredsweald, dense, and if not impenetrable, at least formidable and sparsely populated, the name itself meaning 'the wood where nobody dwells.' This reached inland for a depth of several miles before it met the dry, partially wooded, chalk hills which today we call the North Downs. Along the length of this feature, which sweeps for 120 miles in a great arc from west Surrey to south-east Kent, and terminates in the foothills overlooking the ford on the Great Stour where Canterbury now stands, ran a trackway ancient even in those times. In the medieval period this came to be known as The Pilgrim's Way. This was undoubtedly one of the major trackways in the southern half of Britain, not only because of its value as a trading route but primarily because it linked with the six great ridges of high land, themselves ancient trackways, which radiate from Salisbury Plain. It evolved over a period of time along the southern slopes of the Downs since these, being exposed to the rays of the sun, provided drier walking; but the Roman engineers made no use of its existence when laying out Watling Street on the opposing, northern flank of the North Downs, possibly because the route they selected provided the straightest line from Canterbury, through Rochester, to London, or possibly because this flank gave ready access to their supply train on the river Thames.

The south-eastern extremity of the North Downs, lying between Rochester and Canterbury, a distance of 25½ miles, was thus an area of high military value. Moreover, at the time of the landings in AD 43, it had been politically transformed from the Kent discovered by Caesar, who had found the people of *Cantium* divided in four tribes, frequently racked by inter-tribal strife but, as he learnt to his cost, capable of sinking their differences in time of common danger. In about the year AD 10, Cunobelin of the Catuvellauni seized control of all Belgic territory in south-east Britain and engulfed *Cantium* in the process, sweeping away old tribal boundaries and bringing a period of political stability. Even before this occurrence, this corner of Britain had been a prosperous area, as Caesar described[12] when he wrote that the coast was inhabited by Belgic immigrants

22.   Emblem of XX Legion *Valeria* displaying a boar which was its
symbol.

who came to plunder and make war . . . and later settled down to
till the soil. The population is very large, the ground thickly studded
with homesteads, closely resembling those of the Gauls, and the
cattle very numerous . . . By far the most civilised inhabitants are
those living in Kent . . .

The peaceful conditions created by Cunobelin's unification of the tribes
brought about the abandonment of the old tribal strongholds and a
large Belgic settlement grew up, apparently undefended, astride the ford
in the Stour valley. This was *Durovernum* which eventually became the
capital of the *Cantiaci*, having acquired a preference over Rochester,
despite the latter's commanding position at the mouth of the river
Medway. The accessibility of *Durovernum*, which provided the origins
of the modern City of Canterbury, at the centre of a road, river and sea

communications system, was doubtless a deciding factor in this choice although there is some thought that, due to silting of the river, the mantle of port at this time may have been passed to Fordwich, two miles downstream. By the seventeenth century, the Great Stour was not navigable above this point, due to the number of mills built upon it although, according to Sumner,[13] boats and lighters were still carrying coals and stones from Sandwich to Canterbury in 1699. Whether one accepts that port facilities were available at Canterbury or a short distance away at Fordwich when Plautius landed in Kent, it is most unlikely that he would not have made the fullest use of them at either place, in preference to Richborough twelve miles away particularly since *Durovernum*, upon its surrender, would have become a key civil and military administrative centre possibly under the returned exile, Adminius. For a more mundane, but nevertheless practical reason, an overland supply lift over these twelve miles would have been an unnecessary and wasteful use of his animal transport resources if the river route was available. *Durovernum* was thus an important first objective for the Roman general, after coming ashore with his main assault force and passing through his nearby, securely established and unchallenged bridgehead at Richborough.

Dio's Narrative gives no indication of the length of time it took the Britons to get a force into the field to harass the legions, slow their advance and gain time for their main host to assemble west of the Medway; but it is clear that both Caratacus and Togodumnus led parties against Plautius during the early stage of his advance. Both these sons of Cunobelin were masters of the art of guerilla warfare and, although they must have been commanding hastily raised, scratch forces, they probably struck hard at the Roman lines of communication, as Cassivellaunus had done before them. It is possible, by reading between the lines of Dio's somewhat plaintive commentary on the events,[14] to judge that the Britons enjoyed some degree of success before rejoining their main force assembled on the Medway. Whether they fled, as Dio records, or simply withdrew, as is equally possible, they would appear to have gained the time they sought, although they may well have been roughly handled in the process. Indeed, it may have been this experience which influenced a Dobunnic contingent to surrender: alternatively, the capture of *Durovernum* by the Romans may have persuaded them that the time had come to lay down their arms and gain the best possible terms for their tribe, for they had no binding loyalty to the Catuvellauni, who had absorbed their lands as a client kingdom upon the death of Cunobelin.

If Dio's Narrative gives no information about the resistance of the British to the initial landings of the Romans, it is equally uninformative

23. Tablet with the emblems of II Legion *Augusta*, found at Benwell, Northumberland (see Appendix C).

about the Roman movements, other than to state, as has already been quoted, that[15]

> ... they sailed in three divisions to avoid the delays in landing which might be occasioned by the ferrying over of a single force ...

On the face of it, these words merely record a shrewdly planned phased arrival but they have been interpreted by many experts to indicate three separate assault landings. One, for example, discusses the possibility that a special battle group may have been despatched simultaneously to West Sussex, to reinstate upon his throne the elderly Verica, recently living in Rome under the protection of Claudius as a refugee from Caratacus.[16] Another argues that, to save time and distract resistance, the army landed at three different points, in the natural harbours of Dover and Lympne, as well as the main landing place on Thanet.[17] A third considers the possibility that a decoy force may have been despatched to Dover.[18] On the other hand, Professor Frere expresses the opinion that no general would have dispersed his army initially in this way and there are good grounds for agreeing with this viewpoint.[19] With the obvious lack of information which existed about the whereabouts of the British forces, it would have been imprudent of the commanding general to have risked a secondary landing until a secure foothold had been established by the main force, particularly since his objective was clear. The failure of such a landing would have been intolerable: moreover, the military and administrative organisation required to sustain it would have added greatly to the problems of command and control and would drastically have reduced the resources and effort available to the main operation. Under these circumstances, it must be doubtful that any force with the task of carrying out a secondary landing sailed from Boulogne with the invasion fleet, as an integral part of that operation. Equally, it is barely conceivable that a decoy force was employed since this could only hope for success if the location of the British enemy were known and if it was enabled to make its demonstration off the coast in daylight hours. Dio's Narrative suggests that Aulus Plautius, following the example of Julius Caesar on his earlier expeditions, sailed at night time with the expectations of a dawn arrival, thus achieving a surprise landing. The appearance of a decoy force might have had the reverse effect of destroying this tactic.

Finally, it is impossible fully to discuss the implications of Dio's 'three divisions' without giving consideration to the comparative strengths of the opposing armies and the influence this would have had on the ability of Plautius to fragment his strike force in this way. Due to the lack of any hard evidence on this subject it is again necessary to look for guidance to the decisions and experiences of Julius Caesar.

In 55 BC Caesar's invasion force comprised two legions, with one *ala* of cavalry and possibly some auxiliary infantry. As has already been said, he had not come to stay, he intended to live off the land, he had to provide himself with a force to defend his bridgehead and administrative base but he did not intend to penetrate deep into the hinterland and thus create the need to defend a lengthy line of supply and communication. His arrival was opposed by local Kentish tribes, whose leaders he named later as Cingetorix, Carvilius, Taximagalus and Legovax;[20] additionally, these may have received support from neighbouring territories but there is no evidence to suggest this.

Caesar returned in the following year with five legions, cavalry and supporting troops, with the intention of being self-sufficient in foodstuffs and supplies and, as it transpired, with the aim of establishing friendly links with the Trinovantes. He thus now had the need of a military strength which would be adequate, not only to defend the supply and harbour area within his bridgehead, but also to provide garrisons along the 75 mile line of communication from the coast to the Thames crossing place, where he entered the territory of the Catuvellauni.[21] The bridgehead guard, in Caesar's words, comprised ten cohorts and 300 cavalry; that is to say, its numbers compared with a legion in strength and could possibly have been provided by allied contingents, or by withdrawing two cohorts from each of the five legions under command. By this method Caesar could have allocated a legion (less two cohorts) to secure his river crossing place, after he had moved deeper into Catuvellaunian territory, and another to garrison his rear echelons. Once again the Roman landings were contested by the local Kentish tribes but they quickly realised the task was too great for them to handle alone; they buried their tribal differences and called upon Cassivellaunus, a famous war-lord, to help. The latter formed a confederated tribal force to operate north and south of the Thames, which significantly was not joined by the Trinovantes. In essence, the main opposition was provided by the Catuvellauni and the tribes in Kent, who remained within their territory and by their presence posed a constant threat to the Roman administrative base on the coast. In view of its experiences and commitments, the expeditionary force does not seem to have been excessively large.

Plautius sailed to Britain in AD 43 with four legions, supported by cavalry and auxiliary troops; during the period following the initial landings, until stable civil administration had been established, this force was possibly augmented by elements from other legions, with

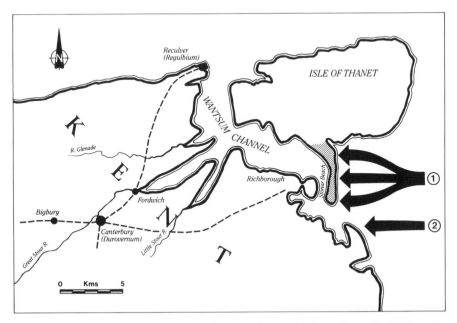

24. The Claudian landings (Phase 1). The first assault wave lands on Stonar Beach (1) as the second approaches Richborough. When this has been seized a harbour area can be safely laid out west of the Stonar Peninsula.

auxiliary cohorts. It was Plautius' intention, as it had been that of Caesar on his second expedition, to be self sufficient in supplies and foodstuffs; he probably resolved his resulting transport problems by operating a waterborne supply route, under the *Classis Britannica*, along the Wantsum channel and the line of the river Thames. Garrisons would still have been required, even by this method, but the animal transport and feed requirement, together with their protective infantry and cavalry screens, would have been greatly reduced. It may be that this measure enabled Plautius to reduce by one legion the strength of the force brought by Caesar and thus lessen an otherwise costly administrative burden. The main opposition to his landing was once again provided by the Catuvellauni but, since the days of Caesar, they had now extended their influence and domination to the territories of the Trinovantes, Atrebates, Dobunni and the Kentish tribes as well as others. In some cases their overlordship had been established for many years and thus, in assessing the strength of the force they fielded, one must assume that all these tribes provided contingents to it, whilst recognising that in some cases their enthusiasm for the task may have been muted. The size of the individual tribal contributions is not easy to estimate but, bearing in mind that they all had their roots in Gaul from

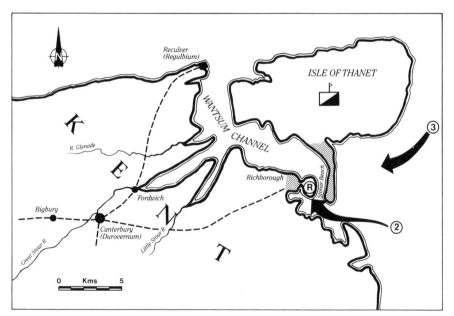

25. The Claudian landings (Phase 2). The bridgehead on Stonar Beach has been consolidated and a harbour area established, whilst the assault force extends its grip on Thanet. The main break-out force (3) is approaching, also carrying stores for the administrative base and heavy equipment.

where some had emigrated only a few generations earlier, it may be fair
to take as a yardstick the numbers provided by the Gallic tribes to the
Belgic uprising in 57 BC.[22] At that time the largest contingent, from the
Bellovaci, numbered 100,000; and the smallest, from the Menapii,
totalled 7,000. On this basis, it may be conjectured that the force raised
by Cunobelin's two sons, Caratacus and Togodumnus, could reasonably have had a strength of 150,000, made up as follows:

Catuvellauni	70,000
Trinovantes	40,000
Atrebates	10,000
Dobunni	7,000
Kentish tribes	23,000
Total	150,000

Webster[23] holds the view that Scapula, in his final battle against
Caratacus, could have coped with odds of four or five to one. If this
proportion is acceptable as a planning basis, although the odds appear
high if success is to be assured, then Plautius should have kept in hand a

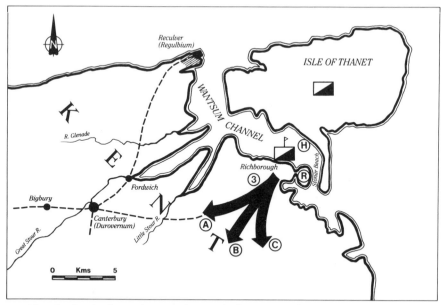

26. The Claudian landings (Phase 3). The main body moves out from the bridgehead. Column A
thrusts for Canterbury, whilst Column B, mainly cavalry, provides flank protection. Column C
heads south to seize Dover for the Roman Navy. When Canterbury has been secured, the main
supply base will move there so as to shorten lines of communication. The Roman Navy occupies
Reculver to complete their control of the Wantsum Channel and establish a presence in the
Thames estuary.

main strike force of 30,000 to 35,000 troops, without taking count of his requirement for troops to guard his lines of communication. When this number is set against the generally accepted estimated strength of the task force (40,000 to 50,000 troops) there seems to have been small scope to fragment the main force to undertake landings outside the immediate operational area.

It is now possible, from the above consideration of the factors which might have affected the military thinking of the Roman general staff, to suggest three operational tasks which would have resulted in the fleet being marshalled in three divisions, as stated by Dio Cassius:

First Division (bridgehead force)
a. To secure the harbour area between the Stonar peninsula and Richborough, by seizing both Richborough and Stonar Beach, and placing both in a defensive position.
b. To exploit in force from both these positions,
   (i) in the case of Richborough, to establish a mainland bridgehead and to locate the enemy.
   (ii) in the case of Stonar Beach, to clear the Isle of Thanet of enemy forces.

Second Division (the main assault force)
   To pass through the Richborough bridgehead and capture *Durovernum*.

Third Division (the follow-up force)
   To provide a reserve force and administrative support: to bring heavy weapons, transport and supplies and also to secure the western flank.

It is easy to imagine that the commanding general, whether or not his mind was working on these precise lines, had some very similar plan of operation. The logistical problems of the campaign have been demonstrated, in particular those associated with the landing, and he will have wished to embark his legions, with their supporting weapons, cavalry and supplies, in groups to enable them to carry out their allotted tasks on arrival. The business of embarkation is always one which calls for careful staff work; in this case it will have been magnified by the sheer size of the requirement and the number and miniscule size of the fleet transports. Pre-invasion packing into echelons was therefore essential and the fact that the fleet sailed in three divisions need in no way suggest that each division was sailing for a separate destination. Indeed, the military facts would seem to demand otherwise.

CHAPTER FOUR

THE BATTLE ON THE MEDWAY

Forget not, Roman, that it is your special genius to rule the people;
to impose the ways of peace, to spare the defeated, and to crush
those proud men who will not submit.

Virgil, *Aeneid.*

In order to retrace the course of the campaign which followed after
Plautius's occupation of *Durovernum*, it is necessary once again to
make reference to Dio's Narrative and to consider his account of events
in the light of the facts which must have influenced the tactical
decision-making of the opposing generals. Dio may frequently pose
more questions than he answers but a study of his writings, in the
context of what the battlefield historian, Colonel A. Burne, termed
'inherent military probability', may help to fill some of the gaps.[1]

Aulus Plautius therefore had much trouble in making contact with
them. When he did so, he defeated first Caratacus and then
Togodumnus, the sons of Cunobelinus, who was dead. (At this
period the Britons were not free and independent but ruled by the
kings of other tribes). When these kings had fled he won over by
agreement a portion of the Bodunni,[2] a people dependent upon the
Catuvellauni, thereupon he left a garrison there and continued his
advance. Then he came to a river. The Britons supposed that the
Romans would not be able to cross it without a bridge, and so had
camped carelessly on the opposite bank. He therefore sent across
Gallic troops who were trained to swim with full equipment across
the swiftest of rivers. Surprise was achieved against the enemy by
this attack: but they did not shoot at the men themselves: instead,
wounding the horses that drew their chariots, they made it impossible even for the charioteers to get away in the subsequent confusion. At this point Plautius sent over Vespasian . . . This force also
succeeded in crossing the river, and killing the barbarians, who
were not expecting them. The rest of the British forces did not

66

retreat, however, but remained to fight on the following day. There was an indecisive struggle, but at last Gnaeus Hosidius Geta (after being almost taken prisoner) managed to defeat them . . . Then the Britons fell back from this position on to the River Thames, at a point where it enters the sea and forms a large pool at high tide. Knowing the firm ground and the fords with much precision they crossed the river without difficulty, but the Roman forces were not so successful . . .

Each separate operation, we are instructed by our guiding principle of war, must be directed towards the achievement of the final result and requires to have a more limited aim of its own. Thus in the furtherance of the ultimate objective given to him by Claudius, namely the establishment of a new Roman province in south east Britain, Aulus Plautius may be expected to have divided this task into a number of phases, each to be regarded as a stepping stone to the next. The first of these phases could only have been the occupation and pacification of the territories of the Catuvellauni, including those they had taken by force over the years, lying north and south of the river Thames, and the seizure of their tribal capital of *Camulodunum* (Colchester); but even this self-imposed division was incapable of achievement in one blow, for logistical and geographical reasons. The river Thames provided a substantial obstacle between Plautius and his target, the tribal capital.

27. A detachment of XX Legion on the march.

This necessitated that first he should consolidate his occupation of Kent, in the main the area of the former tribal kingdoms noted by Caesar, by setting up a system of local administration, establishing a supply organisation for his forward troops and tightening his grip on the trackway and river communications which then existed. None of these things could be achieved satisfactorily if his occupation was opposed and continued to be opposed. Thus his primary task, in each phase of his advance to Camulodunum, was to seek out and destroy the enemy forces opposing him; and all his tactical decisions will have been taken with this in mind (but never forgetting Napoleon's dictum that an army marches on its stomach) and with the aim of progressively consolidating his position as he penetrated inland.

The problems created by the mutiny at Boulogne, and the doubts which it must have sown in the minds of the Roman commanders, if not the rank and file, could gravely have diminished the chances of success of the operation. Paradoxically it did otherwise; for, as we have seen, when the news of the unrest amongst the Roman army filtered across the Straits, presumably to the great joy of the Britons, the latter relaxed their guard. This was a vital failure of commission since Caratacus and Togodumnus could not responsibly have considered themselves out of danger until they had received intelligence that the legions assembled for the assault had been dispersed. The result was calamitous for the Britons, for it allowed Aulus Plautius to achieve complete surprise, an important principle of war often sought but rarely achieved in such an unexpected manner and with such success. As a consequence the British leadership lost its best opportunity of repelling the landing force by striking at it in its most vulnerable moment, as it disembarked on the beaches. The military advantage this would have given them has been well described by Caesar,[3] who was faced with a similar situation in 55 BC:

> The Britons of course knew all the shallows: standing on dry land, they watched the men disembark in small parties, galloped down, attacked them as they struggled through the surf, and surrounded them with superior numbers, while others opened fire on the exposed flanks of isolated units . . .

The outcome of Caesar's battle for the beach could have been in serious doubt had it not been for his superb generalship, his pre-battle briefing of his commanders and his complete control of the situation, even though the larger part of his invasion force was still afloat. He had evolved a good ship to ship communication system, supplemented by messages sent by small boat, and by this means he was able to divert units to reinforce success wherever it appeared. As a result of these tactics, he was able after some bitter fighting to clear a sufficient area to form his legions in battle order; when they charged, the Britons were hurled back and the bridgehead was secured.

There were lessons in this engagement for Caratacus and Togodumnus, whose fighting men – proud, fierce, of strong physique[4] and highly mobile, many being expert horsemen and charioteers – were never more dangerous than when the circumstances of the battle, much as in this case, allowed them the full use of their swords. These were slashing weapons, used by cutting them from side to side and whirling them around the head in a sort of chopping motion. This technique of fighting was totally unsuited to the close quarter, cut and thrust formation drill at which the Roman professional soldier was so thoroughly trained and for which he was so well equipped. He was armed with a short, pointed stabbing sword and a rectangular shield, curved to provide maximum protection. The shield was also useful in hand to hand fighting for Tacitus describes[5] how, in one engagement, Batavian auxiliaries assaulted the enemy with the heavy boss of their shields, simultaneously stabbing for the face, whilst advancing in closely packed lines. It was a tactic which required training, discipline and team-work, qualities not always readily apparent in a haphazardly assembled tribal army. The articulated, and rather intricate, form of plate armour worn by the legionaries was particularly well suited for these well rehearsed battle drills but for individual combat its weight may have proved restrictive. The Britons, other than chieftains or wealthy members of the warrior class, wore little if any body armour. They carried light-weight shields and must have been in little doubt of the futility of involving themselves in a set-piece encounter with Plautius, except upon a ground of their own choosing.

Few options thus remained open to Caratacus and Togodumnus and, if at one stage the brothers had felt fully confident they could drive their Roman invaders into the sea should they set foot in Britain, this confidence must have been badly dented when unexpectedly news of the enemy landing was received. It may be assumed that thought of surrender would never have entered their minds; but if it had been their original intention to defend the coastline of Kent, these new circumstances, now that the Romans were ashore, must have compelled them to reassess their position. Their army had already started to disintegrate, and the presence of the *Classis Britannica* in the Thames estuary posed a threat which was directed, not only at their left flank, but disastrously at *Camulodunum* itself. The loss of Kent would be bad enough but if their tribal capital should fall into Roman hands, this could only mean defeat. They withdrew west of the Medway to regroup and decide upon

28. An aerial photograph of the River Medway taken above Strood. The Batavian cohorts probably crossed the water at the top of the picture, concealed by the bends of the river.

their next move but not until both the brothers had had a sharp engagement with the enemy; indeed, it is sometimes suggested that Togodumnus may either have been killed or mortally wounded during this phase of operations.

If news of the Roman landing was not expected by the British leadership, the lack of opposition to his disembarkation must have been equally surprising to the Roman general, although it cannot have disturbed him unduly; on the contrary, it will have given him the opportunity to get his supplies ashore without harassment and to consolidate his position at *Durovernum* by putting a force on to the high ground beyond the river Stour [the garrison, mentioned by Dio, possibly located at Harbledown as Frere suggests,[6]] by establishing a fortified control point at Reculver in the east and by the occupation of Dover in the west, the responsibility for both of which he may immediately have passed to the *Classis Britannica*. In all this, it must not be overlooked that Plautius probably brought with him from the continent Adminius, the fugitive brother of Caratacus and Togodumnus, who had fled overseas only three years earlier to claim the protection of Gaius Caligula. Webster suggests that this prince ruled over the north eastern extremity of Kent[7] and, if this were so, his local influence, combined with his knowledge of people and the terrain, must have been of considerable benefit to Plautius in this preparatory phase. Finally, although the Roman commander would have wanted to maintain the momentum achieved by the capture of *Durovernum*, he would have wished to satisfy himself, before continuing his advance, of the security of his rear echelons, both militarily and politically – a subject to which we will return – and of the efficiency of the supply system to his forward troops. Plautius cannot fail to have noted the harbouring facilities of the Medway and the suitability of *Durobrivae* as a forward supply base. It would not be unreasonable to assume that this was his next objective.

The shortest route to *Durobrivae* from *Durovernum* lay westwards across the low lying land between the Downs and the Swale, a distance as the crow flies of 25 miles, and a saving of some 10 miles for a wayfarer not travelling by the North Downs Way. Margary[8] denies the suggestion, sometimes mooted, that this trackway provided the line for Watling Street and disappeared in its construction: he considers instead that it may well have run a little to the north of the Roman road, along the broad line of Faversham, Sittingbourne and Gillingham to Rochester. It would have had its disadvantages: the opening stage, after crossing the Stour, ran through the Forest of Blean in which, in any event, the Romans would have had to establish their dominance – it was possibly here that one of their early encounters with the Britons occurred – and thence, as it descended to lower ground, it ran into a belt of occasionally wooded, heavy London Clay, reaching down to the banks of the Thames.

The traditional route westwards to Rochester and beyond, but not, as we have seen, necessarily that taken by people living in the settlement of *Durovernum*, was that provided by the North Downs Way, as it progressed along the lip of the steep southerly escarpment of the Downs, to look across the merged valleys of the Lea, a tributary of the Medway, and the Stour. The latter, flowing at its outset in a southeasterly direction towards the coast at Hythe, turns sharply north at Ashford to pass through a wide gap in the chalk hills on its way to Canterbury and the Wantsum channel, as it then existed. On the

29. Road construction: a Roman army engineer surveys the line of a road.

northerly flank of this ancient track way as it runs westwards, today
skirting such delightful villages as Lenham, is a plateau, then thickly
wooded, which descends gently to the less steep escarpment on the far
side of the Downs, where the trees then give way to open downland.
The North Downs Way had three clear advantages to offer Plautius as
an axis for his advance. It was an established, well drained road,
capable of carrying heavy military equipment: it would lead him to a
narrower river crossing well up the valley of the Medway, thus avoiding
the problems of tidal waters: and it provided the tactical advantage of
high ground. In other ways it left much to be desired; it was more
consuming of logistical resources, since it was a longer route than the

30. A Roman army surveyor aligns a road with the use of a *groma*.

frontal approach discussed above and, more seriously, there was a grave risk that a force marching along this route would have been out of touch with events occurring on the opposite side of the Downs, thus leaving *Durovernum* open to frontal attack and the *Classis Britannica*, in the Thames estuary, out of touch with its commanding general.

A third option open to Plautius would have been to advance along the northern escarpment of the Downs, roughly along the line of the present day villages of Doddington, Bredgar, Stockbury and Bredhurst, from where long views are available to the Hoo Marshes, the Swale and the low hills of Sheppey. This line of advance, which significantly is roughly that of the modern M2 motorway, would have offered him the opportunity of either merging with the North Downs Way near Kit's Coty, and from there descending to the Medway crossings or, alternatively, of turning north to the high ground at Chatham Great Lines, from where commanding views would have been available of *Durobrivae* and Strood Hill across the river. Confirmation of a Roman presence was discovered on this axis in July, 1957, when a hoard of 37 Roman gold coins was unearthed at Bredgar, the latest of the collection being four Claudian aurei, almost in mint condition, dated AD 41. This

31.   A hoard of thirty-seven gold coins buried by a soldier in the Roman invasion force of AD 43,
at Bredgar, Kent. The total sum amounts to more than four years' pay for a legionary, and could
have been concealed as a precaution before a battle.

represented the equivalent of three months pay for a centurion and
Frere suggests[9] that they could have been buried, perhaps prior to an
engagement, as the army moved forward. It is possibly not coincidental
that an old trackway, used for the transport of salt from the north Kent
coast to the Wealden community, is thought to have passed through the
downland woods at about this point;[10] it would therefore have been a
track junction of some tactical importance and could well have
provided the site for the second skirmish between the two armies.

On the sector of the River Medway within the operational area we
are considering, five places have justifiable claims to be the site of the
original passage; these are Aylesford, about eight miles from Rochester
and the furthest point upstream; Snodland, which Thornhill suggests[11]

came into use in later Romano-British times, when the advance of tides upstream forced wayfarers to abandon the crossing place at Holborough; Holborough, close to the northern end of the Holborough cement works wharf, whence a prehistoric trackway ran to Birling Place; Halling, where a ford may have existed between Halling and Wouldham; and, finally, Cuxton, favoured as a site by the Kent County Council but its case appears less convincing than some of the others. Additionally, there is local belief at Rochester that some form of crossing place, either a ford or a bridge, existed a few hundred yards upstream from the site of the present bridges. There is no hard evidence of this, but it may be considered substantiated by the fact that the North Downs Way makes a considerable detour to the Rochester crossing at a point south of Kit's Coty, to descend through Burham and Borstal, before turning back via Cuxton and Upper Halling on the opposite bank to rejoin its original path at Birling Place. There is no evidence of the construction of bridges by Britons but there appears no reason to doubt that they possessed the technology to permit this; indeed, the statement by Dio that the Britons supposed that the Romans would not be able to cross without a bridge, implies the existence of a bridge which had been purposely destroyed. In short, if Plautius' attempt to cross at *Durobrivae* was frustrated, a good choice of alternative crossing places existed upstream, at Halling or above.

It can surely be assumed that Plautius was in possession of all these facts, having obtained them either from his own reconnaissance forces or, more probably, from the leaders of the tribal contingents which had surrendered to him. He would then have considered the advantages and disadvantages of the routes we have discussed above against these facts before issuing his instructions for the advance. He might have listed them as follows:

(a)   The North Downs Way, logistically expensive, would have brought him to an easy crossing of the Medway and well to the flank of his enemy, thus permitting the Roman general room for manoeuvre; but he could not afford to leave his central front exposed and, to avoid this, he would have to detach a force for employment on the direct route between the two settlements. Since the wooded downland ridge would intervene, they would be out of touch with each other and this would be unacceptable. Against this, to leave the North Downs Way unguarded would be to invite a surprise flank attack on *Durovernum*.

(b)   The direct route from *Durovernum* to *Durobrivae* was logistically the most suitable, with proximity to the *Classis Britannica* on the nearby Thames and a short supply line back to the Wantsum. It was also tactically important, since possession of it implied domination of the vitally important belt of land lying between the North Downs and the Thames. It was, however, easily observed and susceptible to attack from the high ground of the North Downs on its left flank.

(c)   The route along the northern escarpment of the Downs offered excellent observation of the low lying land on its right flank and beyond that to the river Thames. It was vulnerable to attack from the woods on the downland hilltops but a force using it would be ideally situated, upon reaching the Medway, to cross the river and outflank the enemy without undue interference. This force could also act as a flank guard to the main body on the lower road.

From a study of these various factors, Plautius may well have put together a plan along the following lines:

The main body (less the escarpment flank guard) to advance along the lower road, with two legions forward, the right flank legion moving along the axis of the road.

The flank guard, comprising at least one legion, one cavalry regiment, with auxiliary cohorts, under the overall command of Gnaeus Hosidius Geta, the army second-in-command, to advance along the northern escarpment of the Downs, to clear the woods and maintain signal communication with the main body and the rear base.

A garrison, withdrawn if need be from Harbledown and replaced there by a fortified signal station, to be stationed on the high ground at TQ 9749, now occupied by a gliding club, to secure the approaches of the North Downs Way to Dover and Canterbury.

In the execution of this plan, it may be imagined that Plautius advanced in three stages: firstly, to the western edge of the Forest of Blean and, having consolidated that position, thence to the line of the 'salt' trackway, running roughly from Bredgar to Sittingbourne. The latter location, so near the Swale, could have been of major importance even if Milton Creek had not then granted access from the Thames. The third stage would have been the army's advance to the Medway on a wide front, with its first sighting of the main body of the British force.

The military significance of the North Downs to an invading army was emphasised in the previous chapter. This great range of chalk downland extends in a sweeping arc from the Downs above Canterbury, and from the Kentish cliff tops between Folkestone and Dover in the east, to Farnham in the west, embracing on its way the dominating feature of Box Hill. At the western foot of this famous beauty spot flows the river Mole, which Cunliffe speculates[12] may have provided the western boundary of the four Kentish kingdoms mentioned by Caesar. The Mole, with its disconcerting habit of 'burrowing' underground and about which Spenser wrote in the *Faerie Queen*

> The Mole, that like a nousling mole doth make
> His way still underground, till Thames he overtake,

is one of five rivers, the others being the Wey, the Darent, the Medway and the Stour, all of which rise in the Weald and have cut their way through the Downs to join the Thames. As they widened and deepened downriver, on their approach to the main stream, they would have provided a series of formidable obstacles to an army of those early days marching westwards, north of the Downs; equally, they could have posed great difficulty to a retreating army, particularly if its enemy possessed sufficient mobility and initiative to deny the crossing places. The valleys which the rivers thus created, slicing through the forested hilltops of the downland as it then was, offered easy communication between the two parts of the kingdoms held apart by the North Downs range. They acted as feeder trackways, linking with the ancient trunk way as it crossed each of them in turn, on its journey westward, descending into the valley to climb the opposing hills. This labyrinth of trackway and river, with its many crossing places, evolved into an area of strategic importance. It was here, in AD 774, that Offa, King of Mercia, battled on the banks of the Darent with Aldric, King of Kent; and, in AD 1016, in a place only half a mile distant from there, Edmund Ironside crushed Canute and his army, pursuing the Dane to the river Medway.

It is a matter of sensible speculation[13] that by the end of the 1st century BC, the population of the two Kentish kingdoms thought to have been located west of the Medway, had drifted to settle in the valleys of the Mole and the Darent; the remaining two, east of the river, had abandoned their hillforts at Bigbury and Oldbury, to occupy open settlements at *Durovernum* and *Durobrivae* respectively, although there are suggestions that Oldbury was reoccupied and refortified just prior to AD 43. This would have been a natural thing to have happened; but the idea put forward by Ward Perkins[14] that it was the later scene of an assault by the Romans, when mopping up after the Medway battle, is perhaps less militarily acceptable.

The geographical partition of the four kingdoms by the river Medway underlined two totally different socio-economic systems,[15] differences which are still emphasised in modern times by those people living on the western side of the boundary claiming to be the Kentish Men and those opposite, the Men of Kent. The people of the four kingdoms seem to have had little in common with the Wealden community but, importantly, the population of north-east Kent does appear to have had cultural links with the inhabitants, across the river, of south-east Essex. This is indicated by archaeological excavation[16] of 2nd and 1st century BC decorated pottery (Mucking-Crayford style) found on both sides of the river Thames but particularly east of the Medway in Kent. These discoveries suggest that there must therefore have been a system of communication, either by boat or by a fordable crossing, which linked the two communities together. Patrick Thornhill[17] has argued the case convincingly for such a fordable crossing to have existed in the lower Thames. The river, unconstrained by the bank enclosures which began with the salt marshes in the 13th century, covered an area three or four times wider than the present channel, depositing alluvial mud to a considerable depth. As has occurred in so many of the great estuaries of the world, when the

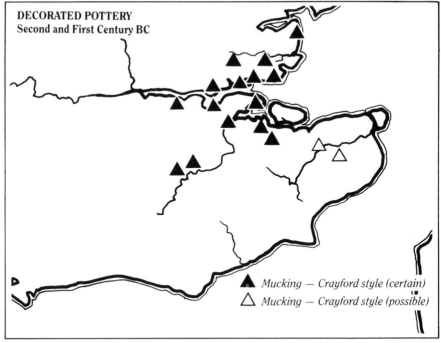

DECORATED POTTERY
Second and First Century BC

▲ Mucking — Crayford style (certain)
△ Mucking — Crayford style (possible)

32. Iron Age crossing of the Thames estuary. Finds of Second and First Century BC Decorated Pottery in both sides of the Thames estuary suggest an Iron Age cross river link by ferry or ford (12). Map reproduced by kind permission of Professor B. Cunliffe.

seaward flow of freshwater was dammed by the incoming tide, the level of water deepened and spread to its full width; when the tide receded the water level dropped rapidly, exposing a wide area of mud flats. In the early Romano-British period an uplift of land took place, the first effect of which was to raise the level of the mud flats above high tide water, thus enabling them to dry out, become desalinated and to be colonised by vegetation. In Thornhill's words,[18] the picture which emerged was

> that of a valley floor laced with stream-channels flowing between densely thicketed 'aits'; it may well have been impassable in winter but negotiable in summer by those who knew the shallow places and the way through the undergrowth – and who knew the tides.

He suggests that, in the passage of time, as the river deepened, due in part to its banks becoming increasingly enclosed, this crossing place disappeared under the water, to be replaced by a ferry. There is evidence that, in the early medieval period, a ferry plied across the Thames[19] between what is now East Tilbury and a point on the opposite bank. The prioress of Higham Priory, located rather more than four miles from the Medway crossing at Rochester on the west side of the river, was deemed responsible in AD 1293 for the upkeep of a causeway and bridge leading across the marshes to the ferry station which then existed. The fact that a causeway existed at that time, the remains of which are still visible today, is significant. The presence of ancient trackways indicate the directions from which it was approached: routes from Cobham, and the Medway valley, converge on Higham Upshire near Gad's Hill, before continuing in the direction of the Priory, to peter out at Church Street. Higham Upshire lies barely two miles from Strood Hill, in the vicinity of which the army commanded by the two British leaders was probably encamped, under the eye of Plautius from a vantage point on the east bank of the Medway. If these facts are linked with the inference to be drawn from the local discoveries of decorated pottery, then the possibility of a fordable crossing over the Thames having existed in this area becomes very real indeed. It is thus a factor which cannot be omitted when considering the circumstances which influenced the tactical decisions of the opposing commanders at this stage.

Dio has described this moment of encounter before battle in the following words, already quoted above,

> Then he (Plautius) came to a river. The Britons supposed that the Romans would not be able to cross it without a bridge, and so had

camped carelessly on the opposite bank. He therefore sent across
Gallic troops who were trained to swim with full equipment against
the swiftest of rivers. Surprise was achieved against the enemy by
this attack.

The Britons were unconcerned about the sudden Roman appearance
on the far bank of the river, possibly because the tide was at the full and
the ford was impassable or, much more probably, because they had
destroyed the bridge over it. They were aware that the nearest fordable
crossing place for Plautius was such a distance upstream as to impose
upon him a delay of some hours before he could get a force across in
sufficient strength to engage them. The Britons had 'camped carelessly'
and, by this description, it may be thought they saw no need to take
defensive precautions; nor, apparently, had they considered it either
necessary or prudent to despatch a force upstream to deny their enemy
a crossing which would put their southern flank at risk. It would
appear, therefore, that they had every intention of evading contact with
the Romans and it could even be possible that they were on the point of
withdrawal. Many of their allies had, by this time, probably defected,
recognising that the battle for Kent was lost. The occupation of
Reculver by the *Classis Britannica* had already placed *Camulodunum*
under threat and the battle for their Essex homeland was about to
begin. The only doubt, from the view point of the military historian, is
in which direction they intended to move. Dio's account of events
implies that the Britons were assembled on the west bank of the
Medway, overlooking the destroyed bridge; the Thames was to their
north and the river Darent approximately 15 miles to their west.
Additionally, the Romans were manoeuvring to outflank them from the
south and, at first sight, it would seem that the Britons had been guilty
of allowing themselves to be boxed into a trap; but this would have
been completely out of character with the skill and nature of Caratacus.
Tacitus, when describing[20] the final battle of the British chieftain with
Scapula, wrote

> his deficiency in strength was compensated by superior cunning and
> topographical knowledge . . . He selected a site where numerous
> factors – notably approaches and escape routes – helped him and
> impeded us.

It must thus be thought that if the British leaders had it in mind to
retreat further westwards along the line of the Thames, before crossing
to its north bank, they would not have allowed themselves to be caught
in the apparently untenable position in which Plautius found them: on
the other hand, the assembly area they were occupying was ideally

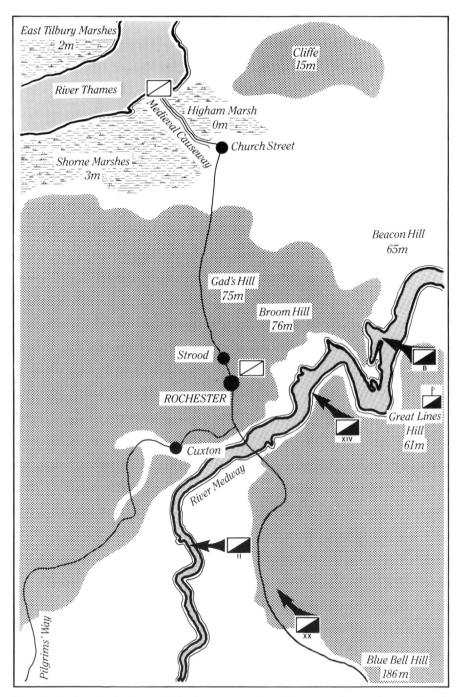

33. The Medway Battle (Phase 1). The shaded areas of land illustrate the boundaries of chalk and beds of sand: unshaded areas, mid-1st century AD, would have been low-lying, marshy land. Plautius on high ground at Great Lines observes the enemy at Strood. The Batavians on right flank, and II Legion on left, prepare to cross the Medway.

suited for a withdrawal northwards, towards the ford over the Thames to East Tilbury. If it is questioned why they were not yet marching towards it, it may be that the tide on the river was operating against them and they were waiting for the water level to fall.

It may be assumed that Plautius was equally aware of the East Tilbury crossing place: if he had not learnt of it from the local population, he would have been told of it by Adminius or his followers. His immediate response upon sighting the Britons appears to have been to throw a contingent of auxiliary troops across the Medway, especially trained in river crossing techniques. Dio refers to this force as 'Gallic' troops of 'Kelts'; but Hassall has argued[21] strongly that they were probably Batavians, famous for being especially skilled in this form of warfare, and that as many as eight cohorts of them may have served with Plautius' invasion force. Even if the Roman general had decided to commit all of these to the operation he had in mind, this number would have been quite inadequate on its own to tackle the assembled British force. It is clear, therefore, that they were allocated to a specific task, most probably to sever the British line of retreat by seizing the important track junction at Higham Upshire. Dio relates that the Batavians made the crossing undetected, presumably well downstream from the normal crossing place and protected from view by a bend in the river; and one can only speculate that they were heading for their objective, or were already in possession of it, when they were observed by the Britons, who reacted sharply to this threat to their escape route by counter-attacking with their war-chariots. The manner in which the Batavians now handled the attack upon themselves was devastating: they directed their fire at the horses, rather than the men, and made 'it impossible even for the charioteers to get away in the subsequent confusion.'

Whilst this action was taking place, Plautius sent a message to Vespasian, commanding general of II Legion *Augusta*, instructing him to cross the Medway with all speed to engage the enemy's southern flank. Thus, whilst the British, in considerable disarray, were distracted by the disastrous action being fought on their northern flank, Vespasian dealt them another severe blow from the south, inflicting heavy casualties. It says much for the morale of the Britons, and the quality of their leadership, that they recovered their balance and fought back with considerable spirit until nightfall, which arrived with no side having gained an advantage. Unusually for an engagement involving tribal forces, particularly in those times, dawn saw the British forces still in position and the battle was renewed. Its outcome was unresolved until the intervention of Gnaeus Hosidius Geta, who by this time had negotiated the Medway to join Vespasian. Even at this late stage of the

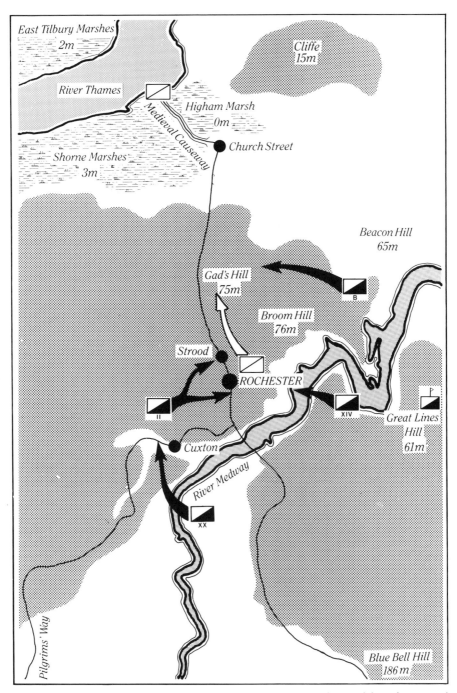

34. The Medway Battle (Phase 2). The Batavian auxiliaries threaten the British line of retreat and the British detach a chariot force to deal with them. XX Legion begins to cross the Medway and XIV Legion demonstrates in front of the British position to hold their attention.

engagement, the level of fighting was still intense and he was fortunate to escape capture. Nevertheless, the part he played was decisive and, in due course, it was recognised by the award to him of *ornamenta triumphalia*, an honour of unusual merit.

The British now fell back to the river Thames, making their way through the undergrowth and the many rivulets without difficulty, and thence over the main stream to the north bank. It is interesting to ponder why they had not withdrawn earlier: possibly they smelt a chance of victory, stimulated by the rather piecemeal arrival of their Roman opponents, whose every action seems to have been directed towards containing the Britons for long enough to enable their destruction. Alternatively, their withdrawal may have been delayed by darkness and adverse tides, for movement through the marshes at night – let alone in daytime – was not easy, as the Romans found to their cost. Then the Batavians once again displayed their aquatic skills and established a foothold across the Thames and

> . . . some others got over by a bridge a little way upstream, after which they assailed the barbarians from several sides at once and cut down many of them. But they were incautious in their pursuit of the rest, got themselves entrapped in impassable marshes, and lost many men.

There has been much discussion regarding the whereabouts of this 'bridge' mentioned by Dio, some archaeologists and historians suggesting it may have been located as far away as Southwark, Westminster, Wandsworth or even Brentford, on the grounds that this was possibly the crossing place used by Caesar in 54 BC. The likelihood of the bridge having been constructed by Roman engineers, from barges towed upstream from Richborough has also been argued;[22] but most of these propositions take little account of the important time factor. Dio, whose narrative admittedly omits much detail, is generally factually correct, and his account of this closing stage of the Medway battle presents a picture of a flowing, running-fight, rather than one which had been interrupted by an outflanking movement of at least two days duration. It appears from a close study of his words that the Batavians, in close pursuit of the Britons, failed to discover their crossing place: they therefore swam across. It is necessary to look at what happened next through the eyes of the Romans. Another party, arriving through the undergrowth on to the banks of the Thames a little way upstream from the Batavians, discovered a bridge, possibly one which the Britons had already used for their withdrawal; they made valuable use of this and got across in strength.

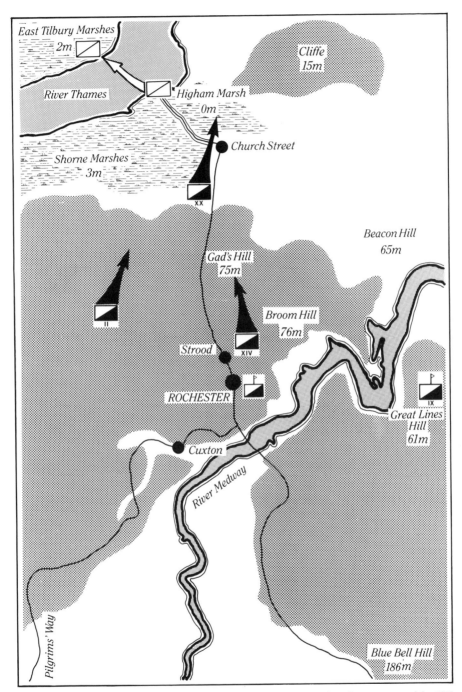

35. The Medway Battle (Phase 3). The British fall back across the Thames pursued by XX Legion. II Legion swings wide to block southerly escape routes. XIV Legion is now across the Medway and becomes army reserve. Plautius has established his Headquarters at Rochester and IX Legion continues as rear guard, watching supply arrangements, located at Great Lines area.

Shortly after this Togodumnus died. Far from giving in, the Britons gathered all the more stubbornly to avenge him. Plautius became alarmed and refused to advance further. Resolved to hold on to the ground he had already won, he sent for Claudius.[23]

The Medway battle is an important bench-mark in the progress of the invasion for, until its outcome was clear, defeat for Plautius by the federated British force was always possible, if not probable. After the Britons had retired across the Thames the campaign, which until that moment had been a full scale invasion, took on the pattern of consolidation and exploitation of the successes achieved. Plautius may have welcomed a pause in which to recover his administrative balance but it is difficult to believe that a commander of his quality could not have found the resources, and did not possess the military ability to recognise the necessity, to thrust forward into Essex and sustain the momentum of his advance. With the presence and help of the *Classis Britannica* a wide range of options were open to him; and one can only assume that his alleged refusal to advance further until the arrival of Claudius was a politically contrived situation, designed to bring credit to his emperor and to provide him with the triumph he was seeking to celebrate in Rome. There is another aspect of the battle which is notable; it was probably the only occasion during the invasion when the four legions comprising the Task Force were employed jointly on the same operation. The positions which they found themselves occupying at the conclusion of this phase, and the roles in which they were then employed, will have provided a platform for the next stage of the operation, and will thus have reflected the subsequent tasks given to them. It is therefore worthwhile to consider what this deployment might have been.

We have already conjectured that during the advance from *Durovernum* Plautius selected the short northern route as his main axis of advance; he marched along it with two legions forward, his right forward legion moving along the line of the trackway, supported by a reserve legion and auxiliary troops. His flank guard, composed of a legion, with a regiment of cavalry and supporting troops, advanced along the northern escarpment of the Downs. The left forward legion of the main body would probably have been first across the Medway to support the Batavians and attack the British southern flank: we know this to have been II Legion *Augusta* commanded by Vespasian. The first troops in action were the Batavian cohorts, who crossed the lower waters of the river. These were later withdrawn from Britain in AD 67, for an expedition against the Albani of the Caucasus, together with XIV Legion *Gemina*, to which they were attached.[24] It is thus possible that

XIV Legion marched with the Batavians to support their crossing of the lower Medway. When Plautius was called from Pannonia to command the invasion force, he brought with him IX Legion *Hispana* which had served there for many years and which must have become proficient in waterborne operations on the Danube: indeed it was possibly because of this proficiency that they were selected. It is noteworthy that this formation seems always to have been employed on the seaward flank in Britain, first on its march northwards to Lincoln along the east coast, and later during Agricola's campaigns in northern Britain, when it operated along the Tay and the Firth of Forth. The *camaraderie* which they had by that time established with the sailors of the *Classis Britannica* was made plain by Tacitus,[25] who described how the war was then pushed forward simultaneously by land and sea, and

> infantry, cavalry and marines, often meeting in the same camp, would mess and make merry together. They boasted, as soldiers will, of their several exploits and adventures, and matched the perilous depths of woods and ravines against the hazardsof storms and waves, victories on land against the conquest of the ocean.

Personal contact of this nature must have bred an invaluable inter-service understanding, which would not have been lightly discarded. In view of the apparently continuous employment of IX Legion in these techniques in later years, it appears justifiable to assume that this cooperation with the Roman Navy in British waters commenced during operations on the Thames, during the advance to the Medway. It is not difficult to visualise the *Classis Britannica* moving upriver parallel with the Task Force and IX Legion marching with Plautius, held under his hand awaiting a river operation should the need arise. By a process of elimination, therefore, XX Legion *Valeria* was possibly providing flank guard under Hosidius Geta, and would have crossed the Medway upon the heels of Vespasian, to attack the Britons on the second day of the battle. This could have been the unit which pursued them through the marshes and discovered the bridge across the Thames. Thus IX and XIV Legions, up to this moment unemployed in the battle, could now have passed to reserve, awaiting the arrival of Claudius, with his entourage, reinforcements and elephants. In the meantime, it is possible to imagine they were employed in the process of consolidation, exploiting forward to the boundary of the river Mole, assisting with road construction and other engineering works, such as bridge building for example (see Appendix C) and generally making preparations for the next phase of the campaign, the advance to *Camulodunum*. XX Legion, having fought its way across the Thames, may be expected to have extended its grip on the bridgehead thus established, and II Legion *Augusta*, possibly responsible for covering the southern flank of the force, may be seen as exploiting westwards along the North Downs Way.

CHAPTER FIVE

THE FALL OF COLCHESTER

It often happens that, when the first phase of a hard fought campaign has been successfully completed and the second is in full swing, the commander will be as much occupied in preparations for the next stage as with the actual fighting then in progress.

A Concise History of Warfare
– FM Viscount Montgomery of Alamein

... nothing has helped us more in fighting against their very powerful nations than their inability to cooperate. It is seldom that two or three states unite to repel a common danger; thus fighting in separate groups, all are conquered.

Tacitus, *The Agricola*

As he paused on the Medway there appears to be no evident reason why Aulus Plautius should have felt displeased with the progress of his campaign at this moment, either with the speed of his advance or with the outcome of his encounters with the British force. He had achieved a successful Channel crossing, despite considerable logistical problems, with a large and balanced invasion force; his landing had been fortuitously unopposed and, indeed, there were early signs of the disintegration of the enemy force confronting him; the forces under his command had advanced with determination and dash to drive their opponents from the far bank of the Medway, northwards across the river Thames into Essex, and he had received news of the death of Togodumnus, who seemingly had either been killed or had succumbed to wounds inflicted upon him. It is true that his regiment which pursued the British across the Thames, into the marshland beyond, may have suffered casualties in the fighting which then ensued but little appears to have happened to justify Dio's statement, already quoted,[1] describing Plautius' state of alarm. Tacitus has described him, as likewise his successor, as a fine soldier, and he was surely in a position to speak with authority for the reason that his father-in-law, Gnaeus Julius Agricola, himself a distinguished soldier, had commanded XX Legion *Valeria Victrix* on operations in Britain during AD 70–73, and later served there for six years as *legatus pro praetore* before being recalled to Rome in AD 84. It would thus be surprising if Agricola was not well aware of the military ability of his illustrious predecessor, the first governor of the province, and had not discussed this knowledge with his son-in-law. It may be that Tacitus provides some guidance to the truth when he suggests[2] that, after the death of the emperor Augustus in AD 14, the rising tide of flattery distorted the accuracy of recorded history. The reigns of Gaius, Claudius and Nero, he tells us, were described 'during their lifetime in fictitious terms for fear of the consequences; whereas the accounts written after their deaths were influenced by still raging animosities'. Elsewhere, he gives us his version of the part played by Claudius when he writes that, although the emperor Gaius unquestionably planned an invasion of Britain[3]

> ... it was the late emperor Claudius who initiated the renewed undertaking. He sent over legions and auxiliaries and chose Vespasian to share in the enterprise – the first step towards his future greatness. Tribes were subdued and kings captured ...

An equally restrained note is struck by Suetonius,[4] a contemporary of Tacitus, who is content to provide a very abbreviated account of Claudius' military participation in the campaign. He does no more than describe the direction of the emperor's march through Gaul to Boulogne, from where he crossed the Channel

> ... and was back in Rome six months later. He had fought no battles and suffered no casualties, but reduced a large part of the island to submission. His triumph was a very splendid one, and among those he invited to witness it were his provincial governors and exiles as well. The emblems of his victory included the naval crown, representing the crossing and the conquest, so to speak, of the ocean ...

There are two important factors which must be remembered when assessing the extent of the military role to be credited to Claudius at this time. Firstly, when he undertook the long journey from Rome to Britain, upon his summons by Plautius, he had already decided that Britain was the country 'where a real triumph could most readily be earned'. A campaign defeat of one of his generals was something he might have been expected to survive but it would have been intolerable for him to have been called forward, in the special circumstances

36. Bronze head of the emperor Claudius (AD 41–54) recovered from the river Alde in Suffolk.

depicted by Dio, and then to have had to return to Rome after an absence of six months to report to the Senate the failure of his mission. Victory had to be a clear outcome, both in his own eyes and those of Plautius, before he set forth on his travels; and once he had set forth there could be no turning back, for all Rome would have been aware of his purpose. Secondly, his stay in Britain was of only sixteen days duration, a very brief time to remain if within that period he was expecting to resolve, with any guarantee of success, the logistical problems of crossing the Thames with an army of about forty thousand men and with several thousand animals, before advancing to seize *Camulodunum* from the hands of a determined enemy. Even if he were a resourceful and thrustful general (which is doubtful, for his biographer, Suetonius, portrays him as a sickly and indecisive man, albeit a good administrator) this would have been a great demand to put upon him. It seems fairer to assume that, when his master arrived to take command of the Roman army then deployed in camps astride the Thames, Plautius had already achieved his immediate objectives in Essex, namely, the destruction of the tribal army confronting him and the capture of *Camulodunum*, for all but the final formalities. Thus it follows that, if there are good grounds for arguing the incredibility of Plautius' 'alarm' upon encountering stubborn resistance from the Britons gathered to oppose his endeavours to get across the Thames, then that resistance must either have been comparatively shortlived or its intensity over-emphasised. Indeed, it has been remarked that the 'implicit ease with which *Camulodunum* and the rest of the Trinovantian territory were overrun at the time of the conquest suggests that the Roman occupation was not unwelcome in some sectors of their society'.[5]

Some explanation of what may have happened is perhaps to be found in the pattern of events which took place after the Romans had completed their conquest of the enemy territory north of the Thames and had brought the Trinovantes and the Catuvellauni under the control of their civil administration. Before the conquest, *Camulodunum*, had expanded into one of the most prosperous and frequented seaports in north-west Europe, its fortunes safe-guarded by the powerful and expansionist policies of Cunobelin. Its wealth had attracted the increasing attention of Rome, who were never likely to forget that Caesar had provided the stimulus for the growth of this great new trading centre; and their interest was redoubled upon the emperor Tiberius' abandonment of his predecessor's expensive schemes for German subjugation, which released a number of legions to be employed in more profitable ventures. *Camulodunum*, however, was also a Trinovantian creation, for, as we have seen, their king, Addedomaros, had moved his centre of government from the eastern headwaters of the river Lea to a new site on the east coast, almost immediately upon his succession to the throne, circa 25 BC. For whatever reason he made his decision, it was one which ensured the cumulative prosperity of the Trinovantian people for nearly seventy years; and it may be judged that during that time *Camulodunum* had become for them a proud symbol of their tribal status and influence. In AD 49, by decree of Claudius,[6] the town was designated the first *colonia* of the new province, to be called COLONIA CLAUDIA VICTRICENSIS – the Claudian Colony of Victory – a title which will hardly have endeared its previous occupants to its new inhabitants, particularly since the new arrivals were ex-soldiers provided with standard areas of land taken, inevitably, from the native Trinovantes. Tacitus describes the ruthlessness with which they were treated, which ultimately caused them to rise in rebellion, along with the Iceni, led by Boudicca:[7]

> Servitude had not broken them, and they had secretly plotted together to become free again. They particularly hated the Roman ex-soldiers who had recently established a settlement at *Camulodu-*

37. A model reproduction of the 1st century AD temple of Claudius at Colchester.

num. The settlers drove the Trinobantes from their homes and land, and called them prisoners and slaves. The troops encouraged the settlers' outrages, since their own way of behaving was the same – and they looked forward to similar licence for themselves.

It is sometimes suggested that *Caesaromagus* (Chelmsford) was given to the Trinovantes at this time as a political gesture to preserve their loyalty upon losing their old capital: and that the name, *Caesaromagus*, the only town name in Claudius' new province to contain the 'Caesar' prefix, implied that this was so, since its translation reads 'Caesar's Market'.[8] If this is a correct interpretation of events, then the Romans subsequently treated their allies in a very strange way. On the other hand, Professor Rivet suggests that an alternative translation might have read 'Caesar's Plain', which could indicate instead that this was the site where the British leaders surrendered to Claudius, and the name was afterwards transferred to the town. Certainly this suggestion is more in keeping with the subsequent actions of the Romans and their apparent insensitivity to the feelings of the Trinovantes: but their treatment of the Catuvellauni, whose city of *Verulamium* is recorded in Ptolemy's Geography, was significantly different.

Post-conquest *Verulamium* was founded about AD 50, probably simultaneously with the grant of *colonia* status to *Camulodunum*, and within a very short time it appears to have been given the rank of *municipium*, whose inhabitants were granted Roman or Latin rights in law, dependent upon the terms of the charter. This was a rare distinction, awarded soon after the conquest and, since London was apparently the only other town or city to be thus favoured (but, if so, at not such an early date), it raises the question – what had the Catuvellauni done to be considered worthy of such an honour? Clearly, if they had offered bitter resistance to the Roman advance, or if they had offered continued hostility, either politically or by supporting Caratacus, they would have been treated very differently. The probability, therefore, must be that at some stage following the Roman defeat of the Britons at the Medway crossing, when the outcome of the battle must have become clear to them beyond doubt, they changed sides and negotiated a separate peace with their enemy. This conceivably happened upon the death of Togodumnus for it is likely that, when Cunobelin had his royal seat at *Camulodunum* and reigned over the two tribes of the Catuvellauni and the Trinovantes, his three sons were allocated their own spheres of responsibility within his kingdom, and Togodumnus, by a process of elimination and some conjecture, probably ruled the Catuvellaunian homeland, with his centre of government in *Verulamium*. In these circumstances, his death could have dealt a considerable blow to the morale of his subjects.

There were, additionally, sound economic reasons why the Catuvellauni could have been persuaded to surrender, for many of them were settled on prime agricultural land, and the more their participation in the campaign was prolonged, the more damage might be inflicted upon their annual food crop, not only with loss to themselves but to the detriment of the whole community; furthermore, they can have had little interest in doing anything to restrict the flow of imported luxury goods into the Braughing area, many of which were probably traded for grain to the benefit of the native aristocracy. Thus when an opportunity was presented to safeguard their future, which might perhaps have been further improved by entering into profitable agreements to supply grain to the invading forces, the Catuvellaunian people may have seen little point in placing their own situation in jeopardy by engaging in a losing battle on behalf of their neighbours, the Trinovantes. Some confirmation of this possibility is revealed in 1st-century burials and cremations, excavated both in Hertfordshire and the Ivel Valley of Bedfordshire, where there is evidence that the tribal aristocracy retained their wealth and status after the conquest.[9] Frere sees no reason to doubt that the Roman administration was widely welcomed by most people in this area, and that a wide spectrum of the population had, within a generation, enjoyed a vast increase in prosperity.[10] A surrender agreement of this nature, guaranteeing to the Romans the neutrality of the Catuvellaunian people, with its implication of administrative support and the unfettered use of local track and waterway communications, would have proved a devastating blow to the Trinovantes. It would also provide a reason for the apparent ease with which *Camulodunum* and the Trinovantian homelands were eventually overwhelmed; and would account for the seemingly scant mid-1st century Roman military presence in Cautvellaunian territory.

There can be little doubt that the Trinovantes would have regarded such a betrayal by the Catuvellauni with great bitterness, and the savage assaults which were later to be delivered upon Godmanchester and St Alban's during the Boudiccan uprising (AD 60–61) were perhaps indicative of this pent-up feeling. There is one matter about which there can be no argument: the death of Togodumnus and the casualties which both sides inflicted upon each other in the fierce fighting which took place in the marshes on the north bank of the Thames, after the battle of the Medway,[11] left both Caratacus and Plautius with some interesting decisions to make. These can best be understood by a brief glance at the topography of Essex, which was then the heartland of the

Trinovantian people, and was shortly to become the next theatre of military operations.

With the exception of the north-west corner of the county, the borders of Essex are almost entirely defined by water. The river Thames lies to its south and the North Sea guards its eastern seaboard. In the north, the boundary takes the line of the river Stour, joining it at Sturmer, at the point where the river enters Essex from the hilly, open country of West Suffolk, and thence follows its course to the coast at Harwich. Similarly, in the west, the boundary has been drawn along the line of the river Stort, from Bishop's Stortford to its confluence with the Lea: from there it runs southwards to join the Thames at Canning Town. There is evidence that, at the time of the invasion, an extensive forest straddled the marshy valley of the Lea, extending westwards to embrace the area of the present Enfield Chase, northwards to a point just short of Bishop's Stortford and south to the verges of Hackney Marshes. It was through this forest that Julius Caesar marched to assault Cassivellaunus' stronghold, 'strategically placed among wood and marshland',[12] and its original extent may still be discerned today from the spread of its surviving areas of woodland, the forests of Epping, Hainault, Waltham, Wintry and Hatfield Broad Oak.[13] The degree to which this combination of river, marshland and forest discouraged lateral movement to and from central Essex may be detected from the pattern of the road system evolved by the Romans, the shape of which, in the first instance, was almost certainly dictated by tactical necessity and the presence of suitable tribal trackways. Within this pattern, three roads of importance command attention as they fan outwards from London:[14]

(a)   Ermine Street, destined to become a valuable strategic trunk road, to the main centres of military occupation at Lincoln and York. It is of little interest to an investigation of the early days of the Claudian invasion, except to note that, significantly, its original alignment was considerably westwards of the Lea Valley, although it was subsequently moved closer to it.

(b)   The main route through Essex, connecting *Londinium* through Chelmsford (*Caesaromagus*) with the old tribal capital of the Trinovantes at Colchester (*Camulodunum*). The route passes through the Hackney Marshes and crosses the rivers Lea, Roding and Chelmer amongst others.

(c)   The road from the east bank of the Lea, opposite Clapton, (tactically probably the most interesting of these three roads) which makes a junction at Great Dunmow with Stane Street, the principal Roman east–west road connecting Colchester and the coast with the road centre of Braughing. In the early part of its journey from the south west of the county, it follows the rough line of the Roding, passing through Chigwell (*Durolitum*) and about three miles west of Ongar.

These highways were all laid out in such a manner as to avoid the Forest, even to the extent that traffic between Colchester and St Alban's was guided via Braughing, although the logical geographical route would have been through Chelmsford, to Ongar and thence westwards.[15]

Braughing was an important settlement in the late Iron Age period for the same reasons that it continued to remain so after the conquest, until its status was diminished by the changes brought about by the new order of administration introduced by the Romans. The settlement probably came into being in the first instance as a trading post, situated at the navigable extremity of the Rib, a northern tributary of the Lea. The Rib is now no more than a stream at most times of the year but recent examination has suggested that, in the 1st century AD, the river was much larger and could have been negotiated by water transport for the whole distance from the Lea to Braughing.[16] Thus the location of the settlement, with its ready access to the Icknield Way and onwards to the upper reaches of the Thames, together with its availability to the rich grain producing areas of Bedfordshire and Cambridgeshire, made it both a valuable commercial and strategic centre. In recognition of this fact five roads radiated from it, including Ermine Street on its journey to the North and, importantly, Stane Street connecting with Colchester: and at least some of these, in particular Stane Street, are thought to have been constructed on already existing native trackways.

When the Romans arrived in Britain in AD 43, they found that the Essex of the Trinovantes was one of the most advanced regions in the country, with great changes in living standards and agricultural techniques having been achieved since the expeditions of Julius Caesar in the 1st century BC. The numerous burial and villa sites uncovered in recent times[17] provide evidence that the wealth of the territory was then concentrated on the fertile stratum of boulder clay, north of Chelmsford, where the relatively high ground (the county nowhere rises to a greater height than 500 feet) acts as a watershed, providing the source of several tactically important rivers of varying size. These mainly flow south or south-easterly into the sector of low-lying, frequently marshy land, composed predominantly of London Clay and fringed with alluvial mud, adjoining the Thames and its estuary: and they include the Lea which, as has already been noted, defines a substantial part of

38. A detachment of XX Legion.

the county border with Hertfordshire, and the rivers Roding, Ingrebourne, Mardyke and Chelmer. These rivers are a factor which
defender and invader alike could not fail to take to account when
making their military plans because at least three of them, the Lea,
Roding and Chelmer, could have created formidable obstacles to the
lateral, cross-country movement of large bodies of troops, and their
crossing places would consequently have become areas of considerable
military importance. The Chelmer, with its fords at Chelmsford and
Great Dunmow held in determined hands, and as the principal river
in Essex, would probably have been one of the most difficult of
these.

   There was one other aspect of these riverways which would greatly
have affected Roman military thinking, namely that at least three of
them were navigable for a considerable distance into the interior. The
Lea was certainly negotiable as far as Ware, and thence up its tributary,
the Rib, to Braughing, although transhipment into smaller craft might
have been necessary at Ware; the Roding was navigable to Chigwell
(*Durolitum*)[18] and probably to Ongar; the Chelmer was open to
Chelmsford and perhaps beyond to Great Dunmow. There must be less
certainty about the possibility of using the two remaining rivers in this
manner, the Ingrebourne and the Mardyke, but they should neverthe-

less be considered. The Ingrebourne runs on a reasonably straight alignment as far as Upminster but beyond that point it turns back upon itself so frequently that its employment as a supply route or means of communication would probably have been impracticable. On the other hand, as late as 1870 the Mardyke, although its appearance today belies the possibility, was being negotiated by shallow-draught vessels poled upstream to Lorkins Farm, the heart of what had been a Romano-Celtic settlement area, after they had been sailed down the main stream of the Thames from Purfleet.[19] The Mardyke bears signs of having been 'straightened' at an early date and Astbury suggests that this may have been done by the Romans to make it easier to get their farm produce to London. No evidence has yet been found to support this proposition and there would clearly have been little opportunity for Plautius to have engaged in engineering work of this nature under the operational conditions which then confronted him, or in the time which was available to him; but the probability that the Mardyke was navigable at the time of the conquest would be difficult to deny. Thus despite the limited access to the interior which both these rivers would have offered, their availability should not be overlooked when discussing the options open to Plautius for the next phase of his campaign, the thrust of which was to seize the Trinovantian capital of *Camulodunum*, to destroy the enemy force confronting him and, if possible, to prevent the escape of Caratacus and other British leaders who might be tempted to take their resistance elsewhere to neighbouring tribal territories.

When the Britons retreated from the Medway battlefield and crossed the Thames, it probably caused them some surprise and no little alarm to discover that their Roman opponents had followed so swiftly and established a foothold on the north bank with such speed. They were almost certainly unaware of the Batavian expertise in this type of operation and they can have had little experience of it in battle; the dash with which the Roman landing was effected could, for this reason, have denied them the time to destroy the bridge they had retained for their withdrawal and one can only conjecture what happened next. Togodumnus was killed in the fighting or died of wounds already received; and Caratacus led a fierce counter attack to retrieve a situation which can have given him little encouragement. Even if he had been successful in driving the enemy back across the Thames, and there is nothing to indicate this was the case, he can have felt little doubt that they would soon return in force, well organised and employing all the resources at their disposal. One of the most important of these resources would have been the *Classis Britannica*, the presence of which in the lower Thames not only menaced *Camulodunum*, as has already been suggested, but also threatened to outflank the British host gathered around the Roman bridgehead. Additionally, Plautius had it within his capability, now that Kent was under his domination, to march upstream and cross the river almost at leisure and there must consequently have been considerable uncertainty in the British camp as to where the next blow might fall. At the end of the first phase of his invasion operation, however, the Roman general was seeking a period in which to consolidate his gains and was in no immediate hurry to press home his advantage. He was probably pleasantly aware that simply by his presence, supported by his navy with its fleet transports, he was already creating problems for the British leadership without any need to bestir himself further.

The situation confronting Caratacus was more complicated. He was in danger of being outflanked, either from the sea or by a speedy land operation launched from the west. He had lost the majority of his fast-moving chariot force in the battle for the Medway crossing and the forces remaining under his command were inadequate to guard a lengthy coast and river line against attack. He had succeeded in containing the Romans in the area where they had gained a foothold on the north bank of the Thames but he must have been very conscious that the forward position he was occupying in order to do this rendered the whole purpose of his defensive operation extremely vulnerable. On the other hand, to have pulled back his army to defend the tribal capital itself, if unsuccessful, might have resulted in the pillage and destruction of the town which Cunobelin had built and developed with such pride. There were doubtless many Trinovantes who would have wished to avoid a disaster of this nature, which could have ruined their fortunes made from the operations of the seaport, and who would rather, as Rodwell suggests,[20] have welcomed occupation by the Roman army. It is not inconceivable that, as the realisation of his situation came to him, after the death of his brother and perhaps the defection of the Catuvellauni, and as intelligence reports produced increasing evidence of the preparations being made by Plautius to launch an offensive upon the arrival of Claudius, Caratacus dispersed his followers to their homes, retaining a hard core with which to conduct a guerilla style campaign against the enemy's lines of communication. It is more probable, however, that he would have found it difficult to persuade both himself and his henchmen to accept such a decision until the threat had developed to a more critical stage. Indeed, Dio's Narrative leaves no doubt that one more battle took place before the fall of *Camulodunum* and, whilst there is no evidence that Caratacus was present on that occasion, it would have been out of character for him to have been anywhere else. Equally, it may be believed that, with a plan for prolonged resistance already in mind, he would not have delayed on the battlefield to suffer heavy casualties, once the outcome was clear.

No historical record of these events gives any hint as to the locality in which this encounter took place but we can make a rough guess, from our knowledge of the problems confronting Caratacus at that moment and the topography of the land in which the campaign was being conducted. The British chieftain was seeking a defensive position which would enable him to contest the enemy's advance from the west but which would be so close to *Camulodunum* that he could march to its support should it become the target of a seaborne assault from the south-east coast. He did not have far to look for he must have been well aware of the defensive qualities of the river Chelmer and the strategic importance of its crossing place, adjoining the confluence of that river with the Can, where two Iron Age trackways are thought to have converged,[21] one of which later provided the line of the main Roman highway between London and Colchester. It is pure conjecture to suggest that Claudius' victorious encounter with the 'barbarians' took place on this site, for no material evidence has yet been produced to support the possibility; but militarily it appears to be a reasonable supposition, given some credence by Rivet's theory that *Caesaromagus* may be translated as *Caesar's Plain* (see above).

Plautius, with Kent under his control and the *Classis Britannica* operating in his support, had three possible courses of action for consideration:

(a)   to make a seaborne landing across the mouth of the Thames, possibly using Reculver as a supply port, thus outflanking the Britons to his west and directly threatening their capital, *Camulodunum*.

(b)   to exploit the foothold already established on the north bank of the river, build up strength within its area and break out in a thrust towards the Trinovantian capital.

(c)   to cross the Thames upstream in a move which would simultaneously establish a supply base for the forthcoming operation, block the escape route south of the Forest and threaten the flank of the Britons confronting the bridgehead.

The option of a seaborne landing in the Thames estuary, whilst at first sight appearing attractive, would have contained many serious disadvantages. For example, not only would the operation have left open the western escape route from Essex for Caratacus and his followers but it would have required the eastward withdrawal of the bulk of the Roman army after its victorious march westwards, an apparent evacuation of territory which Plautius, for obvious reasons, must be expected to have regarded with disfavour: but, more importantly, the distance across the estuary, an area subject to sudden variations of weather, wind and tide, was considerably greater than that already undertaken by the invasion force a few months earlier, when it crossed the Channel from Boulogne after much preparation. An attack across the waters of the estuary, therefore, would not only have contained an unacceptable degree of uncertainty, in view of Claudius' hopes for a speedy conquest, but would also have required considerable staff and logistical support, possibly withdrawn for the purpose from other deserving areas. It is thus improbable that the Roman general would have considered this to be a viable choice of operation.

Plautius' second possible course of action, namely to build upon the foothold already established on the north bank of the Thames, offered only limited tactical and geographical advantages. His bridgehead force, due to its proximity to Rochester and the Medway, enjoyed a short line of communication for the movement of supplies and reserves across the river and, by its occupation of a compact area, it offered the sort of opportunity for a concentrated military effort at which the Roman soldier excelled. If Plautius could occupy the low gravel ridge which looked down upon his positions, the stage would then be set for him to thrust the remaining three or four miles to seize the ancient ford on the Mardyke at Stifford:[22] by this means he could not only outflank the Britons confronting his bridgehead (if they remained to allow him to do this) but would also open up a possible waterborne supply route from the Thames, up the Mardyke to Stifford. The way would then be prepared for a major advance to Chelmsford but, if he wished to take advantage of the benefits of a waterborne supply route, his progress would be limited by the restricted navigability of the Mardyke compared, for example, with the Lea or the Roding. There are other factors which should be remembered when considering this option. The bridgehead area was not of Plautius' choosing: he had arrived in it whilst pursuing a retreating enemy, its fringes consisted of heavy marshland, severely inhibiting his mobility, and he was probably under constant observation. Thus any attempt to use the bridgehead as a launching-pad for an assault on Essex would have lost the benefits of surprise and mobility, and would have done little to prevent the westward movement of Caratacus and his men should they have decided that the time had come to go.

A number of sub-rectangular earthwork enclosures have been identified along the length of the gravel ridge overlooking the Thames in this area and they have been stated to have had defensive origins in the

39. An *onager* in action: the two legionaries by the machine are applying torsion. The sling on the throwing-arm has yet to be loaded. Each legion had ten *onagri*.

mid-1st century AD; but this possibility is being increasingly discarded by authoritative opinion. Three of them, at Mucking, Gun Hill and East Tilbury, are tactically sited on high ground with a view over the river. Another earthwork of similar construction is located further inland at Orsett: and it is described by Rodwell as being situated[23]

> . . . perhaps not without significance, on the highest piece of land for some miles around (35m OD) and (is) alongside a ridgeway, now the A 13, at least of Roman and possibly earlier origin.

He adds his opinion that this earthwork, together with those at Mucking and Gun Hill, was a short lived defensive construction, built around the time of the Roman conquest. Babbidge[27] disputes this viewpoint, believing that the sites 'reflect nothing more grand than the farmsteads of single families', since 'it is very hard to see a Roman inception for any of them', and he adds

> The strategic nonsense of a large number of small isolated defended strongpoints is obvious, and indeed such a concept was against the

whole Belgic military philosophy which, according to classical
authors, demanded set-piece battles.

Whilst admitting that considerable doubt must remain about the
purpose of these earthworks until further evidence is uncovered, it does
appear that this statement is over conclusive. Strategy deals with the art
of war and the conduct of a campaign, tactics with the deployment of
troops: it might thus have been tactical nonsense to deploy so many
defended strongpoints as suggested by Babbidge but equally there may
have been sound military thinking behind their provision. If, for
example, Plautius had pulled back to the river simply to defend the
Thames crossing place, he might have pushed forward strong standing
patrol groups of 300 to 400 men, dependent upon the size of the
enclosure being discussed,[25] to occupy the high ground in this manner
to safeguard his position. Alternatively, and not improbably, he might
have withdrawn his force from the bridgehead in its entirety and have
been content to watch over the southern end of the crossing, whilst
consolidating his position in Kent. An action of this nature might have
produced so much uncertainty in the British camp that it could have
resulted in their withdrawal to the line of the Chelmer, whilst leaving
these positions overlooking the Thames to report on Roman movement. Finally, it is arguable that Belgic military philosophy, at least as it
applied to Britain, did not demand set-piece battles, for this was an art
of war at which they were greatly inferior to their well-rehearsed
Roman opponents. Cassivellaunus, after one or two battlefield encounters with Julius Caesar, soon learnt that it was a more profitable tactic
to harry the Roman line of communication than to confront the legions
in serried ranks. There are clear indications from the pattern of the
campaign after Plautius' landings in Kent, that Cunobelin's two sons
had also grasped this lesson, perhaps from handed-down knowledge of
Cassivellaunus' experience. Tacitus gave some indication of this when
he wrote about the prowess of Caratacus[26]

> . . . whose many undefeated battles, and even many victories, had
> made him pre-eminent among British chieftains. His deficiency in
> strength was compensated by superior cunning and topographical
> knowledge.

This, surely, is the description of a man who was an expert in irregular
warfare; and it is an interesting statement in another way, for it raises
the question of whether Caratacus played any part in harassing the
Roman advance across southern Britain after the fall of *Camulodunum*,

before his emergence in Wales, and whether this advance was completed as swiftly as is popularly believed.

The broad outline of Plautius' third possible course of action is plain enough but, when discussing the factors affecting it, there are two questions which must also be considered, namely, what are the known facts surrounding Claudius' arrival. and how was the final capitulation of the Trinovantes brought about?

It may perhaps be assumed that Claudius and his entourage followed the pattern set by Julius Caesar, in his two expeditions of the previous century, and of Plautius himself earlier in the year, and sailed from Boulogne about midnight to arrive off the Kentish coast in the early morning. Claudius would not have been encumbered by numerous fleet transports, since the reinforcements of troops and elephants he is said to have brought with him almost certainly would have preceded his arrival, else they would have slowed his rate of progress considerably; but the status of the emperor could not have been allowed to be diminished and it may be guessed that he crossed the Channel in an especially equipped fleet vessel, closely escorted by an appropriate number of ships of the *Classis Britannica*, which would have been responsible for the comfort of his travel and his safe arrival. Claudius' prime objective was to preside over the conquest of the Trinovantes and the capture of *Camulodunum*: he had, moreover, just completed an arduous land and river journey to Boulogne from Italy. The road journey from Richborough to Rochester, which now lay in front of him, covered a distance of some 38 miles; but if he disembarked at Canterbury he could reduce this to 30 miles approximately. By this time, however, his army almost certainly would have been assembled in its marshalling area on the Thames, upstream of Rochester awaiting his arrival. It may thus be imagined that, if Claudius had opted to travel by road, he would have been required to undertake a long and tiring two-day journey, along a roughly constructed tactical road (see Appendix C), an arrangement which would have demanded considerable logistical and military support which, at this juncture, might have been more profitably employed elsewhere. It is more likely that his planning staff arranged for him to continue his way by ship, under naval escort and travelling through the night if necessary, to rendezvous with his army in the field. This proposition implies that Plautius had already prepared detailed plans for the operation which, by this time, had been set in hand and were well advanced. These plans would have included arrangements for the move across the Thames, the seizure of river crossing places and other ground vital to his success, the deployment of the legions on to their start lines prior to an eastward thrust towards *Camulodunum* and the establishment of an assured logistical supply system.

Plautius need have had no worries that his passage of the Thames would be contested for if, as may well have been the case, the Catuvellauni had already defected to him, he could have landed without opposition anywhere in their territory west of the Lea and the Hackney Marshes. The most probable crossing place in these circumstances would have been at Southwark, where considerable archaeological excavation has been conducted in recent years and opposite which, Chapman suggests,[27] there may later have been a fort on the river bank upstream of the bridge, using the Walbrook as protection for its western flank and the river Thames on its south. The facts that only small evidence of Roman military activity has been uncovered on the south bank, opposite the City of London, and that the contemporary Roman roads leading to the southern end of the bridge are shown to have been built c. AD 50 and not AD 43, need not necessarily discourage this thinking, for it may be assumed that the assault force would have moved speedily eastwards from there to take hold of the fords across the Lea in the Hackney Marsh area and thence, almost

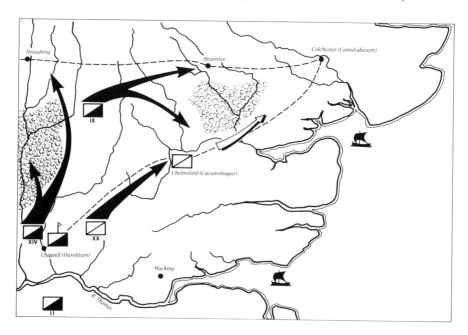

40. The assault on Essex. The map shows how the collapse of British resistance in Essex might have been achieved. XIV Legion aims to close the escape routes westward through the Essex Forest and through Braughing to the Icknield Way. IX Legion outflanks the British at Chelmsford (Caesaromagus) and cuts the track between Braughing and Colchester (Camulodunum). XX Legion crosses the Chelmer and pursues the British as they fall back on Colchester. The Roman Navy in the Thames estuary poses an additional threat.

without delay and so as to rid itself of the military dangers of the surrounding marshy land and the neighbouring forest, to the line of the river Roding. Once in this position, with its right flank based on the mouth of the Roding at Barking, probably secured by the *Classis Britannica*, and with its left flank gripping the ford across the Roding at Chigwell (*Durolitum*), the southern escape route from Essex was effectively blocked and one part of Plautius' task had been achieved. His next act would have been to cast forward strong fighting patrols to locate the enemy and safeguard the front of his assault force as it was deployed along the river line. When this manoeuvre had been carried out he would now have provided himself with a valuable waterborne supply route certainly as far as Chigwell, where an advanced supply depot could have been established preparatory to the next phase of the operation and which he could later have extended through to Ongar. The meaning of *Durolitum*, the fort at the ford, seems to have a special significance which dovetails with a scenario of this nature.

The ease with which this style of operation could have been executed, probably without opposition, and the likelihood that Claudius arrived by ship to join his army, poses the question whether Dio telescoped his account of these events when he wrote[28]

> ... he joined the legions which were waiting for him near the Thames. And taking command of these he forced the river and, engaging the barbarians who had gathered to face his attack, he defeated them in battle and captured *Camulodunum*, Cunobelin's royal seat.

There can be no doubt about the meaning of Dio's opening sentence. He is not telling us that Claudius joined his waiting army in Kent or on the south side of the river but in their positions *near* the Thames: that is to say, his legions could have been deployed either north or south of the river, or on both banks. This possibility has been well recognised: Merrifield[29] implies that both banks were already held in strength by Plautius at the time of the emperor's arrival when he argues that the Roman general employed his army in the construction of a substantial bridge during the period covered by the summoning of Claudius from Rome and his ultimate assumption of command. If, therefore, it can be agreed that the Roman army was occupying both banks of the Thames in strength at this historic moment, then there could have been no apparent military need or purpose for Claudius to disembark upon the far bank of the river and then to cross it, unless for purely symbolic reasons. It is more likely, assuming that he came by ship, that he followed the long established trade route up the Thames, from the

41.   *left:* Gold *aureus* of Claudius (AD 41–54) commemorating his triumph over Britain.
right: A silver *didrachm* struck to commemorate the Claudian conquest of Britain.

Wantsum Channel, and was then carried up the Lea, or more probably the Roding, to the point where his army was assembled, poised for the final push. It is not difficult to imagine his ceremonial progress along the course of the river, being acclaimed by his legions, before landing at *Durolitum.*

It is less easy to accept Dio's next statement that Claudius, taking command of his legions, 'forced the river', if by these words he intended to suggest that the emperor attacked across the river Thames. Professor Frere, who has been kind enough to interpret the above passage for me, is in no doubt that Dio's words should be taken exactly as they stand unless there is some good reason why the original Greek can be construed in a different way. Chapman, obviously detects a sense of ambiguity in Dio's version of these events when he suggests[30] that his reference to a river crossing is at variance with the accounts in Suetonius and recorded on Claudius' triumphal arch in Rome; he adds that, since at that stage of the operation the Thames must be presumed to have been occupied on both banks, the statement that he forced the river, engaged the Britons and defeated them in battle, must refer to another river, either the Lea or the Chelmer. This proposition is so close to what Colonel Burne, the well known military historian, used to call the 'military probability' that it leaves open only two other possible explanations. One is that Dio misunderstood the account of the operation contained in the archives from which he drew his information. Or it could be that the official document, which he used as his source of information, was one of those papers about which Tacitus complained when he wrote that the reigns of Gaius Caligula, Claudius and Nero were described 'during their lifetime in fictitious terms for fear of the consequences . . .' Indeed, if it can be accepted that Claudius' campaign in Britain was a carefully staged political event, as we have suggested, directed towards the attainment of his much-wanted triumph, then it must be clear that the official war diaries of the invasion can have done nothing else but support the official line, if only by the cloudy recording of events.

By the time of Claudius' arrival, the Britons had already been defeated in all but deed: all that was now required was for a legion to be despatched northwards in the direction of Great Dunmow, there to cross the Chelmer, thus turning the flank of the opposition at *Caesar-omagus*, impeding movement along the main tribal trackway between *Camulodunum* and Braughing and, simultaneously, opening up a new supply route with the rich grain producing areas of the Catuvellauni.

Caratacus would not have stayed to fight to the finish. He had other things in mind.

CHAPTER SIX

CARATACUS' FIGHTING WITHDRAWAL

Oh, yesterday, our little troop was ridden through and through,
Our swaying, tattered pennons fled, a broken, beaten few,
And all a summer afternoon they hunted us and slew;
But to-morrow,
By the living God, we'll try the game again!

John Masefield[1]

The speedy and successful conquest of any large area of heavily populated territory, such as existed in central and southern Britain in AD 43, ultimately depends upon the early restoration of firm government. Indeed, in any major campaign, whereas in the opening stages the whole attention of the commanding general is directed towards the conduct of the battles in which his forces are involved, it is later inevitable, as peace returns to the lands he has either liberated or conquered, that his duties will absorb more and more civil responsibilities. The planning of this aspect of war is one which sometimes tends to be neglected, perhaps because it consumes vital resources of manpower and material which might otherwise be directed towards the furtherance of operations; but its consequence to the outcome of a campaign can be as important as victory on the battlefield itself, as much so in ancient times as it is today. Field Marshal Sir William Slim has recorded that in 1945, when his XIVth army debouched from the Chin Hills on to the Burma plains in hot pursuit of the Japanese, he was confronted 'with startling suddenness with the need to administer to the cares and problems of the civil population'.[2] His task of restoring a framework of government was hampered by an acute shortage of qualified officials, of whom 'too many were held in India under the exiled Burmese Government' or had been posted elsewhere because the necessity of their presence at this crucial moment, despite otherwise punctilious military preparations, had not been anticipated. Slim was able to patch together an increasingly functional organisation by using Burmese members of the pre-war administration, who had gone into hiding on the arrival of the Japanese and now emerged as the tide of battle flowed past them, to help with the process of national reconstruction.

The conditions found by XIVth Army, although proportionately much greater than those encountered by Plautius in AD 43, cannot have been very dissimilar in appearance. Great acreages of land had gone out of cultivation; much of the population, many of whom had taken to the jungle, were living in destitution and were short of such necessities as clothing and food; starvation was rife; towns and villages had been burnt; houses were deserted and pillaged and, in the normal sequence of events, violence and banditry were commonplace. In short, all the man-made disasters which follow in the wake of war were present. Clearly, if the power of civil authority was to be restored, and pending the re-creation of the national para-military police force, substantial military assistance was needed, albeit for a limited period: thus the size of Slim's field army, available to him for the continuance of further operations, was reduced. It is possible to see in these events a mirror of the situation which confronted Plautius, who seems to have planned his invasion of Britain in a number of clearcut phases. Each one of these contained different problems but, although in some areas there was deep hostility, and at least three tribes, the Iceni, Dobunni and Durotriges, appear to have been divided in varying degrees in this respect, the Romans had astutely been able to negotiate helpful alliances at almost every stage. In doing this they were drawing upon years of experience for, in their earliest expansionist period, they had quickly learnt the benefits to the State of arrangements of this nature, in terms of both financial and manpower economies. Thus if neutral areas could be defined, capable of being isolated from theatres of operation or of acting as buffer states in frontier locations, or if dependable rulers could be found to whom liberated or conquered territories could be entrusted in 'freedom' under the protection of Rome, then many of the problems of conducting a war on the extremities of empire could be resolved, whether strategic, logistical or economic. Rome achieved the answer by a process of transition,[3] first, by the appointment of 'client kings' with whom treaties were made and the process set in hand and, second, by the encouragement of local self-government as mutual confidence was established. The ability of the 'client' to maintain law and order was thus implied and for this purpose a reasonably sized body of armed men in certain instances must have been permitted but not, presumably, in doubtful areas where resistance to conquest had been strongest.

When Plautius' term of office came to an end, and he returned to Rome to be honoured for the success of his campaign in Britain, a frontier zone was already being established on the western boundary of the new province and a network of auxiliary forts had been created on the lines of communication leading to it.[4] Webster has suggested[5] that these forts, located at major trackway junctions and river crossing-places (each fort being a day's march from another), not only had the task of safeguarding the flow of traffic but also to restrict the mobility of the subject population and thus impede its ability to muster a resistance force. In a study designed to gauge the scale of such a deployment in Britain, and based upon a projection of already discovered sites, he has estimated that more than 130 forts would have been needed for this purpose during the Plautian period, although perhaps not all of them would have been manned simultaneously. If it is assumed that each garrison broadly consisted of a total of 150 men (some would undoubtedly have been much stronger than this and others possibly smaller) then this would have posed a requirement for nearly 20,000 soldiers, without taking to account the numbers required to administer the force in the field. This figure is the equivalent of the total number of auxiliary soldiers, including cavalrymen, who are estimated to have landed in Kent in AD 43 with the invasion force.

It is inexplicable that the Roman high command should apparently have been willing, even at a time after the cessation of open hostilities, to fragment their reserves in this logistically expensive way and, by so doing, reduce their ability to respond quickly to a hostile situation. There can be no better example of the weakness of this tactic than that provided by the failure of the Romans in AD 60 to respond effectively and instantly to the Boudiccan rebellion. The General at that time, Paulinus, had already the precedent of the AD 47 uprising under the leadership of the Iceni from which to learn, and he should have been aware of the resentment towards their conquerors which smouldered fiercely below the surface of British tribal affairs. In turn his predecessors, Scapula and Plautius, should have learnt something from Caesar's costly experience in Gaul, where his speedy conquest of the country was followed by some six years of tribal warfare, as confidence returned to the conquered. Each of these rebellions had a common factor, namely, they occurred when Roman resources were stretched to capacity and their forces were thus greatly disadvantaged. Tacitus has given us some idea of Paulinus' dilemma when he writes,[6] perhaps with some exaggeration of the scale of the rebellion but none of its ferocity, that

> the whole island rose under the leadership of Boudicca, a lady of royal descent ... they hunted down the Roman troops in their scattered outposts, stormed the forts and assaulted the colony (Camulodunum) ...

When Paulinus received news of these disturbing events he was campaigning in northern Wales with the main weight of his army, and was far distant from the centre of the trouble. He had just defeated the British forces, stimulated as they were by 'Druids', in a final bloody battle on Anglesey: he immediately disengaged from the battlefield and hastened eastwards with his supporting cavalry, leaving the infantry to follow at their best speed. It was two weeks before he could muster a force of some 10,000 men with which to confront and destroy the rebel army, which is said to have suffered a loss of 80,000 men in the resulting battle. It is a figure which is sometimes disputed but nevertheless, even if over estimated, it leaves no doubt that the tribes had managed to assemble a considerable host, apparently unhindered if not unnoticed. If it had not been for Paulinus' quick response on receiving tidings of the disaster, Britain, according to Tacitus, 'would have been lost'. The network of forts established by Plautius east of the Fosse Way border area was therefore a highly vulnerable method of occupying enemy territory, which must have become increasingly so as he pushed his frontiers further and further westwards. Conversely, his grip on the more compact area of conquered tribal lands immediately following the fall of *Camulodunum* was tenacious and impenetrable.

It was arrangements of this nature, such as the institution of 'client' kingdoms, the military occupation of other areas and, by implication, the re-establishment of law and order, which Dio attributed to Claudius in a somewhat flattering passage probably based on the account rendered to the Senate by the Emperor upon his return to Rome. As a result of their appreciation of it, they granted him the honour of a full triumph and he awarded himself a *corona navalis*, along with a *corona civica*, in recognition of his victory over Oceanus upon crossing to Britain. Dio relates that, as a result of the victorious outcome of Claudius' campaign in Essex[7]

> ... he brought over many of the Britons, some by negotiation, others by force, and was therefore hailed *Imperator* many times, contrary to custom. He proceeded to disarm these natives and entrusted them to Plautius, whom he instructed to bring the remaining territory under Roman control.

The 'remaining territory' in this context may fairly be assumed to refer to the unconquered lands as yet to be occupied in order to complete the Roman province of Britannia, the creation of which Claudius had given to Plautius as the objective of his campaign. Its area included all of Britain to the east of a line from the mouth of the River Exe to the Humber estuary. The whole area was bisected by the valley of the river

42. A detachment of XX Legion on guard duty.

Thames and thus provided Plautius with two operational sectors, one north and the other south of the river.

The varying political and operational problems which these two sectors presented to Plautius are reflected in the proportion in which he deployed his legions within them. He allotted one Legion, II Legion *Augusta*, to the southern sector: his remaining three legions, IX Legion *Hispana*, XIV Legion *Gemina* and XX Legion *Valeria*, were given operational tasks north of the river. This significant division of duties was almost certainly made for one or both of two reasons: the extent of his trust in the loyalty of the tribes peopling his respective operational sectors and the urgent need for continuous military action against Caratacus and his followers for, until he could be seized, the British king was bound to be a source of unrest. The operations in the southern sector, with Vespasian's campaigns against the tribes of the West Country, will be discussed in greater detail below: but the ease with which the Kentish kingdoms, with the lands of the Atrebates, fell under the Roman hand is at once recognisable and remarkable. The security of the area, which appears to have survived intact despite the traumas of the Boudiccan rebellion of AD 60, provided a continuing mainstay of

Roman support and could not have been maintained in such a fashion, with such apparently slim military resources, unless its governance had been carefully pre-planned. The Romans had, of course, as a matter of policy, established close links with all tribes in south-east Britain whose lands were safely accessible from the continent. It was, as we have seen, these moves which sparked a reaction from Caratacus and Togodumnus and brought about the flight to Europe of many British princes friendly to Rome. Amongst these was Verica, the elderly ruler of the Regni, whose brother was Tincommius of the Atrebates. It would thus be surprising if the Romans had not landed with a leavening of British princes to reassume, under their political guidance, the tribal leaderships which they had been forced to vacate in earlier years.

A ruler who emerged at this time as a powerful prince loyal to the Roman cause was Cogidubnus. His origins and family background have been the subject of much speculation and have been widely and authoratively discussed elsewhere. His name is frequently associated with the great palace of that era which is continuing to be excavated at Fishbourne, near Chichester, but the area over which he ruled is uncertain. Tacitus records that[8]

> ... certain *civitates* were granted to *Cogidubnus* – he remained most loyal right down to the period of our own recollection – in accordance with an ancient and long-established practice of the Roman people of using even kings as instruments of servitude.

Professor Barrett considers that these *civitates* may have comprised the old kingdom of the Atrebates which, towards the end of 1st century AD appears to have been divided into three self-governing *civitates*: the Regni, in whose territory lay Chichester, the *civitas Atrebatum* with its capital at *Calleva* (Silchester) and the *civitas Belgarum* with its capital at *Venta Belgarum* (Winchester).[9] It is unlikely that the Romans would have given Cogidubnus wider responsibility than this upon his initial appointment as a 'client king' for, at a time when the restoration of stability to the tribal homelands was of prime importance, it would have been an action bound to create unnecessary friction and have risked provoking the resentment of the other British princes, traditionally proud and quarrelsome, who had returned with him for the same purpose. Nevertheless, the possibility cannot be denied that, in later years and at the height of his power, the influence of Cogidubnus extended across the breadth of south-east Britain, from the banks of the Hampshire Avon to the eastern coastline of Kent.

The theory that Cogidubnus was additionally awarded extensive military powers has recently been discarded[10] but there is no suggestion that he did not have under his command a considerable force of native troops to assist him in the restoration of law and order and to defend the frontiers of his kingdom. Boon, in his report on the excavations of Belgic and Roman Silchester (1954–8), discussed the Inner Earthwork revealed there which he considered to be traditional, Belgic and un-Roman in style throughout. He had little doubt that it could be seen as 'the work of British allies controlling considerable manpower and enjoying full Roman trust' and was probably the work of Cogidubnus, constructed at a time when Caratacus was on the rampage in the Upper Thames valley and Roman reserves were required elsewhere for defensive purposes. In fact, evidence has yet to be discovered of any substantial Roman military presence in the area of *Calleva* during mid-1st century AD, despite the excavation of some early pieces of equipment, such as a skillet of Italian make and fittings from a *lorica segmentata* (breast-plate). It would not, on the other hand, be surprising if Plautius had provided a training team of Roman regulars for the instruction of the native troops under Cogidubnus. It would also have been out of character if he, involved in a fierce guerrilla war in his northern sector with a highly mobile enemy, had permitted his southern flank to be weakened by any lack of proper military and political organisation. The situation called for some senior officer who would be responsible for the careful coordination of political affairs, military operations and supply administration in the southern sector, so as to lift these burdens from Plautius, north of the Thames, and Vespasian, soon to be deeply involved in a campaign in south-west Britain against the Durotriges and other hostile tribes. Professor CFC Hawkes has indicated who this man might have been.[11]

Plautius was quite clearly the senior military officer who sailed with the task force to land in Kent; but a later historian than Dio, Eutropius, names with him a second general officer who sailed with the expedition, a consul, Cnaeus Sentius. Hawkes visualises this officer leading a splinter invasion force to land in west Sussex, whilst Plautius was seizing Kent, but we have already considered and discounted the feasibility of simultaneous, separate landings. It is much more probable that his allotted task would have been, in the first instance, to administer the occupied territories whilst his commanding general got on with the business of conquest; and secondly, to assume command, under Plautius, of the affairs of the southern sector of operations.

It is a strange paradox that the difficulties which were to confront Plautius after his victorious landings in Kent, and his occupation of Trinovantian territory, arose almost directly from those successes. Until that moment Caratacus had been concentrating on the defence of his tribal homelands and, in particular, *Camulodunum*. With the attainment of these objectives by Plautius, the initiative passed to Caratacus who, now released from the necessity of defending static targets, appears to have launched a prolonged and aggressive campaign of subversion against his more ponderous enemy. His mobile guerilla force probably enjoyed a lot of local sympathy north of the Thames and certainly possessed an invaluable knowledge of the local terrain. These were the ingredients for success: indeed, the effect of Caratacus' opposition to the Roman advance from Essex is demonstrated by the fact that, despite Plautius' best efforts which earned him an ovation on his return to Italy in AD 47, the general military situation which he handed over to his hapless successor (who was to die within a few years, possibly of a heart attack induced by stress) could only be described by Tacitus as 'chaotic': and the frontier along the line of the Fosse Way with which Plautius' name is associated, was even then insufficiently established to prevent the Britons breaking through into Roman territory. As has been noted, it was not until Scapula had made hurried military and political rearrangements after his arrival that his western boundary was secured and a brief period of rather shaky stability was achieved within Rome's newest province.

The Roman occupation of southern Britain was thus not completed by a simple rapid movement as legions fanned out from *Camulodunum* to seize positions for themselves on the western boundary of this territory: it was, rather, a steady, coordinated advance with a military and political admixture, over a period of years, aimed at pacifying the areas being overrun and restoring them to stable government. It is possible to imagine that Plautius divided his campaign into a series of systematic phases

(a) the conquest and pacification of the Kentish kingdoms.

(b) the occupation of Trinovantian territory and the capture of *Camulodunum*.

(c) the pacification of the lands of the Catuvellauni and the Atrebates, and the establishment of the *civitates* of the Belgae and Regni.

(d) the final advance to a western boundary defined by the line of the river Exe, the southern shore of the Bristol Channel and the rivers Severn and Trent.

In this manner, as each phase of Plautius' advance was completed, the western boundary of the territories occupied by him would have been pushed further and further outwards to yet another defended frontier

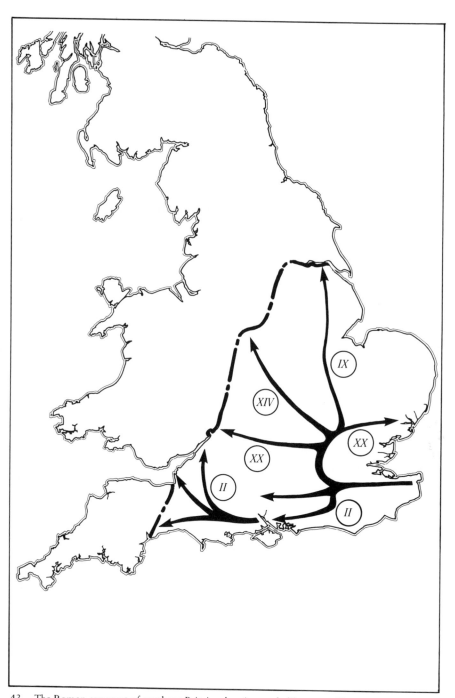

43. The Roman conquest of southern Britain, showing probable areas of legion responsibilities.

line, with coordinated movement in both northern and southern sectors, behind which the army could tackle anew the task of restoring the rule of law. Plainly, Caratacus would have exerted every effort to disrupt this process.

The territory at the western extremity of Plautius' northern operational sector was occupied by the northern faction of the Dobunni, under the chieftainship of Boduoccus. The northern frontier of the sector, aligned with the rivers Severn and Trent, ran through the lands of the Cornovii, with a capital later at Wroxeter; the Coritani, with a capital at Leicester, and the Iceni, whose domain reached from the eastern borders of the Coritani to the North Sea, south of the Wash, but separated from their neighbours by a great area of fen land which extended southwards to Cambridge. This was to be described as[12]

> . . . a most dismal fen of immense size, which begins at the banks of the river Granta not far from the camp which is called Cambridge and stretches from the south as far north as the sea. It is a very long tract, now consisting of marshes, now of bogs, sometimes of black waters overhung by fog, sometimes studded with wooded islands and traversed by the windings of tortuous streams.

Some, if not all, of the leaders of these kingdoms would have witnessed at close hand the downfall of the Trinovantes and were probably already contemplating submission to the Roman invaders. It would therefore have been tactless, if not tactically unwise, for Caratacus to have looked in their direction for help at that moment. Four years later, when the Iceni and the Coritani were simmering on the verge of revolt, the situation was to be different but even then the Brigantes, a primitive, pastoral tribe, ruled by Queen Cartimandua, had shewn themselves sufficiently dependable to have been granted the status of 'client kingdom', perhaps as early as AD 47.[13] It thus figures that Caratacus, when reorganising his forces and operational plans after his withdrawal from Essex, would have expected little support or hospitality from the tribes in the north and probably none at all from those south of the Thames and east of the Hampshire Avon. Plautius had enjoyed a valuable period of some months after his victorious Medway battle, and before the arrival of Claudius, in which to bring stability to this important base area. West of the Hampshire Avon, Caratacus might have been more welcome amongst the tribes of Salisbury Plain or the southern Dobunni, whose territory reached from the Mendips and eastern Somerset to the borders of southern Gloucestershire; but there is little evidence as yet to suggest that they put up much more than a

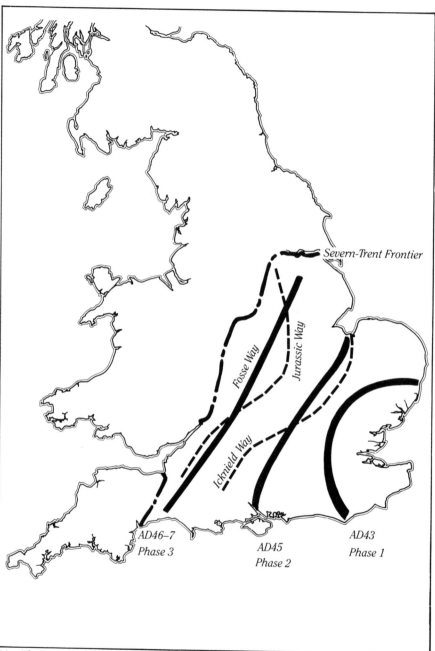

44. The Roman employment of ancient trackways. The map demonstrates the positions of the Jurassic and Icknield Ways in relation to the final frontier position established along the line of the rivers Trent and Severn. It illustrates how easily these might have been used to 'service' the Roman advance.

token resistance to the Roman advance if, indeed, they did not maintain a neutral stance.

It is thus plain that, at an early date, Plautius was successful in gaining the neutrality, if not the total friendship, of tribes located on the flanks of his advance, leaving him free to push his western frontier forward on an ever widening arc. Roman military thinking appears to have recognised that regiments thrust forward to defend exposed frontier areas needed to be mutually supporting, in order to counter the risk of being isolated by enemy raiding parties infiltrating cross-country; because of this, in order to maximise their manpower and for reasons, doubtless, of command and logistical necessity, they evolved a system of 'service' roads, running parallel to their operational frontiers, which permitted the speedy movement of mounted infantry or cavalry to reinforce outposts in cases of emergency. The development of Stanegate, south of Hadrian's Wall, provides one classic example of this: the tactical road constructed by Vespasian between Hamworthy and Bath was perhaps constructed for the same purpose: and the Fosse Way, which remarkably runs from Exeter to Lincoln without deviating more than six miles from its alignment, was almost certainly built for the same tactical reasons. The philosophy behind this idea is reflected in the thinking of Domitian, who introduced a similar technique in Germany at the end of 1st century AD.

'Service' roads thus played an important part in Roman military operations: but they took time to construct and, until provided full use would have been made of existing trackways. The Fosse Way, for example, was laboriously engineered, over a considerable distance, with well marked side ditches and, more often than not, several layers of metalling. It is not easy to believe that it could have been constructed in this manner in a hostile environment, even if a protective screen had been deployed forward of it to safeguard the workforce. A task of this nature, necessarily for a lengthy time, would have deflected Plautius' army from its more important objective, namely, the elimination of Caratacus and the destruction of his guerrilla force. Thus it must be judged that the Fosse Way was built after the withdrawal of the British host across the river Severn into Wales: and, if the Roman general staff were seeking to follow the principle of 'service' roads when selecting the western boundaries for the various phases of their advance, then they would have had to make use of existing trackways. In fact, two ancient trackways were to be found, and may still be traced, in Plautius' northern sector, which would have suited his purpose very well. Both of these slanted from the east coast, diagonally across the country in a south-westerly direction: both were subsequently straightened and developed by the Romans for their own purposes to an extent which emphasised their importance to their plans. These were the *Icknield Way* and the *Jurassic* Way.

The Icknield Way which, it is sometimes suggested, derived its name from the Iceni. It runs from East Anglia, along the western slope of the Chilterns and then continues south-west to a point between Moulsford and Streatley in Berkshire, where it crosses the Thames to join a system of Ridgeways which connect the West Country with the Straits of Dover. Plautius may be expected to have sealed this crossing place, together with those at Staines and Dorchester-on-Thames, at the earliest opportunity. Likewise, he would probably have wished, as soon as circumstances permitted, to control movement along the Way by the occupation of the militarily important areas of Dunstable and Baldock, covering this move with a flank guard near Worsted Lodge. It would have been to his advantage, to complete this phase of his advance by probing forward, without delay, to take positions at Alchester, Towcester, Irchester and Water Newton, hingeing his advance on Dorchester-on-Thames. Dr. Webster[14] sees the line connecting these places as a major route which has so far escaped attention. It should be emphasised that, despite large scale excavations, no evidence of early forts has been discovered at either Baldock or Dunstable; but the military advantage which Plautius would have gained by their occupation is undeniable.

The Jurassic Way, which is named after its geological origin, runs from the southern shore of the Humber, broadly to Lincoln and Grantham and thence it uses the raised ground which forms the watersheds of the streams flowing north-westerly into the Trent, until it links with a low ridge upon which sit Rockingham, Naseby and Daventry. From here it takes a curving, south-westerly course to the Cotswolds and then continues in a southerly direction along the Cotswold Edge, across the Avon at Bath, to the ridges in the South-West. The importance of the Jurassic way to the Romans is reflected in the comment by the editors of the Ordnance Survey Map of Roman Britain, who omitted details of its course from the map because it appeared to 'have been largely superseded by the Foss Way as a connection between the South-West and the Humber'.[15]

The north-west corner of Plautius' northern sector was a strategically vital area since within it lay the gap or 'land-bridge' between the Severn and the Trent valleys, which permitted movement in and out of the sector, to and from Wales and the North. The Romans were well aware of its importance for they stationed within it the equivalent of vexillation-strength standing patrols, or battle groups, at Wall, Kinvas-

45. The River Severn at Ironbridge, 60 miles north of Gloucester as the crow flies, would have presented a formidable obstacle to the Roman legions in pursuit of Caractacus.

ton and probably Metchley. Frere[16] believes that they came, with supporting auxiliaries, from XIV Legion *Gemina* in about AD 48, as part of Scapula's enhanced campaign. It is equally possible that Plautius had already been moving forward in this direction prior to that date. What is of interest, when endeavouring to piece together the Roman overall plan of campaign, is that they identified this area as one of great strategic importance and took these steps to close it firmly.

Similarly, in the sector's south-westerly extremity, the domination of that stretch of the Way reaching from the Bristol Avon to a point near Cheltenham would have been militarily equally desirable. The threat of this area as an invasion route into Wessex was seemingly recognised by a tribal leader in the post-Roman period and countered by the construction of the Wansdyke, which was positioned to cover the gap between the headwaters of the rivers Avon and Kennet. The number of battles which occurred within it bear witness to the accuracy of his appreciation. 'Arthur' repulsed a Saxon invasion at Mount Badon, in the Upper Thames Valley, circa AD 490; the West Saxons destroyed a British host, and slew three princes, at Dyrham, six miles north of Bath, in AD 577; but perhaps the most significant raid through the gap was made in AD 878 by Guthrum, the Dane, who, supported by a fleet sailing up the Bristol Channel, advanced from Cirencester to seize Alfred's winter headquarters at Chippenham, thus forcing the Saxon king's flight to Athelney. Guthrum's subsequent defeat, and the rise to pre-eminence of the Kings of Wessex, is well known. It would be surprising, if the Roman general staff, which identified so readily the strategic importance of the north-westerly 'land-bridge', should have failed to recognise the perhaps greater importance of this south-western area to their operational plans.

But whatever they chose to do ultimately depended upon the behaviour of Caratacus.

There is little evidence of the movements of Caratacus after the British defeat on the Medway and, indeed, even his presence there at that moment remains a matter of pure conjecture, although it is improbable that someone of his heroic nature would not then have been present, if circumstances allowed, playing a full part. When Togodumnus died, the British reacted sharply and, 'far from surrendering . . . gathered all the more strongly' to avenge the death of their leader. This was not the behaviour of a leaderless, beaten force and one can only judge that Caratacus was at their head, inflicting the maximum punishment upon his enemy but probably already secretly aware of the impossibility of defeating Plautius in conventional battle. The next indication of his whereabouts is presented to us by Tacitus, who writes in his *Annals* that, when Publius Ostorius Scapula arrived in Britain in AD 47, to succeed Plautius as Governor,

> . . . a disturbed situation met (him), enemy forces having poured into the territory of the allies, all the more violently because they did not imagine that a new general, with an army of unknown quality, would go out to meet them at the beginning of winter.[17]

Scapula immediately took action to restore the position by advancing into the troubled frontier zone with a light column of selected auxiliary battalions and forced the withdrawal of the insurgents. He next turned his attention to the crisis developing in his rear echelons, where matters had been deteriorating rapidly in the months before his arrival: what he found there resolved him to disarm all the tribes behind the frontier area whose loyalty was suspect. His intervention provided the necessary spark. The Iceni, who until now had cooperated fully with their Roman conquerors, were the first to revolt and they were quickly joined by others including, almost certainly, the Coritani, whose territory covered the broad area of present day Lincolnshire and the East Midlands. Frere suggests[18] that the trouble amongst the Iceni was confined to the western branch of the tribe, since Prasutagus, king of the eastern faction bordering the coast,survived the rebellion to be appointed ruler of the whole of the Iceni and thus presumably must be judged not to have participated.

Scapula wasted little time in putting down the uprising, despite some very tough fighting in which his son, Marcus, was awarded a *corona civica* for gallantry. Tacitus expressed the view[19] that Scapula's prompt and determined action had the affect of 'quieting others who were wavering between war and peace'. There must, therefore, have been a good deal more than a general sense of unrest amongst the tribes north of the Thames at this time: and it seems that the newly arrived commanding general, by a quick and accurate appreciation of what was happening, intervened before they had the opportunity to muster at full strength. The revolt, far from being a spontaneous outburst of tribal anger at the removal of their weapons, appears rather to have been a carefully conceived operation, possibly under the guidance of Caratacus, designed as a final and concerted effort to eject the Romans from Britain, whilst their forces were dangerously extended and a change of command was in progress. This moment, in AD 47, provided a rare occasion when total victory by the British might have been achieved but it is improbable that the tribal chieftains involved in the uprising would have committed themselves to the enterprise if they could not have seen clearly that it stood a reasonable chance of success. They doubtless felt that Caratacus, who by now had earned a considerable military reputation, could offer this to them. Again, when describing the British leader's arrival as a captive in Rome, and the interest demonstrated by the crowd as they gathered to watch his procession through the streets, Tacitus noted that the war in Britain was then in its ninth year and that[19]

the reputation of Caratacus had spread beyond the islands and through the neighbouring provinces to Italy itself. (The) people were curious to see the man who had defied our power for so many years.

The picture presented by these words is that, after the fall of *Camulodunum*, Caratacus conducted a relentless, probably continuous, frequent-

46. A British coin inscribed CARA, minted by Caratacus. The reverse side shows an eagle grasping a serpent.

ly successful campaign against the Roman occupying force and inflicted several defeats upon it;[20] the fact that he sustained its momentum for a period of nine years, when considered in the light of the resources of men and material available to his enemy, is remarkable.

Caratacus' first task upon extricating himself from Essex, must surely have been to find a firm base where he could once again raise his standard. From here he could reorganise, attract others to his cause and despatch harassing parties to obstruct Plautius as he strove to extend his area of occupation, with the intention of making the latter's task so costly in terms of resources that he would, like Caesar, be compelled to withdraw. The site he was seeking would have needed to be sufficiently close to his area of operation so that his patrols would not waste unnecessary time in travel. It was essential, therefore that it should be well concealed, that its approaches should be defensible and that it should lie east of the river Severn. It would be reasonable to assume that he initially used the Savernake Forest area, near *Calleva* but it has been persuasively argued[21] that later he withdrew to a site near Stroud, in Gloucestershire, where a complex of fortifications at Minchinhampton, could have provided a stronghold large enough to accomodate a considerable force, with camp followers, flocks and herds and much equipment. The position is defended by steep escarpments, which rise a sheer 600 feet from the valley below, on all sides except the south-east: here formidable earthworks have been erected, with the ditches cut out of rock. The ramparts are in some cases built from stone and revetted with dry stone walls. The site, if occupied by Caratacus, would have provided him with a speedy withdrawal route into South Wales and with access to the mineral resources of the Forest of Dean, thus furnishing the means for the repair and manufacture of weaponry.

A perplexing aspect of the proposition put forward by Mrs Clifford is that the British general should have selected a site for his stronghold so close to Bagendon, then conceivably an *oppidum* of the northern Dobunni but almost certainly a prosperous tribal trading centre established, Cunliffe suggests,[22] some time just before the invasion of AD 43. It will be recalled that it was this element of the tribe led by Boduoccus (Bodvoc), which had defected to the Romans soon after their landings in Kent and had thus contributed significantly to the British defeat by their behaviour and treacherous example. The terri-tory of the northern Dobunni probably included all Gloucestershire, with frontier areas in Worcestershire and Herefordshire: their eastern boundary extended to north Oxfordshire, where the river Cherwell delineated their border with the Catuvellauni. Excavated finds at Bagendon indicate that the area enjoyed a brisk trade with the Catuvellauni, importing luxury goods from *Camulodunum* such as wine, Arretine pottery from Italy and red glazed ware from southern Gaul, in exchange for a variety of bartered merchandise, amongst which precious metals, wools, hides and slaves probably figured largely.[23] It was doubtless this mutual interest of trade which, in the first instance, persuaded Boduoccus to throw in his lot with the Catuvellauni in an effort to repulse the Roman landings: when he saw the scale and organisation of the Roman operations he was quick to submit, an act which would not have been easily forgiven by Caratacus. Equally, he would not have been lightly abandoned by the Roman high command. It may therefore be imagined that Boduoccus, upon hearing of the arrival of Caratacus in the lower Severn basin, with a tough, battle experienced army, would not in the circumstances have waited to feel the force of his anger. It is likely that he would have abandoned his kingdom to his opponent and fled westwards to seek the protection of his Roman masters who, at this moment, would have been pushing their western frontiers towards his territories.

The extent of land thus abandoned by Boduoccus to Caratacus, if we are right in assuming that this was the pattern of events, would have stretched southwards towards the southern Dobunni, who were poss-ibly more friendly to the British cause, perhaps even to the banks of the Bristol Avon. Eastwards, it probably reached to Lechlade and Bourton-on-the-Water, where it would have included the *oppidum* at Salmons-bury, which lay at the point of intersection of a number of tribal trackways thus giving it control over the passage of goods and command of the trading routes. Salmonsbury was a large, militarily valuable, Iron Age stronghold, sited amidst rich, low-lying pasture land and would have had much to offer Caratacus as a forward outpost. The British commander would surely have wished to bring this flank under his control for, apart from its plentiful grain resources, its occupation would have provided early warning to him of any enemy movement along the axis of the upper Thames valley.

No clear alternative has yet emerged to take the place of Mrs Clifford's proposition that Caratacus used this area as a base to gather his followers and mount his continuing operations against Rome. It remains to be seen whether her imaginative and militarily practical theory will stand the test of time: but there can be no doubt that the Minchinhampton complex and the surrounding terrain would ideally have suited the needs of the British commander, particularly its proximity to his Silurean allies to whom he could have looked either for shelter or reinforcement in case of emergency. If he did not occupy the Minchinhampton complex, then he would have needed to find something very similar to it.

The domain of the Silures, who were described by Tacitus as a 'strong and warlike nation', extended along the north shore of the Bristol Channel, possibly as far as Swansea. Their centre at Llanmelin, a few miles west of Chepstow, suggests that they maintained links across the Severn estuary by ferry boat, for this is a natural crossing place. A similar Roman link is shown in the Antonine Itinerary, between Caerwent and Sea Mills.[24] It may thus not be over imaginative to suggest that the Silures possessed a sea-going capacity which posed more than a casual threat across the Bristol Channel. Their ability to raid the opposing coastline would have made considerable demands upon Roman military resources and, until the arrival of the *Classis Britannica* to establish complete control of those waters, would inevitably have delayed the course of the Roman campaign in both its northern and southern sectors. One is reminded of the guile with which Cassivellaunus struck at Caesar's beach-head, whilst that general was operationally involved in the interior. Caratacus would surely not have missed such an opportunity to create trouble for his enemy by extending the combat area, whilst using the minimum of manpower resources. Likewise, one may assume that the Roman general staff would have foreseen such a possibility, calling for the presence of their Navy in the Bristol Channel if the western boundary of their new province was to be safely secured.

To summarise: the situation which existed at the time of the handover of command between Plautius and Scapula was probably as follows: XIV Legion *Gemina* had been allocated the task of closing the north-western 'land-bridge' but it could not have been kept remote from the operations further south, if only because of manpower shortages. At least some elements may be imagined to have pushed down the line of the Severn, through Droitwich, to link with the southern battle group in sealing the crossing-places over the river. A reserve force, to fill the vacuum thus created in the XIV Legion area and to act as back-up for the forward troops, was probably found by the eastward move of the greater part of IX Legion, perhaps as far as Leicester and High Cross: it would have been a wise precaution but it could not fail to have signalled to the Iceni and Coritani that the Roman garrison was being stretched to its limits. The central battle group, advancing along the Thames valley, had four vital objectives lying to its front, three of which – Cirencester, Andoversford and the ford across the river at Kingsholm, north of Gloucester – demanded occupation at the earliest moment. The main strike force of this group, was probably provided by XX Legion *Valeria*. The fourth objective, lay at Sea Mills, situated on rising ground overlooking the vital ferry route across the Bristol Channel to the hostile territory of the Situres.

In the light of these possible circumstances it is no surprise to learn that a tombstone excavated in Cirencester attests to the presence there, in mid-1st century AD, of a trooper of *Ala Thracum*, a cavalry unit of 500 men which probably accompanied XX Legion when it landed in Britain in AD 43: and that two military tombstones were discovered a mile from Kingsholm, one a memorial to a trooper of Sixth Cohort of Thracians, a unit which campaigned with XIV Legion, and one which commemorated a trooper of XX Legion. A fortress was built at Kingsholm by XX Legion circa AD 49 but the site was almost certainly occupied two or three years earlier by an auxiliary unit, conceivably the Sixth Cohort from XIV Legion, which then handed over its duties to XX Legion as we have suggested, so that its parent formation could reassume its original deployment area. It is probable that Sea Mills was handed over to II Legion *Augusta* as part of this rationalisation.

CHAPTER SEVEN

THE CAMPAIGN IN THE WEST

> Apart from the perils of navigation, especially on the Chindwin, there was one serious obstacle to the use of these rivers as our line of communication – we had no boats ... One hot day at the beginning of the advance, I took Bill Hasted, my quiet spoken Chief Engineer, a little upstream of Kalewa and said, 'Billy, there's the river and there are the trees ...'
>
> *Field Marshal Sir William Slim*[1]

Flavius Vespasian was about thirty-two years of age when, upon the accession of the Emperor Claudius in AD 41, he received command of II Legion *Augusta*. Vespasian's sculptured likeness confirms the description of him given by his biographer, Suetonius.[2] He was a good-looking, well proportioned man of commanding appearance, the line of whose jaw hinted at considerable leadership qualities. As a soldier he demanded high standards of discipline. When some legionaries complained to him about the quality of their footwear, he made them march without sandals, presumably because he doubted their dedication: but, if this seems an unreasonable attitude, Suetonius assures us that, as Governor of Rome's African Province and then as Emperor, his rule was characterised by great justice, modesty and dignity. In AD 43, he landed in Britain with the invading expeditionary force and, as described in an oft quoted extract

> ... he fought thirty battles, subjugated two warlike tribes and captured more than twenty oppida, beside the Isle of Wight (*Vectis*). In these campaigns he served at times under Aulus Plautius, a commander of consular rank, and at times directly under Claudius ...

130

47. Vespasian: commander of II Legion *Augusta* under Aulus Plautius and Emperor Claudius,
AD 71–79.

During the decisive battle on the Medway, in the opening weeks of the
invasion, Vespasian was despatched upstream by Plautius to cross the
river and outflank the British. We also know, although we are not
aware of the date when the happening occurred, that the capture of the
Isle of Wight was attributed to Vespasian by Suetonius. It thus seems
logical to assume that II Legion, under his command, did not, like the
others in the invasion force, cross the Thames in pursuit of the British
host as it withdrew towards *Camulodunum.*

Although we may be certain that the major part of the British force
withdrew successfully across the river after the two day fight at the
Medway, we can have equally little doubt that a considerable number
of stragglers, and perhaps even some units, were cut off and prevented
from doing so. This is to be expected in operations of this nature and

TABLE IV
Suggested Roman Command Structure
Phase IV – The advance to the western frontier of the Province – AD 46–7

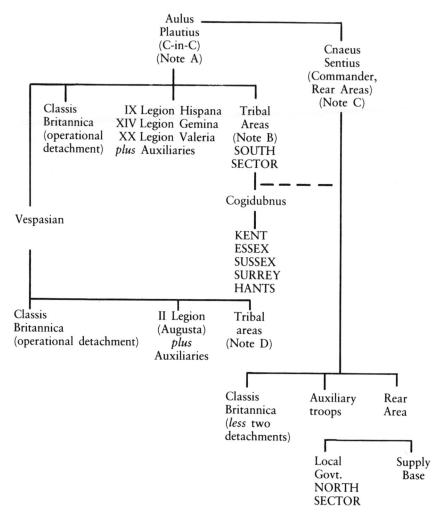

Notes: A. Suitable Headquarter Bases would have been DORCHESTER-ON-THAMES or ALCHESTER from command viewpoint.

B. By AD 46–7 control of the civil southern sector could have been decentralised to Cogidubnus, with operational control remaining with Plautius but a watching brief for 'client kingdom' behaviour remaining with Sentius (or second-in-command).

C. Headquarters probably LONDINIUM.

D. The areas of southern Dobunni and Durotriges.

there is no reason to assume that circumstances in this instance would have been any different. The chariot force, which suffered heavily when it was detached from the British position to deal with the Batavians seeking to cut their line of retreat, would probably have contributed largely to these numbers. They would have found little help if they had retreated east or south: their homes, in the main, lay either in the west or north of the Thames and their only hope would have been to find an unguarded crossing-place further upstream. In the confusion of the battle there is no reason why the Romans should have been aware of the whereabouts of Caratacus, although they may have judged he would have remained with the main body: nor would they have wanted any of his army to escape to fight again another day. Their pursuit of these fugitives would therefore have been thorough and relentless. Plautius would have given one of his formation commanders the task of coordinating this effort and blocking, with the utmost speed, all known crossings over the Thames, lying within a sensible operational area. This restriction would have been necessary, for if his follow-up force had over-stretched itself, it would not only have created unwanted supply problems but would have become increasingly vulnerable to counter-attack. The Legion commander with a force most suitably positioned for this task was Vespasian. It was an important task, worthy of Vespasian's energy and known military efficiency.

We are told by Suetonius that Vespasian at times also served directly under the orders of Claudius. The Emperor was in Britain for a limited period of about sixteen days and may be deemed to have had a full programme, including ceremonial arrival, treaty discussions with local chieftains, a battle for the capture of *Camulodunum* and victory celebrations. It is thus improbable that he would have had either the time or the opportunity to do much else or travel further. Upon arrival in Britain he found his army north of the Thames, poised to continue its advance under his command. To the south of the river, Cnaeus Sentius, if such he was, would by now have established a permanent base from which to supply land and riverine transport units servicing the forward troops; a civil administration, questionably under Adminius, would have already commenced the task of restoring political stability to his old territory; and Vespasian, who it may be imagined by this time had already completed his mopping-up operations, would have been awaiting the arrival of Claudius before moving to his next task. Vespasian as operational commander south of the Thames, would have commanded that area under orders of Plautius, before the coming of Claudius. When the Emperor arrived as commander-in-chief, he would have taken over Plautius' role as commanding general and Vespasian would then have looked directly to Claudius for instructions. Various other

explanations of Suetonius' words have been suggested but it is not easy
to find another which fits both the operational situation and the
restrictions of time and space. If this is a correct assessment of
Suetonius' meaning, then II Legion may be deemed to have been
situated at that moment somewhere in the area of present south-west
London, having already established its influence well beyond those
bounds, as we will see.

The next evidence we have of the whereabouts of II Legion is
Suetonius' already quoted statement that Vespasian 'captured twenty
oppida, beside the Isle of Wight', which implies that his battle group by
that time, either in whole or in part, had reached the south coast. A
comment by Professor St Joseph, when writing about an air reconnaissance of Roman sites in southern Britain, is relevant when considering
the possible movements of the Legion and the circumstances whereby it
arrived at Chichester, where a supply base has been attributed to it. He
remarks that, generally,[3]

> . . . in the south, evidence of early Roman sites is of the slightest. It
> has long puzzled air observers why more early temporary forts and
> camps have not come to light, though there are instances, as at
> Richborough and Great Chesterford, where buried ditches of the
> kind are known to exist but have apparently never been seen as
> crop marks. Only near Dorking in Surrey (TQ 143492) and at
> Wighton in north Norfolk have enclosures been seen that may be
> small temporary camps.

This lack of evidence may have been induced by events. We have
visualised a situation where Vespasian was given responsibility for the
conduct of mopping-up operations south of the Thames and blocking
the crossing places over the river, probably as far west as the Mole. We
are also aware that at some stage he established a legionary fortress at
Chichester before subsequently invading the West Country; but it is
difficult to imagine that operational necessity would have brought him
south at this juncture, away from his watchful position as flank guard
to the main operation, until he could have been relieved of this task by
Plautius. He had also to assure himself of the political stability of the
tribal grouping at Winchester (later *Venta Belgarum*, a *civitas* capital)
and of the old tribal centre of the Atrebates at Silchester (*Calleva*), until
recently the headquarters of Caratacus and the probable home of his
family. A factor unknown to us but vitally important to him in all this
could have been the whereabouts of Cogidubnus at this time. His local
knowledge and influence would have been invaluable to Vespasian, and
the likelihood is that they would both have wished to work together as

a team. Boon has suggested, as we have seen, some indication of the presence of the native chieftain at *Calleva* at about this time. The discovery there of some hinges and other fittings of a *lorica segmetata* (Roman articulated body-armour) also suggests a Roman military presence but, despite considerable local excavations, no signs of a fort have yet been uncovered. It is thus not impossible that, whilst awaiting the arrival of Claudius, Vespasian despatched Cogidubnus, with native levies and supported by a contingent of Roman regular troops, to occupy the northern town and seal its traditional tribal crossing-place over the Thames.

When discussing the timing of the possible movements of Vespasian's II Legion, there are two other important dates to be remembered, the accuracy of which are generally accepted:

(a) Plautius handed over command to his successor, Ostorius Scapula, in AD 46/7, presumably on the completion, or near completion, of his task by reaching his allotted western boundary.

(b) there is datable evidence to show that the Mendip lead mines were in production in AD 49, under the administration of II Legion *Augusta*.[4]

Both these dates point to the possibility that II Legion had achieved its military objectives in the West Country by AD 47, a generous three and a half years after the Medway battle. During this time, and ignoring any resistance which he may have encountered in the Kentish kingdoms, it would seem that Vespasian constructed military installations and a substantial supply base at Chichester and another fortified supply base near Wimborne, in Dorset. There is no suggestion from this of a hasty thrust to his final phase-line, but rather of a steady advance, probably coordinated where possible with Plautius' other legions, north of the Thames. Nevertheless, it should not be overlooked that at the end of the campaigning season of AD 43, Vespasian would have been seeking a suitable site for quarters during the coming winter. It would be pure conjecture to suggest that he found this in his operational area south of the Thames or that he had by then been enabled by events to move to the south coast and establish them there. Militarily, his presence appears to have been required in the Thames valley: logistically, and looking forward to his next campaign, the need to set up a secure administrative base on the south coast was becoming important. He may, of course, have reached a compromise solution which enabled him to divide his resources, by making full use of the loyal Cogidubnus to whom, as soon as possible, he would have wished to hand over the

48. An aerial view of the Charterhouse area of the Mendip Hills looking north-north-west. The circular earthwork in mid-distance was probably a small amphitheatre. The ramparts of a small 1st century AD fort, probably of II Legion *Augusta*, lie in the foreground.

government of these conquered lands, under the watchful eyes of the rear base commander, Cnaeus Sentius.

Upon arrival at Chichester there would have been much to be done. There were supplies to be arranged for immediate consumption and to be stocked for the coming campaign in Dorset and Somerset: there was accomodation to be constructed for his men, defences to be provided, a naval base to be built, the Isle of Wight to be neutralised and roads to be made. Any mopping-up to be done in the Wealds of Kent and Sussex, and in the Andredsweald Forest, would not have been formidable in scale and could probably have been left to the *Classis Britannica*, which would have doubtless sought to divert local iron making resources towards their ship repair and building requirements. If the Navy had required military support, they might perhaps have sought it from Vespasian but more probably it would have been provided by allied levies or the Richborough garrison. With all this work to be done in AD 44, and the slow rate of advance by Plautius, it must be doubtful that II Legion would have planned to commence its westerly drive into Dorset earlier than the Spring of AD 45.

Before we examine the Legion's plans for the invasion of the West Country, it is important to understand the nature of the terrain which lay before them. Its eastern boundary was the Hampshire Avon, a wide strong flowing river, with its watershed in the chalk Downs south of Savernake Forest. The river swells in size significantly at Salisbury, where it is joined by the waters of the Ebble and the Nadder, the latter having already been enlarged by its tributary the Wylye. John Taylor, in 1623, had dreams that the Avon might be made as navigable as the Thames but there was never any chance of these being realised[5] although Defoe, for example, found it to be so to within two miles of the City. Nevertheless, the notion provides an indication of the size of the river and the nature of the obstacle it would have presented to lateral movement in the country lying between Salisbury and the sea. There is one other interesting possibility mooted by Sean McGrail[6], who writes that from Christchurch

> the tributaries of the Avon and Stour are especially wide-ranging, and with a portage from the Wiltshire Wylye to the Somerset Frome there is a theoretical access to the Bristol Channel and the Mendip and Cotswold regions. Whether inland river journeys (in those days) were indeed possible is difficult to decide . . . Travel upstream may have involved towing heavily laden boats . . .

It is the latter possibility, and the speed of the current of the river on its way to the sea, which might have deterred the Romans from using it as a riverine, overland short-cut. It is not at all impossible, that much of the lead from the Mendip mines was transported by this means in the opposite direction. It would have been a much more economic mode of transport compared to cart-loads of lead, of about seven hundred-weights each, being pulled across the steep, rolling Wiltshire downland, along the so-called 'lead' road to Winchester and beyond, to the south coast. Equally, it would have been an incomparably more efficient and less hazardous method of transport than that envisaged by those who suggest it may have been shipped by sea, round Land's End. Apart from the problems of the wind, tide and current, this route would have been very susceptible to interruption by rough weather and would almost certainly have been unusable for this reason during a six month period in every year. It is noteworthy that even today, when the waters of the Bristol Avon have been brought under man-made controls, the river is still tidal as far upstream as Keynsham Weir when seasonal high tides are experienced. In its original, untampered state, it could have been tidal as least as far as Bath. In the mid-19th century the tow-paths between Bristol and Bath were well used by horse-drawn barges. The

49. A Roman Merchantman.

50. Two Durotrigan coins found in Wales: the
possibility of inter-tribal contact with the Silures
across the Bristol Channel thus exists.

possibility that in Roman times the Bristol Avon, the Frome and the Wylye were used for this purpose, as suggested by Sean McGrail, cannot be ignored; but with the main burden of goods and stores, in the early part of Vespasian's West Country campaign, being required to be transported in the opposite direction against the main flow of current, it would have been a difficult operation for the commander of II Legion, drawing extravagantly upon his resources of manpower.

Beyond the valley of the Hampshire Avon lay the lands of the Durotriges, who shared a western frontier with the Dumnonii of Devon and Cornwall. The tribal territory of the Durotriges included the whole of modern-day Dorset, with southerly parts of Somerset and Wiltshire. The north-western boundary, according to Allen[7], probably followed the southern slope of the Mendip Hills and allowed access to the Bristol Channel through a bottle-neck of land drawn between the mouth of the Brue and the estuary of the Parrett. This conclusion, which has been reached as a result of a field study of the find-points of tribal coinage, is of great interest. The coastal Durotriges were a sea-going people who probably numbered among those about whom Julius Caesar complained when he wrote in *De Bello Gallico* that, throughout nearly all his Gallic campaigns, the British had rendered assistance to his enemy. The maritime interest and involvement of the Durotriges appears further confirmed by the discovery of an Iron Age anchor and chain at

51. An Iron Age anchor recovered from Bulbury Camp, near Lytchett Bay, Dorset.

Bulbury Camp, a few miles inland from Lytchett Bay in Poole Harbour. It would thus be surprising if this secure anchorage had not been used by them as a centre for cross-channel trade, as well as Hengistbury, providing an additional outlet for goods from North Somerset and the West Country, perhaps even extending across the Bristol Channel to Silurian territory. It would probably be an overstatement to suggest that two Durotrigan coins currently on display in Cardiff in the National Museum of Wales, and unearthed in South Wales, provide some evidence of a connection of this nature.[8]

The settlement at Combwich, at the mouth of the Parrett, could be expected to have played a large part in this enterprise, located as it would have been at the end of a trade route extending from the headwaters of that river, along the Hardway to the source of the Stour and thence, passing under the eyes of Hod Hill and Spettisbury to Badbury Rings. From here goods could have been transported either to Poole Harbour or Hengistbury Head. An equally satisfactory and important route could also have been operated from the Parrett to Maiden Castle and thence to join the Stour route to Poole Harbour or Hengistbury: for speedier shipment a port of substantial capacity, from which, firstly, Maiden Castle and, subsequently, Dorchester possibly derived their importance, must have existed somewhere in Weymouth Bay. The coastline and sea levels have changed substantially since Roman times but Radipole, at the head of Backwater, behind Weymouth, remains the most likely place for this harbour despite doubts which are sometimes expressed. The direction of the Roman road from Dorchester to the sea, and the occasional find of Claudian material in the area, confirms this likelihood.

The authors of the Victoria County History for Wiltshire suggest that the eastern section of the boundary described by Allen lay along the Wylye and they argue, on the basis of the many univallate forts in the area datable to mid-1st century AD, that the people of the chalklands west of the river Test 'joined the Durotriges in their stand against the advancing Romans'[9]: but this is a viewpoint which might not be generally shared. Cunliffe,[10] for example, believes that Wessex could have remained quite peaceful during this period and that even the great hillfort at Danebury, of which he has particular knowledge, appears to have been by-passed as II Legion pushed forward. Occasional finds of pieces of military equipment, in the same manner possibly as in Sussex, Surrey and Hampshire, simply reflect the passing of the army. In the matter of the boundary, Grinsell[11] places it, rather, in the Vale of Wardour and the Ebble Valley.

Salisbury Plain is a plateau which lay in the north-east corner, and on the fringes, of Vespasian's possible operational area: it rises to a height of more than 600 feet and covers an area of approximately 250 square miles. Savernake Forest, on the north-eastern edge of the Plain, is some 30 miles march from Silchester (*Calleva*) and would have provided an ideal refuge and base for Caratacus and his followers, possibly with their families. If *Calleva* had been Caratacus' provincial capital in the days leading up to the invasion,[12] when his father, Cunobelin, was still alive, it would be logical to expect he would have returned there after his defeat in Essex: but he would have been under pressure and could not safely have remained. From the security of Savernake Forest, he would have been able to lead raids against the Roman enemy as they pressed forward in his pursuit along the Ridgeway Path and the Icknield Way, seeking to regain contact with him and his army.

Frere suggests that Salisbury Plain at that time was inhabited by a loose grouping of tribes which appear to have broken away from the Atrebates, possibly because they disagreed with the pro-Roman policies of Tincommius,[13] then tribal chieftain. It is not inconceivable that they offered to help Caratacus at this moment, stopping short of hard military support. If they were prepared to look after his material needs then, from his hiding place, he would have been well postioned to frustrate Plautius' efforts to extend Roman influence into the Upper Thames Valley. It is not difficult to carry this line of thought still further and suggest that the Roman general would have been quick to neutralise the British source of supply and, either by political or military means, possibly a mix of both, to mete out punishment to those involved. There is some indication that this is what may have happened. In pre-Roman times[14] the Plain was still a highly productive, well populated farming area, although there are signs it may have entered a state of some decline by the late Iron Age; but later, after the conquest it failed to follow the pattern of urban and villa development displayed elsewhere. At Old Sarum, for example, an important junction of trackways and future Roman roads, where a village or town might have been expected to develop, little of substance materialised.

There is as yet no firm evidence that any large scale military operations, comparable to those in Dorset against the Durotriges, were conducted against the inhabitants of Salisbury Plain. Stray finds of military equipment and weaponry have been unearthed at Wilsford, Bulford and Rushall Down, and a small quantity of Claudian military material has been recovered from Casterley Camp but these provide little evidence of a major campaign. This may yet be revealed but, either way, one clear fact emerges: if there had been troubles with the tribes grouped together on Salisbury Plain which involved the employment of II Legion, they would have needed to be resolved before Vespasian commenced his operations against the Durotriges and before Plautius, north of the Thames, continued his advance further westward. The most likely solution may have been, as has been suggested above and particularly in view of the subsequent creation of the 'civitas' of the Belgae at Winchester, that the problem was passed to Cogidubnus to tidy up, possibly with the support of garrison troops left in the area, both for this very purpose and for the task of road construction.

Finally, there is the whereabouts of the western frontier to be considered, which the Durotriges shared with the Dumnonii. Paul Bidwell, writing in 1980[15] suggested this could have been drawn very approximately along the courses of the rivers Axe and Parrett, but recent archaeological finds have revealed a mid-1st century AD Roman military presence, to the west of this line, at Hembury Hill, on the river Otter,[16] and at Wiveliscombe, north-east of Exeter.

If, alternatively, the boundary was drawn along the line of the Exe, then not only would Hembury Hill and the fort at Wiveliscombe have been within Durotrigan territory, but also the Claudian fortlet or signal station at Old Burrow, overlooking the Bristol channel. This solution would mean that II Legion prudently respected Dumnonian neutrality at this sensitive early stage, only moving across the boundary at a later date, and that it was as part of this later advance that the garrison at Old Burrow was transferred to Martinhoe and a small mixed battle group to North Tawton, 17 miles west of the Exe. At North Tawton aerial photography has revealed a fort, some marching camps and the corner of a partly discernible fortress.[17] By c. AD 54 the Romans had reached Nanstallon, where a *Cohors equitata* was established, apparently to provide a base for prospectors searching for local mineral resources.[18]

These, then, were the frontier areas which, together with the southern coastline extending from Christchurch Bay to the mouth of the river Exe, enclosed Durotrigan territory. One must assume that once Vespasian had entered their tribal kingdom, his aim would have been its total subjugation and that the end of the first phase of his West Country campaign would have been achieved upon his arrival at the western frontier with the Dumnonii, having suppressed all resistance during his advance. He would then have wished to consolidate his gain before moving forwards towards his final objective. But what was his final objective? It does not appear at this moment to have involved the Dumnonii: indeed, as Bidwell has rightly commented,[19] nothing in the overall strategic situation before c AD 60 suggests a date when it would have been advantageous to II Legion to advance into their territory. On the contrary, it would have been an unnecessary risk to have done so; the very size of the Dumnonian kingdom could have consumed the resources of II Legion *Augusta*, particularly when it is remembered that the tribal area of the Dubonni still lay unconquered to its north.

There are three important conclusions to be drawn from these matters:

1   The inter-tribal boundary between the Dumnonii and the Durotriges probably followed the line of the rivers Exe and Lyn.

2   The Romans had seemingly established no military presence west of this boundary, in the kingdom of the Dumnonii, until sometime in the period AD 50–60.

3   There was no obvious military advantage to be gained by II Legion advancing into Dumnonian territory upon the conclusion of the Durotrigan campaign: the Dumnonii were a scattered tribe, apparently quiescent, and posed no threat to Roman operations. On the other hand, for II Legion to have crossed the Exe at this juncture would not only have over-stretched its manpower but would have also reduced its contact with Plautius' forces to the north. Additionally, the extensive marshy area of the Somerset Levels would have dangerously interposed between the two armies with each westward mile advanced.

From these conclusions other questions arise for our consideration. If II Legion chose not to cross the Exe at this moment, but seemingly paused for some two or three years before doing so, why did they attack the Durotrigan territory at such an early stage in the overall campaign, when the Legion's manpower might have been more gainfully employed elsewhere? Were the Durotriges planning an uprising which would have posed a threat to Plautius' operations? If they were not doing so, then it must be judged that Vespasian had been given a deeper objective than the simple subjugation of the Durotrigan people. It is for answers to these questions we shall now be seeking.

Vespasian, with II Legion *Augusta*, its supporting auxiliary cohorts, cavalry and the full paraphernalia of war, including heavy artillery catapults, the light pattern *carroballistae* and a total force of about 10,000 men, entered the lands of the Durotriges in the Spring of AD 45. The army is unlikely to have arrived by sea for it would have been easier with a force of this nature, accompanied by a large number of animals and much equipment, to have crossed over the Hampshire Avon rather than to have embarked for a seaborne landing which might have been opposed. Apart from this, an advance along the general line of the coast with the added flexibility of manoeuvre this offered, would have avoided the unwanted publicity inevitably attracted by the assemblage of a large fleet. It would also have afforded Vespasian the opportunity, should he have required it, to take care of the promontory fort at Hengistbury Head, if it had been showing signs of hostility.

Hengistbury Head lay almost precisely on the eastern boundary of Durotrigan territory and dominated a natural harbour, fed by the joint estuary of the Dorset Stour and the Hampshire Avon, lying to the west of Christchurch Bay. In the half century before Caesar's expeditions to Britain, the Hengistbury community had achieved a climax of trade with the continent, whilst seemingly conducting its affairs somewhat along the lines of a twentieth century 'free-port'. The scale of business handled[20] by its inhabitants is demonstrated not only by the numbers of *amphorae* uncovered on the site, with the implication that the port was in direct contact with the shippers of Italian wines, but also by the quantities of coinage excavated, much of it indicating trading links with north-west France. The geographical position of the Hengistbury settlement provided its people with considerable local, political and economic influence; and there are signs that they shared their prosperity with their neighbours, the Durotriges, by permitting them to operate a market within their commercial centre.

In the century following Caesar's adventures in Britain, the reputa-

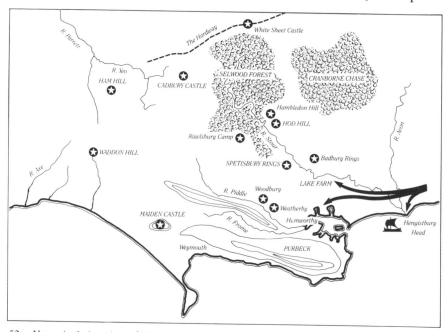

52. Vespasian's invasion of Durotrigan territory (phase 1). Vespasian crosses the Hampshire Avon, having first ensured the neutrality of the occupants of Hengistbury Head. He establishes a base at Lake Farm and a port at Hamworthy.

tion of Hengistbury as a hub of international trade diminished to that of a port for the use of the tribal peoples of the West Country. The growth of Colchester, and the attractive opportunities of trading with the Trinovantes, whose empire was fast expanding, had persuaded Roman dealers, and those under their influence, to take their business to the east coast of Britain. Cunliffe,[21] however, believes that Hengistbury was still commercially active, and may indeed have been positively defended, when Vespasian commenced his attack on Durotrigan territory. The leaders of the community, however, cannot have been blind to the preparations being mounted by II Legion nor to its intentions: and since there is no sign that they received any military support from the Durotriges, it is surely unlikely that they would have wished to stand alone against such a formidable force.

Vespasian quickly established a base camp at Lake Farm on the banks of the Stour at Wimbourne: in due course this appears to have been linked to a naval supply point at Hamworthy, in Poole Harbour. The Lake site was shrewdly chosen, for at one blow it cut the Stour valley trackway link to Bradbury and Hengistbury Head: it gave the Romans command of the important lower and navigable reaches of the

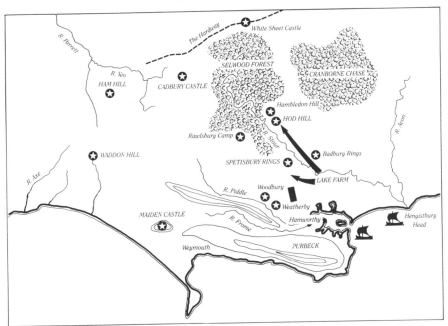

53. Vespasian's invasion of Durotrigan territory (Phase 2). Vespasian moves out from Lake Farm to neutralise British resistance at Spettisbury Ring, Badbury, Hod Hill and Hambledon Hill, thus seizing control of the Stour valley. Whilst doing this he probably would also have pushed a force forward to contain any intervention from the camps at Weatherby and Woodbury.

Stour, thus enabling them to be resupplied from Christchurch Bay until the Hamworthy base in Poole Harbour was safely in their hands: and it placed Vespasian in such a position that he could, without delay, move to the next phase of his operation.

Vespasian's immediate aim at this stage was the conquest of the Durotriges and the seizure of their land, with its control resting fully in his hands. It was springtime and stocks of grain held by the British would have been kept from his grasp where possible but in any event would have been seasonally low. It would therefore have been necessary for him to transport his own supplies with him and so to arrange his campaign that they flowed to him easily and were readily available. The two Roman roads built from Hamworthy to Badbury and Bath, and from Weymouth to Dorchester and Ilchester, are almost certainly military roads: they illustrate clearly how II Legion resolved its administrative problems and point to the main axis of advance, probably along the Purbeck Hills. But Vespasian would have been unable to undertake any movement in this direction until the threat to his northern flank, posed by the hillforts of the Stour Valley, had been eliminated.

The courses of action open to the Durotriges, as they watched the military force assembling within their south-eastern frontier were simple: they could combine their tribal armies to resist the invasion of their territory or they could surrender. As so often happens in war, when things are rarely so clear cut as might be hoped, they opted for a third, seemingly illogical and certainly unsuccessful alternative: they resisted the Roman attack, hillfort by hillfort, settlement by settlement, in some cases with considerable loss of life. There is little evidence of a Roman assault on Badbury Rings but the presence of a legionary fortress at Lake Farm can only imply that it fell into their hands at an early date, either by surrender or as a result of direct attack. There is less doubt about the actuality of the assault on the neighbouring hillfort, Spettisbury Rings, on the opposing side of the Valley where, in 1857, during the construction of the Central Dorset Railway, some eighty or ninety skeletons were recovered from a pit, together with several pieces of weaponry and a fragment of binding from a legionary shield.[22] After their victory, the Romans established a small fort, one mile south-west of Badbury, of which air photographs have revealed ditches at Crab Farm, Shapwick. The fort was ideally sited, being positioned to keep watch on two hillforts, guard the crossing place over the Stour and safeguard the movement of barges on the river, which at that point is still some 35 feet wide.[23]

With the subjugation and probable eviction of the inhabitants from the Badbury Ring hillforts, which had stood sentry either side of the

54. The Iron Age hillfort at Hod Hill, near Blandford, Dorset. The Roman fort constructed within it (top right) probably housed a garrison of one cohort with a detachment of cavalry.

Stour at the entrance to the chalkland (the people were possibly employed as slave labour for the construction of the dramatic highway of Ackling Dyke), the way was now open for Vespasian to push further upstream to Hod Hill, a formidable feature which, from about 300 BC to the eve of the invasion, had been defended by a single rampart. Additional defences were then hastily flung up but some of these appear to have been incomplete when Vespasian launched his attack. Sir Ian Richmond has argued that the occupants of the hillfort were surprised by the speed of events and made 'feverish preparations' for their defence.[24] There is no evidence of heavy fighting at Hod Hill, even after careful excavation: on the contrary, the signs are that resistance crumbled speedily when a rain of artillery bolts was directed, possibly from a siege-tower, at the chieftian's group of hutting within the settlement. The pattern in which artillery bolts have been recovered from the interior of the hillfort, suggests that the strike of bolts ranged either side of the target until finally it was brought to bear on the hutting, with salutary effect. When surrender was complete, the Romans sited a fort on the north-west corner of the summit of the hill. Its garrison is estimated to have numbered about 800 men, comprising one cohort of infantry and a half *ala* of cavalry.

It is likely that Vespasian, after these successes and with the limited resources available to him, might now have felt he had done enough to secure his northern flank and that he was free to concentrate his attack upon Maiden Castle without fear of interference from this quarter. Doubtless, with a larger force at his disposal, he might have been tempted to advance further up the Stour, to establish a watchful presence on the strategically important Hardway, perhaps in the area of Alfred's Tower, overlooking the Somerset plains. The uncertainty of the behaviour of the Dobunni and the northern element of the Durotriges, the latter occupying an imposing multivallate hillfort at South Cadbury, on the Dorset-Somerset border, could well have persuaded him to do this. In the event, the inhabitants of South Cadbury stood back from the fighting which had developed,[25] possibly because Vespasian's advance along the south coast carried the war past them or possibly for purely political reasons. It has been suggested that the Durotriges of North Dorset survived as client state for a number of years, until they were brought directly under Roman control.

Maiden Castle, which was an unambitious earthwork in its early existence, was originally occupied about 500 BC. During Julius Caesar's Gallic Wars, many Veneti are thought to have fled across the Channel to seek refuge in southern Britain. They were a warlike tribe, and the possibility that they brought with them the slingstone weapon, which seems to have emerged in Britain about this time, is something which must be considered. The technique of slingstone warfare required taking a new look at the defensive construction of hillforts and it is no surprise that the ramparts of Maiden Castle should have been enlargened in these years. They were again refashioned, far more comprehensively c. AD 25, to provide four great circular ramparts and to make the Castle one of the most famous of the Durotrigan hillforts. Thomas Hardy illustrated its massive strength when he described the ramparts covering its entrances as overlapping 'like loosely clasped fingers. between which a zig-zag path may be followed – a cunning construction that puzzles the uninformed eye'. The official guide

55. Maiden Castle: Thomas Hardy described the western entrance as a 'cunning construction that puzzles the uninformed eye'.

56. Maiden Castle: the backbone of a defender, pierced by an arrow during the Roman assault.

57. 'That night . . . the survivors crept forth from their broken stronghold and, in the darkness, buried their dead . . .' (*Mortimer Wheeler*, 1943).

book,[26] compiled by Sir Mortimer Wheeler, sees the sevenfold ramparts of the western gate as a 'veritable cascade of banks and ditches through which the visitor winds his way'.

Wheeler has provided a vivid reconstruction[27] of the Roman attack on the Castle: as a renowned archaeologist and a distinguished soldier of the Second World War, he has brought to life in exciting detail, an event which took place nearly 2,000 years ago. He is describing the Roman assault on the eastern gate:

> What happened there is plain to read: the regiment of artillery, which normally accompanied a legion on campaign, was ordered into action, and put down a barrage of iron-shod ballista-arrows over the eastern part of the site. Following this barrage the infantry advanced up the slope, cutting its way from rampart to rampart, tower to tower. In the innermost bay of the entrance, close outside the actual gates, a number of huts had recently been built; these were now set alight, and under the rising clouds of smoke the gates were stormed and the position carried. But the resistance had been obstinate and the fury of the attackers was aroused. For a space,

confusion and massacre dominated the scene. Men and women, young and old, were savagely cut down, before the legionaries were called to heel and the work of systematic destruction begun . . .

That night, when the fires of the legionaries shone out (we may imagine) in orderly lines across the valley, the survivors crept forth from their broken stronghold and, in the darkness, buried their dead as nearly as might be outside their tumbled gates, in that place where the ashes of their burnt huts lay warm and thick upon the ground . . . At daylight on the morrow, the legion moved westward to fresh conquest . . .

A recent article[28] has rightly queried some of these conclusions: is it likely, for example, that Vespasian, having fought savagely for possession of this strategically and politically important stronghold, would have moved out next morning to continue his advance, leaving the inhabitants of Maiden Castle unguarded and still in possession of their hillfort? It would not only have been unnecessary for him to have acted with such urgency: it would have been logistically unwise and probably impossible. He still had the rest of Durotrigan territory to conquer and this would have been an ideal spot upon which to consolidate his

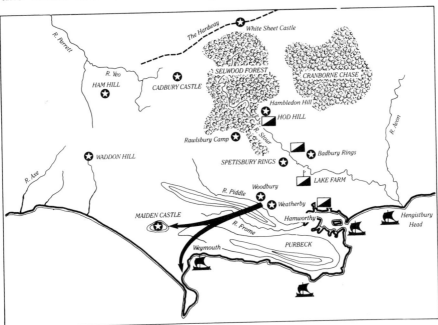

58. Vespasian's invasion of Durotrigan territory (Phase 3). Having secured his main base at Lake Farm against possible attack from its northern flank, the main body could now advance westward to occupy Maiden Castle and open up a forward supply port at or near Weymouth.

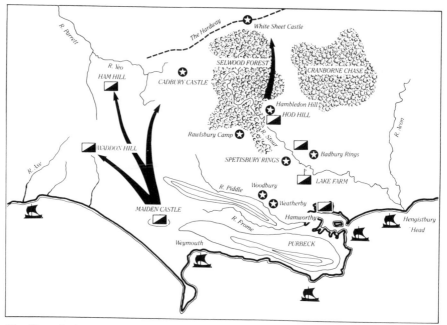

59.   Vespasian's invasion of Durotrigan territory (Phase 4). After the capture of Maiden Castle
Vespasian would probably have moved westward to positions at Ham Hill and Waddon Hill from
which he could watch the frontier with the Dumnonii. He could now consolidate his position in
the territory he had occupied by moving northwards to the headwaters of the Parrett and by
seizing the ancient Hardway, which gave access eastward to Old Sarum and Silchester.

position whilst he opened a new supply link at Weymouth, before
advancing to the western frontier and the seizure, amongst other places,
of the hillforts at Waddon Hill and Ham Hill. A Roman fort has been
attested at Waddon Hill and it is almost certain that another was sited
at Ham Hill, where much military material has been recovered but the
location has been destroyed by heavy quarrying for stone. Ham Hill,
looking out towards Vespasian's westward frontier and situated near
the south-western end of the Hardway, where it bends towards the
mouth of the Devonshire Axe, would have been an invaluable
acquisition.[29] From here was a short distance to the nodal point where
Ilchester now stands, astride the Hardway, with access down the
Parrett to the Bristol Channel and controlling the established tribal
trade routes from the Mendips, in one direction to Maiden Castle and,
in the other, to Hengistbury Head. Above Ilchester lie the Somerset
Levels, flanked on the north by the Mendip Hills and on the south-east
by the Quantocks. To the south and south-east of the Levels lie the
Blackdown Hills and the Oolitic escarpment which carries the Jurassic
Way, after its crossing of the river Avon, near Bath. The Somerset

Levels in general, then as now, were a marshy area scattered with various islands of high ground and two or three prominent ridges, such as Curry Rivel and the Polden Hills. Occupied by a hostile force, the Levels could have provided a lot of trouble for II Legion. When the Fosse Way was finally provided, it was driven in a straight line from Ilchester to the ford at Bath, keeping well clear of this hazardous area and the broad downstream waters of the river Avon.

Some small indication has been found of 1st century AD Roman defences at the Yeo river crossing: these have not been significant and one must believe that the site of a substantial military fort is still waiting to be discovered in this area. Such a fort would have served as the hinge for the defence of the northern boundary of the operational zone we have defined for Vespasian, for which the Hardway could have been used as a 'service' road: its eastern end might have been anchored by another similar fort in the locality of White Sheet Castle (ST 8035) or Alfred's Tower. Behind these frontiers, Vespasian would have been able to commence his process of consolidation and one of his prime tasks may well have been the construction of the southern part of his military

60. The Hardway skirts the edge of White Sheet Castle and then crosses the centre of the picture to pass beneath Alfred's Tower (skyline) before descending to the Somerset Levels.

road to Bath, well to the east of the Stour valley, and in a comparatively peaceful area to the flank of the fighting zone. Once these tactically important places had been occupied, Vespasian could have been certain that his grip on the Durotriges was complete.

The question remains to be answered why Plautius felt it necessary to undertake this foray into the West Country at a time when his forces elsewhere were apparently being increasingly stretched to cover his operational area. The danger he was courting, and the uprising he could have been inviting, was to burst upon his successor Ostorius Scapula barely eighteen months later. Plautius' alternative strategy would have been to use all of his four legions in the troublesome war being fought with Caratacus north of the Thames. II Legion, operating in harmony with the others under his command, could have been given responsibility for an early move on Bagendon and Sea Mills, at the mouth of the river Avon, and for eliminating enemy resistance in the Lower Severn basin. This action could have threatened Caratacus' southern flank. Additionally, if the southern element of the Dobunni had displayed sympathy for the British cause, it would have isolated them from the Briton and lessened the risk of their help reaching him.

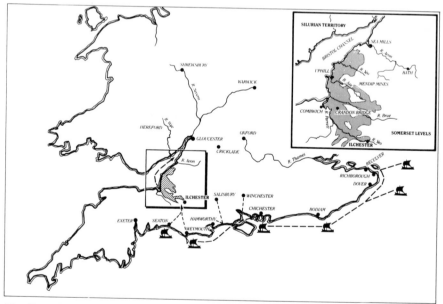

61. Vespasian's invasion of Durotrigan territory (Phase 5). Vespasian's conquest of Durotrigan territory provided the Romans with a short portage from the south coast to the headwaters of the Parrett and thence waterborne access to the Bristol Channel. This route would not only have made considerable savings in time and logistical resources but would also have avoided the hazardous waters and tides around Land's End.

The fact that Plautius did not adopt this strategy, which fits well with the sound principle of *concentration of force*, suggests that he either feared trouble from the Durotriges, and possibly the Dumnonii, or that he was pursuing some other aim. Yet it was to be another decade before the Romans concerned themselves seriously with the Dumnonii; and as for the Durotriges, they appear to have been a reasonably prosperous trading, seagoing and farming people who, despite an undoubted hostility to the Romans, had stood back from involvement in the war, apparently to the extent of taking no part in the initial British resistance to the landings in Kent. In short, the Durotriges were not the assailants: they were the assailed, and one must judge that Plautius' aim was not so much their subjugation as the occupation of their territory, with the opportunity it offered of an existing, and functional, land and riverine route from Weymouth, then down the river Parrett, linking the English and Bristol Channels.

This route would have cut out a wasteful and frequently hazardous passage of some 300 miles around Land's End. A Roman ship making for the Bristol Channel would have been looking for very special conditions of wind and tide. The navigator would ideally have been seeking for an ebb tide in the English Channel, with a light or following wind, and for a rising tide in the Bristol Channel. The skilled Roman

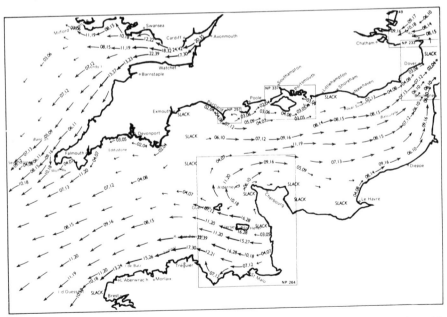

62. Navigating around Land's End. Reproduced from Admiralty Tidal Stream Atlas with permission of HMSO.

oarsmen could have manoeuvred naval craft around the promontory to take advantage of the current flowing up the Channel and, given the benefit of a south-west wind, might have been able to hoist the auxiliary sail to gain added speed. Clearly most sailing ships would not have enjoyed the manoeuvreability of naval vessels, and, besides, the tidal habits of the English and Bristol Channels do not fit easily into this scenario. In practice, optimum conditions are found for one period of two hours in every twelve, as Table VII illustrates.

It was obviously feasible for the Romans to negotiate the waters around Land's End but they would have been subjected to considerable and frequent delays in dangerous waters whilst awaiting tidal and weather changes. The likelihood of this can be appreciated when it is realised that the journey between the Isle of Wight and Mounts Bay,

TABLE VII
Tidal Ebb and Flow

Hours after/ before High Water, DOVER	English Channel		Bristol Channel		Suitable
	Ebb	Flow	Ebb	Flow	
After					
1	x		x		
2	x			x	yes
3	x			x	yes
4		x		x	
5		x		x	
6		x		x	
Before					
1	x		x		
2	x		x		
3		x(a)	x		(a) a lot of slack
4		x	x		water
5		x		x	
6		x		x	

Authority: Reed's Nautical Almanac, 1985

sailing at an estimated speed of 2½ knots, would probably have taken six days to complete, assuming that the passage was made in daylight hours only.

The rate of probability of finding a fair wind, when travelling down-Channel in a westerly direction, has been graded at 32 per cent: the rating for the return journey, which benefits from the general set of the wind up-Channel from the south-west, is a much more favourable 86 per cent.[30] It is thus likely that the down-Channel journey in overall time may have taken an average 10 to 12 days and the return passage could have been made in a rather better 7 or 8 days. Since the shipping we are discussing would have been seeking to trade into the Bristol Channel, then it would have been looking for a favourable wind, as it rounded the peninsula, to carry it up the Bristol Channel, along the northern coastline of Cornwall, Devon and Somerset, probably for an equal distance, making a possible voyage duration of 20 days in each direction. This figure takes no account of the time to be allowed for the passage around Land's End, from Mounts Bay to St Ives Bay: given reasonable conditions this might have been achieved in one or two days but it is difficult to believe that sailors newly arrived in these strange and unpredictable waters would have had sufficient skill, or indeed the local knowledge, to have picked up a fair tide without the benefit of a pilot. The employment of pilots is not improbable, but the dangers of missing a favourable tide would still have existed, with the unwelcome consequence either of awaiting its change on an inhospitable coastline or returning to Mounts Bay.

These conditions would have made it essential that safe harbours were available on the north and south coasts of Devon and Cornwall, with the implied willingness of the Dumnonii to allow their use, or, alternatively, the application of substantial military pressure if Dumnonian permission was not forthcoming.

Land transport was both economically and administratively expensive unless a generous proportion of river traffic could be utilised. Diocletian's Price Edict of AD 301[31] shows that a 1200 pound wagon load of grain would double in price after a road journey of 300 miles: shipping the grain the length of the Mediterranean was cheaper than taking it 75 miles by road. Thus a mixed land and riverine route, as described above, could have cut out the dangers and dead haul of supply by ship around Land's End and would have reduced the economic costs and the calls upon military administrative resources.

As well as these advantages, however, there was another factor which required the Romans to gain access to the waters of the Bristol Channel at this moment. Our judgement may perhaps be influenced by the fact that II Legion deemed it necessary, as mentioned above, to construct the fortlet cum signal station at Old Burrow on the North Devon coast, which Frere suggests was designed to watch for Silurian raids and 'to act as the eyes of a fleet'. The fortlet was later replaced by a more permanent construction, further westward along the cliffs, at Martinhoe. Both stations are thought to have provided accommodation for 65 to 80 men, and both were located where they could obtain the widest views of the Bristol Channel, close to possible landing places. Frere's comment is of double interest; first, because he visualises the possibility of Silurian raids across the sea from South Wales and, second, because he suggests that the Romans operated a fleet in the Channel. Indeed, the first eventuality would inevitably have led to the second.

The Silures undeniably had the capability of carrying out raids of this nature, for their native craft was the *curragh*, an adaptable and easily constructed vessel, sometimes still to be seen on the west coast of Ireland. It was apparently successfully used in Spain by Julius Caesar, c. 49 BC, for he afterwards wrote[32]

> I therefore directed the troops to build a number of boats, modelled on some I had once seen in Britain. The keels and ribs were made of light timber, the rest of the hull was of wicker-work covered with hides. When they had finished, each one was loaded on a pair of wagons, and the whole lot was taken by night to the river, which lay about twenty-one miles from the camp. An infantry detachment went across in these vessels . . . Later a whole legion went over to join them . . .

Craft of this nature could, with equal ease, have similarly served the Silures had they wished to transport a force across the Channel to come to the aid of the British on its southern shores. The vessels were frequently 24 feet long but they could, without difficulty, have been built larger than this. Tim Severin[33] sailed a 36 feet *curragh* across the North Atlantic in 1976 to demonstrate the feasibility of a legend that Irish monks had been the first to discover the Americas. Experiments with her showed that, with a 10 man crew and a coasting load, moving up and downstream on the lower Charles River, in a westerly Force 3 wind with a current c. 1.3 knots, she was capable of 5.03 miles per hour. When the crew was reduced to 4 men, she was capable of c. 4 miles per hour downstream but could make no headway upstream against the tide. The vessel behaved well in heavy weather, possibly because of a ballast of fresh water stowed beneath the floor boards: under sail, she went well before a moderate following wind but her performance was otherwise restricted and sometimes dangerous in fresh weather.

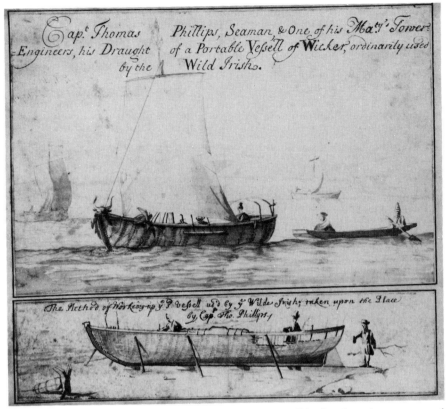

63. The *curragh*, a lightly built boat of Celtic origin, may still be found on the west coast of Ireland. It is here described by Captain Thomas Phillips (*c.* 1683) as a 'portable Vessell of Wicker . . . used by the Wild Irish.'

In the face of this threat, it may be assumed that Vespasian would have provided himself with a fleet to combat it: moreover, he would also have required barges for use on riverways, patrolling coastal waters and for the riverine transportation of infantry and supplies. These would probably have taken the form of flat-bottomed river craft, frequently employed by the Romans on the rivers of Gaul and Britain.[34] It is unlikely that they would have been risked, any more perhaps than the ships of the *Classis Britannica* at this early stage, in the hazardous weather conditions and dangerous tidal currents around Land's End. It is more probable that they would have been constructed on a local river, in a manner possibly imitated later by Suetonius Paulinus in AD 60, when he built infantry landing craft on the river Dee, in Cheshire, for his attack on Anglesey.[35] There could have been no more suitable river for Vespasian's purpose than the Parrett, where there is plenty of evidence of Roman usage, three ports of varying capacities having been revealed along its length, at Combwich, Crandon Bridge and Ilchester.

Combwich, connected to Roman Ilchester both by road and river, lay closest to the sea: it was, according to Rahtz,[36] the site of a Roman settlement which should be interpreted as a port, possibly Ptolemy's *Ischalis*, in general use from 1st to 4th centuries AD. A minor tributary of the Parrett, the Pill, drains into the estuary at this point and creates a natural harbour for light coastal shipping. In the later Roman period, the water level rose some 18 feet, flooding a considerable area of low-lying land and drowning much valuable evidence of the port's existence. Nevertheless, the location speaks loudly for the importance of the site, which connects in one direction with Ilchester, where a small river port and the remains of Roman quays appear to have been identified west of the town, and in the other, with the sea lanes of the Bristol Channel.

The third port, at Crandon Bridge, is significantly located at the most easterly point from which it could have had access inland along the Polden ridge. The site is now more than a mile from the Parrett, due to the construction of a new channel in 1677, when it most probably stood on the edge of deep water and alongside a smaller stream which drained into the river at this point. Excavations carried out on the site in 1971 were unfortunately necessarily hurried since road construction works by the County Council were imminent but, in the limited area which was tackled, the finds were of great interest:[37]

> The stone bases of 10 Roman structures were partly excavated and their plans recorded. They were all rectangular and all aligned on the same north to south axis, up and down the south-falling slope. None were definitely domestic buildings and, whilst the smallest can be said with some certainty to have been a lavatory, some seem best interpreted as warehouses, in particular the latest corridor-type structures, examined in some detail at the East end of the excavation . . . where, below the water table, the earliest structures were timber buildings associated with 'Durotrigan' pottery, and occupation had spanned the Roman period from 1st century AD onwards.

The assumption of the excavators was that they had probably discovered the remains of a Roman port and there is without doubt a marked similarity between the description of the various buildings uncovered here and the various finds on the river Dee, where Paulinus built his landing craft. The Roman fortress at Chester occupied a position near the river which, at that time, seemingly washed very close to its walls. Granaries existed just inside the west gate but, outside, traces of warehouses and administrative buildings have been noted, with some remains of a timber wharf. A short distance upstream an area has been found upon which, in 1st century AD, a small collection of huts had stood, possibly used as workshops or by metal workers.

There are some parallels between these two river ports which indicate that at one time they both fulfilled the same sort of administrative roles, including warehousing and the bulk distribution and storage of supplies. No mention was made in the report on the Somerset excavation of the discovery of a workshop building but time did not allow for a thorough examination. It is not impossible, indeed it is probable, that still to be revealed at Crandon Bridge lie the remains of a shipwright's yard from which Vespasian launched his Bristol Channel flotilla. There are three pointers which may be thought to support this possibility:

1   sources of iron supply in the Kent and Sussex Wealds were in large scale production by mid-1st century AD: it was, from the beginning, essentially a sea-based operation, closely associated with the *Classis Britannica* and distributed through the Rother and Brede estuaries.[38]

2   a dedication to a temple of Minerva and Neptune, found at Chichester in 1723, implies that it was erected by a Guild of Ironworkers, *Collegium Fabror(um)*. Webster[39] suggests that the combination of these two deities indicates that the donors were prosperous shipbuilders, who had profited considerably in 1st century AD through contracts with the Roman army.

3   the intensive use of the river Parrett by the Roman administration is apparent from a very early moment in mid-1st century AD. The route from Weymouth to the river, and thence downstream, was almost certainly already in use by the Durotriges: the transport of shipbuilding stores along the south coast, overland to Ilchester and then down the river to a shipwright's yard would have presented little problem.

If this is a correct interpretation of Vespasian's intention when he crossed into Durotrigan territory about AD 45, then it would be wrong to suggest that the action was forced upon him by Silurian raids on the Devon and Somerset coastline, for he was seemingly already committed to operations in the south and west much earlier than this moment. If, as has already been suggested, Durotrigan behaviour was not the reason for his attack upon them, and he had no interest at that moment in the Dumnonii, then one must assume that his task was the seizure of their important trading route, cutting across the West Country peninsula and linking the two Channels, for Roman use. It is apparent that he must have been given this task when his II Legion *Augusta* was mopping-up south of the Thames, and already detached from the main body of the army. It is possible that the tactical road which he constructed between Hamworthy and Bath (where the Bristol Avon gave access to Sea Mills, at the mouth of the river Severn) was an interim measure which fell quickly out of use once the Parrett route had been opened up. It was apparently never developed as a highway and could have been abandoned at an early date because of the long and administratively expensive portage to and from Poole.

CHAPTER EIGHT

DEFEAT FOR CARATACUS

But when won the coming battle,
  What of profit springs therefrom?
What if conquest, subjugation,
  Even greater ills become . . .?

Bret Harte

The military task given to Aulus Plautius by Claudius was the establishment of a new Roman Province in south-eastern Britain, the boundaries of which we attempted to define in the previous chapter. Seemingly Plautius considered he could not secure his western boundary unless he could achieve naval dominance in the Bristol Channel: additionally, he needed the means of ensuring that all resistance had been extinguished in the Somerset Levels, an ideal area for irregular warfare, and that no flames had been left smouldering that might revive it. The craft we suggest were built by Vespasian would have given him the ability to complete both these tasks by the end of the campaigning season of AD 46: they would then have been ready for operations under the hand of Ostorius Scapula in the following year.

The newly arrived Scapula was promptly diverted from any plans he may have prepared to continue the logical sequence of operations being pursued by Plautius: and to say this is not to place any responsibility on his shoulders for the events which were about to happen, for the forces handed over to his command were severely overstretched. Scapula had hardly set foot in Britain when hostile tribes from beyond his western frontier burst through into the territory of his 'allies'. He hastily assembled a force and dispersed them but was at once confronted with rebellion in eastern Britain, led by the Iceni. He suppressed this vigorously and is next to be found marching against the Deceangli of north-east Wales, an inexplicable and isolated operation which apparently bore no relationship to any obvious, established plan. It was possibly a punitive expedition in retaliation for their part in the tribal raid which sparked this unhappy series of events but it was a mistake in priorities. The Brigantes had been watching his force disappear over the Welsh border and, in their turn, took to arms. News of this latest disaster reached Scapula when, according to Tacitus[1] he 'had nearly reached the sea facing Ireland'. If his position has been correctly reported then, under all the circumstances, it is not easy to see what he was hoping to achieve by this plunge into Welsh territory. His response to the recall was immediate: the Brigantes were soon brought under control, the ringleaders executed and others, less implicated, were pardoned. It seems that only the western element of the tribe had been disaffected, the furthest from Cartimandua, their Queen and 'client' of the Roman administration. The greater part of the campaigning season of AD 47 would, by this time, have been consumed, and Tacitus tells us that Scapula now determined to put all thoughts of further expansion on one side until his conquests had been secured. It seems clear from this talk of expansion that Scapula had already decided on the conquest of Wales and the pursuit and destruction of Caratacus.

As the Roman general gazed across the Severn into the Welsh interior, he must soon have become aware of the enormity of the task he was about to undertake. He had no friends across the border and, in particular, he had a dangerous, determined and dedicated enemy in the Silures, whose loyalty to Caratacus had already been proven. It is necessary to remind ourselves of the extent of Silurian territory. In the west, it reached at least as far as Swansea; in the north, it included the ranges of the Black Mountains and the Brecon Beacons; and in the south, it was bounded by a fertile coastal strip overlooking the Bristol Channel. Scapula would have been particularly interested in the terrain of the eastern boundary, which lay across his front as he sought to advance westwards. Here the tribal border probably extended as far as the Severn, for it would have been strange if they had not brought the Forest of Dean, with all its natural resources, under their influence at this time. In addition to the obstacle imposed by the Forest, Scapula's path was also obstructed by three major rivers, the Severn, with its tributaries the Wye and the Usk, both of which joined the main stream at its mouth, where it flowed into the Bristol Channel. All three rivers presented formidable obstacles to any advance by land along the line of the coast but were navigable for considerable distances. A Silurian *oppidum* lay situated at Llanmelin, on ground to the west of Chepstow, lying between the Wye and the Usk, with clear views across the Severn estuary to the mouth of the Avon. It is thus evident that as long as the

64. A detachment of XX Legion prepare to march.

Silures occupied this position and dominated the forest areas between the Usk and the Severn, then the use of the latter river would be a constant source of troubles to the Romans. Scapula's prime task must have been to seize this area.

It would appear that in order to do this he had three courses open to him:

1 *He could outflank the forest and river obstacles to his front by marching north and then thrusting south-west via Monmouth to Usk*: to have taken the traditional route into Wales, along the Severn valley would have carried him away from his objective of cutting tribal withdrawal lines from the Forest. The disadvantages of this course are obvious, for his own lines of communication and supply would themselves be vulnerable to attack by the Silures. Additionally, a lot of preliminary preparation would be required, setting-up supply bases and constructing roads into forward area, all of which would be expensive in terms of manpower and resources.

2 *He could land on the north bank of the Severn estuary, seize Llanmelin and clear the river route to Kingsholm*. This alternative has evident advantages, for it would strengthen the frontier defences

and at the same time retain contact with reinforcements and westerly supply routes.

3   *He might have combined the two options* but, bearing in mind the military principle that success should normally result from the concentration of a superior military force, he would probably have discarded this for the reason that it was not a viable alternative.

Tacitus tells us that when Scapula invaded Silurian territory, Caratacus moved to the country of the Ordovices indicating that when the Briton withdrew from the southern area of Wales, he did so in a northerly or north-westerly direction, possibly from the coastline of the Severn estuary where, it will be recalled, he is thought to have been based with his followers and families after pulling out of his Cotswold stronghold (Chapter VI). All of these apparently marched with him to a new hideout in the territory of the Ordovices (his own wife and daughter were soon to be captured in that area by the Romans) and the indications are that he was falling back, in the face of pressure from the south, to a battlefield of his own choosing. If this is a correct interpretation of his actions then it would seem likely that Scapula had chosen to attack along the northern flank of the Severn estuary and had broken through to the line of the Usk, enveloping the vital forest area, possibly as late as AD 49 or 50. It is important to remember the time factor, for the rear elements of XX Legion did not march out of *Camulodunum* until some time in AD 48 and the forest battle zone we are discussing was a difficult area, fiercely defended and could not have been instantly overrun.

Caratacus, at this time, was almost certainly aware that this was his last opportunity in Wales to snatch victory from the Romans and he was probably already planning to return eastwards to revive resistance there. There was growing restlessness amongst the Brigantes and if this could be coupled to the implacable determination of the Silures, Scapula's cup of trouble would be full. Caratacus' standing amongst his followers increased, not only with every success but also with every year for which he managed to prolong his campaign of resistance. His reputation and courage were renowned throughout Europe and, like the German Field Marshal Rommel in the Second World War, he had also won the admiration of his enemies. Even after eight years of war, men who 'found the prospect of a Roman peace alarming' were still flocking to his colours and, given a modicum of luck, he could have provided the catalyst to unify the British tribes.

The capture of Caratacus and the destruction of his army remained a main objective of Scapula's plans. He pursued the British leader into

Ordovician territory, probably with XIV Legion, leaving XX Legion deployed amongst the Silures, holding the line of the Usk and maintaining pressure upon them by threatening to take immediate advantage of any move they might make in a northerly direction to aid the British chieftain: additionally, Scapula had to be careful to allow the Silures no opportunity to break through eastwards into Roman-held territory, since this would have been a catastrophic event at this juncture, placing the whole of his operation in jeopardy. Indeed, one must admire Scapula's initiative in pushing forward at this moment with such determination, for Wales was apparently a tinder box which could have ignited with little encouragement. Caratacus was doubtless kept well informed of all these preparations and, as the Roman column edged nearer to him, with its cavalry patrols seeking out his whereabouts, he decided to give battle. His wisdom for doing so must be questioned but it is possible that he was influenced by the size of his administrative column which, now that he was being pushed into a corner, was becoming increasingly vulnerable. It would inevitably have been a slow-moving, attractive target, with families, possibly wounded, and cattle.

> He selected a site where numerous factors, notably approaches and escape routes, helped him and impeded (the Romans). On one side there were steep hills. Wherever the gradient was gentler, stones were piled into a kind of rampart, and to his front there was a river without easy crossings.[2]

Dr St Joseph[3] had identified a position west of Caersws, which fits this description and where earthworks still exist, strengthening his claim.

When the Roman advance was brought to a halt by the river obstacle, the commanders gazed with some dismay at the sight of Caratacus' defensive position, with its dark, overhanging cliffs and at the obvious thoroughness of his preparations. It seemed to them that tribesmen stood upon every rock, brandishing their weapons and shouting angry defiance. They had been enflamed by their clan chieftains, who had described vividly how their women and children would suffer if the day was lost: for 'this was the day, this the battle, which would either win back their freedom or enslave them forever'.

Scapula promptly sent out patrols to both flanks in an effort to discover a less formidable approach and, having received their reports, he plunged into the river, leading his troops in a frontal attack. They crossed through the water without difficulty but, when they came up against the first line of stone ramparts, they suffered heavy casualties. It

65. The hillfort of Caersws in Central Wales, where Caratacus possibly fought his last battle.

66. The cropmarks of the Roman fort which stood at Caersws are clearly visible in this photograph (centre).

was at this moment that the superior training, discipline and equipment of the Roman soldiers began to reassert themselves. They adopted the famous *testudo*, or tortoise, formation, with shields locked over their heads as a protective roof and, under this cover, they demolished the embankment with their hands and stormed up the hillside. The fast moving auxiliaries led the way, armed with javelins, and behind them came the heavy regular infantry in close formation. A general melee took place on the top of the hill, probably a 'forlorn hope' last stand by the British, which covered Caratacus as he made good his escape. Scapula would have wasted little time in pursuing the fleeting Britons, particularly since the British leader was amongst their number, and he doubtless soon found their main base, where Caratacus' wife and daughter were seized and his brother was captured.

Scapula claimed a great victory and received an honorary triumph. As for Caratacus, even discounting some of the pro-Roman embellishments of Tacitus' version of events, it is not easy to believe that the day went as he had hoped or planned. In view of the hard-fighting qualities of the Silures, which time was to show were far from extinguished, it remains a mystery why he should have moved away from the security of their kingdom, unless he was already intending to open a second front in north Britain, where there seems always to have been latent unrest. If this was the case, then Caratacus' next move was incomprehensible, for he apparently fled from the battlefield to Cartimandua, Queen of the Brigantes and a known Roman sympathiser, to seek her support.

Cartimandua, according to Tacitus, was a princess of high birth and great influence: by her actions she also showed herself to be arrogant, ambitious, ruthless and treacherous. The domain over which she ruled, according to Ptolemy, extended from sea to sea and the tribal population was numerically the largest in Britain. Her friendship was therefore vital to the Roman cause as they pursued their campaign of conquest in southern Britain, for her territory provided a buffer against interference from the north. She did not enjoy whole hearted support amongst her people for her pro-Roman attitude: the tribesmen of her western region had already demonstrated this in AD 48, when they rose in delayed sympathy with the rebellion of the Iceni. Scapula had been quick to offer the Queen military help to stamp out the insurrection and she was indebted to him for this demonstration of support, which greatly enhanced her tribal authority. Under these circumstances it is strange, to put it no stronger, that Caratacus should have found his way to her Court, whether it was in an effort to persuade her to join him in his resistance or simply to seek sanctuary. Cartimandua had no hesitation: she arrested him and gave him to Scapula, who sent him at once, with his family and kinsfolk, to Rome, where he was marched through the streets in chains, to the gratification and interest of the population.

Cartimandua's consort was one, Venutius, who until this moment had been content to follow his wife's policy of cooperation with the invading Romans and to enjoy with her the many benefits it brought. There may be some significance in the fact that, after the Queen's betrayal of Caratacus in AD 51, the royal couple split up, Venutius emerging at the head of a faction hostile to the Roman presence and in open conflict with his wife. It is possible to read into this that Venutius was sickened by Cartimandua's act of treachery, which may have been even deeper than appears at first sight, and that Caratacus was deliberately tricked into her hands by an offer of military help, before being cast into irons. It is notable that Tacitus refers to a ruse by which, on some other occasion, the Queen 'had astutely trapped Venutius' brother and other relatives',[4] so she was not averse to this sort of devious behaviour.

On the other hand, Tacitus also provides another reason why the couple may have parted, although which came first would not be easy to answer. The Queen, with the new found wealth heaped upon her as a reward for her part in the capture of Caratacus, tired of Venutius and gave her hand and kingdom to his one-time armour bearer, Vellocatus. It is not surprising that the resulting scandal rocked the royal household to its foundations and the Brigantian people, with the willing help of neighbouring tribes, rallied to the support of Venutius, who quickly found himself heading a revolt, contesting her right to the throne. Cartimandua appealed to the Romans for help and, after some desperate fighting, they managed to extricate her from her dangerous predicament and left the field to Venutius. Tacitus described the outcome of the operation neatly, when he wrote

'Venutius inherited the throne, and we the fighting'.

By whatever means Scapula achieved the elimination of Caratacus from the British scene or however much he may have felt his situation would improve through the removal of the British commander from the theatre of operations, he was to be proved wrong, with dramatic suddenness. Venutius now assumed the role of Caratacus and kept the flame of resistance burning in northern Britain for nearly thirty years: and in Wales, the Silures, seemingly enflamed by the capture of their leader and inspired by his example, descended upon the Roman soldiery occupying their territory with a savage and destructive competence, using all their guile and local knowledge and maintaining a momentum of raids which must have caused the Roman commanders considerable concern. Troops engaged in the building of a fort were attacked and only saved from annihilation by the arrival of reinforcements from neighbouring bases which had been alerted to their plight. Despite this intervention, a divisional chief of staff, eight centurions and the pick of the men engaged on the work were slain.

Seemingly on the same day as this occurrence, the tribesmen were also successful in ambushing a foraging party and then, turning fiercely, they repulsed the cavalry which had ridden to the rescue of the working party. By this time Roman military headquarters must have been in some confusion, for the auxiliary cohorts which Scapula had thrown forward to prevent the situation from developing into a rout, had failed to do so. He next committed his regular infantry and regained some of the initiative but they inflicted little damage on the Silures, who faded away into the darkness, largely unscathed. Encouraged by these successes, the tribesmen now took to the forests and to the marsh areas, from where they conducted a sustained campaign against their enemy. The Romans were thus compelled to abandon their set-piece battle drills and adapt themselves to this new form of unsavoury warfare. Battle, according to Tacitus, followed battle: some were chance encounters on a woodland path, some were skirmishes in low lying marsh land, others were carefully planned operations, with the purpose of seeking out enemy strongholds in the heart of the forests and the swamps. In none was Scapula seen to enjoy success and the morale of the normally well disciplined Roman soldiery began to suffer. The native troops in particular, who so often bore the brunt of the fighting, may well have begun to question the reasons for their presence in this unproductive war. Two of their cohorts allowed themselves to be surprised by the Silures whilst on a looting foray: they had failed to put out pickets and suffered heavy casualties. If it is true that there are no bad soldiers but only bad officers, then the officer corps must be blamed for having allowed this situation to develop and were themselves probably suffering from the same malaise.

The reason for the decline in general discipline may perhaps be attributable to the fact that Scapula was in increasing ill-health. In AD 52 he died, 'exhausted by his responsibilities'. The Silures greeted the news as a great victory and lifted their efforts of resistance to even greater heights. They were to remain a thorn in the Roman side for another five years and even then were not entirely subdued until Frontinus brought Wales under control in his decisive campaign circa AD 74.

CHAPTER NINE

THE PROTAGONISTS

AULUS
PLAUTIUS

Jesus Christ was crucified some ten years before the Claudian invasion of Britain, in the reign of the Emperor Tiberius (AD 14–37). When Aulus Plautius returned to Rome about AD 47, to be received in triumph by Claudius and be granted an *ovatio*, an honour normally restricted to members of the Imperial family, he was not to know that within a few years his wife, Pomponia Graecina, would be charged with observing foreign superstitions, by which it was probably meant that she had adopted the Christian faith. Tacitus relates that[1] 'in accordance with ancient tradition he decided her fate and reputation before her kinsmen and acquitted her' of guilt. By this act he became responsible for her future behaviour and this may explain why the gallant general seemingly disappeared from front of stage at the height of his career, when his future looked so promising; but more troubles lay ahead for Aulus Plautius and his family, for his son, who bore the same name as himself, was to fall foul of Nero (AD 54–68), with fatal results. This irrational Emperor, who distrusted his mother, Agrippina, and ultimately was to plot her assassination, persuaded himself that she was in love with young Aulus Plautius and had seduced him into making a bid for the throne.[2] It is not possible from this range in time to make a judgement whether he was right or wrong in his belief except to comment that anything, no matter how seemingly inconceivable, was possible in mid-1st century Rome. The outcome was not in doubt: young Aulus was instantly and unpleasantly put to death.

NARICISSUS

Narcissus, the ex-slave, whose eloquence on behalf of his Emperor so amused Plautius' mutinous army at Boulogne, was ultimately appointed Secretary-General and

Head of the State Department. Despite his devious nature, and the fact that he appears to have been continuously enmeshed in intrigues, his loyalty to his master never seems to have been in doubt, probably because he could see clearly that their destinies were closely interwined. Claudius (AD 41–54) encouraged the Senate to heap money and honours upon his servant to such an extent that, when the Emperor was heard to complain how little cash was left in the Imperial Treasury, it was suggested to him that he would experience no shortage 'if only his two freedmen (Narcissus and his friend, Pallas) took him into partnership'.

It was largely through the insistence of Narcissus that Claudius took notice of the infidelity and political miscon- duct of his wife, Messalina, which so nearly cost him his throne. Tacitus remarks that[3] the Emperor was inclined to show her mercy but his First Secretary could see clear dangers to them both unless immediate action was taken. He gave instructions for her execution. Claudius

CLAUDIUS

> was still at table when news reached him that Messa- lina had died; whether by her hand or by another's was unspecified. Claudius did not inquire. He called for more wine and went on with his party without interruption.

The Emperor next married Agrippina, the ruthlessly ambitious mother of Nero, now Claudius' stepson. Agrip- pina at once persuaded him to adopt Nero into the Imperial family and wasted no time in conspiring so that Britannicus, his rightful son and heir, should be brought increasingly under the control of herself and her nominees. Once again, the perceptive Narcissus was in no doubt as to the purpose of these intrigues and endeavoured, without success, to forestall them. He incurred the displeasure of the Empress by his opposition to her ambitions and, when Claudius died in AD 54, seemingly from poison, he committed suicide to avoid his inevitable execution. Claudius was declared a god at his death and Nero (AD 54–68), who was then only sixteen years of age, upon being informed that his step-father may have died from eating poisoned mushrooms, wittily remarked that 'mushrooms must indeed be the food of the gods'.

It may be imagined, without difficulty, that Britannicus was to be the next to die. He was only fourteen years of age but was gaining considerable sympathy from the populace for the treatment he had received from his step-brother and for his displacement from his father's house and throne. He was fed poison whilst seated at the children's table in the royal[4] banquet hall. Nero watched unconcernedly as he ceased to breathe and, lying back on his couch, remarked that this sort of fatal seizure often happened to epileptics.

MARCUS OSTORIUS SCAPULA

Nero was also responsible for the death of the son of yet another Roman general who had governed in Britain during the invasion years, Ostorius Scapula. It will be recalled that Marcus Ostorius Scapula was awarded the *corona civica* in AD 48, to honour his gallantry in battle during the revolt of the Iceni. Marcus was insufficiently indiscreet as to cultivate the friendship of an untrustworthy tribune, Antistius Sosianus, and to permit him to read a poem offensive to Nero, whilst at a dinner party in his house. Antistius was exiled and, in order to reestablish himself in the eyes of his Emperor, he avowed he had proof that Marcus Ostorius and a friend were plotting against the Empire. The outcome was reminiscent of Hitler's assassination of Rommel:[5]

> . . . a staff officer of the Guard was dispatched to kill him rapidly. The reason for this haste was Nero's fear of attack. Always cowardly, he was more terrified than ever since the recently discovered conspiracy. Besides, Ostorius was of huge physique and an expert with weapons – his distinguished military record included the oak-wreath for saving a citizen's life in Britain. The officer arrived; and closing every exit from the house, he told Ostorius of the Emperor's orders. The courage he had so often demonstrated against the enemy, Ostorius now turned upon himself.

VESPASIAN

Vespasian was more fortunate, although he did not escape Nero's displeasure. When he returned to Rome, after performing the duties of Proconsul of the African Province 'with great justice and dignity', he fell asleep during one of his master's interminable song recitals, and was disfavourably noticed. Agrippina also distrusted him but, in her case, it was because he had received command of II Legion *Augusta* from Claudius upon the preferment of Narcissus whom, as we have seen above, she regarded with an implacable hatred. Vespasian sensibly, in modern parlance, adopted a 'low profile' and retired to the country from where, in due course, he was to be called to compete for the Imperial throne. He succeeded to the throne in AD 69 and Rome then settled down to a period of fair-handed rule, such as it had not experienced for many years.

Evidence of Cogidubnus' life and activities remains obscure but the outcome of events during the invasion years, and later during the Boudiccan rebellion, testify to his loyalty to Rome and the thoroughness with which he established his 'client' kingdom. Tacitus, in a well-known and often quoted passage[6] wrote that King Cogidubnus

COGIDUBNUS

> maintained his unswerving loyalty right down to our own times – an example of the long established Roman custom of employing even kings to make others slaves.

Tacitus' words are generally interpreted as meaning that the British king survived until some point in the early to mid-sixties. There can be no doubt that the part he played in bringing political stability to the south-eastern kingdoms of Britain made a major contribution to the success of the Roman conquest.

The last word of the story must surely rest with Caratacus. The occasion was the spectacle in Rome when the British prince, with his brothers, wife and daughter were marched in chains through the city, to be displayed to the populace and brought before Claudius. As he passed among the crowds he looked around him in disdain, ignoring the frightened appeals for mercy being made to the spectators by his relatives. His reputation as a courageous warrior king had spread throughout Europe and his carriage and behaviour on this occasion did nothing to diminish it. He mounted the dais and, allowing his eyes to pass over the splendours of the surrounding buildings, in front of which the Praetorian Guard had been marshalled, he addressed Claudius and those gathered around him in the following words,[7]

CARATACUS

Had my lineage and rank been accompanied by only moderate success, I should have come to this city as a friend rather than a prisoner, and you would not have disdained to ally yourself peacefully with one so nobly borne, the ruler of so many nations. As it is humiliation is my lot, glory yours. I had horses, men, arms, wealth. Are you surprised I am sorry to lose them? If you want to rule the world, does it follow that every one else welcomes enslavement? If I had surrendered without a blow before being brought before you, neither my downfall nor your triumph would have become famous. If you execute me, they will be forgotten. Spare me, and I shall be an everlasting token of your mercy.

According to Dio, he asked, waving his arm in the direction of the splendours of the city, 'When you have all this, why do you envy us our poor hovels?'

Claudius responded by pardoning him, his family and brothers and, when they had been released from their chains, they offered their gratitude and homage, first to the emperor, who had granted them freedom to live out their lives in Rome, and then to his wife, Agrippina, mother of Nero.

Caratacus, the first British hero, then descended the dais and walked away from history.

APPENDIX A

Caesar's Invasion, 54 BC

Suggested route of advance inland
Watling Street to Chelsea

Route 101	Sandwich to Canterbury	12½
1(b)	Canterbury to Rochester	25½
1(c)	Rochester to Greenwich	28½
	Greenwich to Chelsea Bridge	8½
	Total mileage	75

Reference: I.D. Margary, *Roman Roads in Britain* (1955, rev. 1967)

Alternative route
North Down Way to the Thames between Wandsworth and Chelsea

1.	Caesar's bridgehead to R. Stour	12	12
2.	R. Stour to R. Medway		
	(i) R. Stour to Charing	4	4
	(ii) Charing to R. Medway	16	16
3.	R. Medway to Otford	11	11
4.	Otford to Titsey Hill, Westerham	10	
5.	Titsey Hill to Thames	21	
	or, alternatively		
4.	Otford to Tandridge Hill		13
5.	Tandridge Hill to Thames		18
	Total mileage	74	74

Reference: C.J. Wright, *A Guide to the Pilgrim's Way and North Downs Way* (1971, 2nd ed. 1977)

NOTE: The mileage from Caesar's bridgehead is as recorded by him (Caesar: *Gallic War*, V): distances from Thames to Titsey, Tandridge and Greenwich are from HM Ordnance Survey Maps.

APPENDIX B

The Medway bridges at Rochester

References

A.K. Astbury, *Estuary: Land and Water in the Lower Thames Basin,* (1980), 159–160

2. J.J. Robson, Origins of Rochester Bridge, *Archaeologia Cantiana,* xxxv

Chronology

1.	AD 43–45	Construction of Roman Bridge.
	AD 960	Documentary evidence exists that an ancient bridge, probably Roman, was pulled down for safety reasons and rebuilt in reign of King Edgar.
	AD 1264	Wooden superstructure of bridge burnt by Simon de Montfort in war of Barons against the King.
	AD 1281	Bridge less its piers and abutments carried away by floods, to be replaced by a wooden bridge.
	AD 1387–92	Wooden bridge, weakened by traffic resulting from capture of Calais, replaced by stone structure.
	AD *c* 1850	Stone bridge replaced by 19th century structure.

Original foundations

2. The 19th century engineer responsible for the construction of the existing bridge at Rochester, recorded removing the foundations of an ancient bridge from the river, which had been sunk by the use of 20′ wooden piles, made mostly from elm and shod with iron. He excavated more than 10,000 of these from the river bed, making a total of 250,000 cubic feet of timber. The piles were sunk to a depth of 13′ to 25′ thus making it probable that the bridge it carried was constructed of stone.

3.   In 1115 it was recorded that the existing bridge was carried by nine
     stone piers, 43′ from centre to centre, implying a total span of
     about 475′.

67.   The demolition of the old bridge at Rochester by the Royal Engineers in 1856. More than
20,000 wooden piles, sunk by the Romans, were discovered during subsequent rebuilding work.

APPENDIX C

Roman Logistical Matters

THE TASK FORCE[1, 2]

Legions

a. **II LEGION AUGUSTA**
Served in Spain until c. AD 9, when it was transferred to Upper Germany. It was awarded two emblems, *Capricorn*, indicating its reconstitution by Augustus, and *Pegasus* the significance of which is not clear but Holder suggests it was awarded for service under Vespasian.

b. **IX LEGION HISPANA**
The legion had a prolonged history of garrisoning Spain. It was transferred to Illyricum (Pannonia) some time before AD 6, and thence to Britain in AD 43.

c. **XIV LEGION GEMINA**
The legion sprang from the amalgamation of two other legions, hence its cognomen, *Gemina*. Raised after Actium by Augustus, it was stationed at Mainz in Upper Germany from AD 9. It was awarded the emblem *Capricorn* (see sub para a above). XIV Legion was especially honoured for its conduct during the Boudiccan rebellion in AD 60–61, by being granted the additional title *Martia Victrix*, or Martial and Victorious.

d. **XX LEGION VALERIA**
Probably raised after the battle of Actium and, after service in the Balkans (?20 BC–AD 9), it was then transferred to Lower Germany. Until recently it was thought to have taken its title from Valerius Messalinus, under whose generalship it served in the Illyrican War. Keppie suggests it was awarded the title *Valeria Victrix*, or Valiant and Victorious, for service in the aftermath of Boudicca's revolt.[3]

Supporting Arms

It is not possible to be so specific about the regimental titles or numbers of units which embarked in support of the legions. There is some indication that these were allotted to legions as 'divisional troops', in much the same manner as modern practice. A skillet, for example, unusually marked with the name of *Ala 1 Thracum* had recently been unearthed at Caerleon, in South Wales, a legionary fortress associated with II Legion *Augusta*. There are, as Boon has pointed out, many explanations for the presence of the vessel. It would, however, be understandable that legion commanders would have wished to have units operating in their support of whose training and battlefield performance they had first hand experience. Additionally, it would have been of mutual benefit that the commanding officers of those regiments knew the mind of their commanding general. The Roman war machine, above all, would have appreciated the value of this sort of team work.

The following cavalry regiments appear to have served in Britain in the early years of the invasion:[4]

e. ALA INDIANA GALLORUM
Raised in Gaul in AD 21 and is known to have served in Upper Germany in the pre Claudian period. A tombstone at Cirencester, erected in the reign of Vespasian, suggests the regiment may have arrived in AD 43 or 61.

f. ALA I HISPANORUM ASTURUM
The regiment was raised from the Astures of north west Spain shortly before AD 43 and may have formed part of the invasion force.

g. ALA HISPANORUM VETTONUM CR
Raised from the Vettones of Central Spain shortly before AD 43 and is also presumed to have formed part of the invasion force. It is attested on the tombstone of a trooper at Bath and also at Brecon Gaer at the end of the first century.

h. ALA I PANNONIORUM SABINIANA
i. ALA I PANNONIORUM TAMPIANA
Both of these regiments were raised in Pannonia (broadly modern Hungary) and possibly arrived in Britain in AD 43.

j. ALA I THRACUM
This regiment was raised in Thrace (broadly modern Bulgaria) and is presumed to have landed in Britain with the invasion force in AD 43. It is attested in Colchester in the reign of Claudius.

Cohorts

Some cohorts may have been embarked for front line service with legions to whom they were probably attached as 'divisional troops'. Others almost certainly will have come ashore to take their part in garrison duties or guarding lines of communication, and yet others, such as the Batavians, skilled in river crossing techniques, or the archers of Cohors I Hamiorum, may have been held directly under the hand of the Army Commander. Once again, no firm order of battle has been handed down to us but the following are amongst those units which may have disembarked:[5]

		Inf.	Eq.	
k.	Cohors I Alpinorum	1		
l.	Cohors I Aquitanorum Eq.		1	
m.	Cohortes I–VIII Batavorum	8		
n.	Cohors III Bracaraugustanorum	1		
o.	Cohors III Breucorum	1		
p.	Cohortes I–IV Delmatarum	4		
q.	Cohortes I and II Delmatarum Eq.		2	
r.	Cohors IIII Delmatarum	1		
s.	Cohortes I–V Gallorum	5		
t.	Cohors I Hamiorum	1		Archers
u.	Cohors VI Thracum Eq		1	
v.	Cohors VII Thracum	1		
	Total cohorts	23	4	

Strength and composition

It must be said at once that the lists of *alae* and *cohortes* produced above, in the absence of factual evidence, depend in many cases upon probability and judgement. Nevertheless, they do provide a guide line for calculations: on this broad basis, the 'teeth' arms sailing with the invasion force conceivably had an effective strength as follows

Legions	4	or	19,200 men
Cavalry Regiments	6		3,000
Mounted Infantry (Eq.)	4		2,000
Infantry (Inf.)	23		11,500
			35,700 men

To this figure should be added a further less easily calculable number to allow, at unit level, for employed men (the bane of the sergeant-major's life) or *immunes* as the Romans termed them, and at Force Headquarters for *immunes* and specialists such as engineers, medical and transport personnel, including the handlers of river transport and shore-based detachments of the *Classis Britannica*. In general, the *immunes* were those who had their own special duties to perform and were thus exempt from general duties: by the second century AD these had emerged clearly as a class of their own, within the army, and their range of duties is defined comprehensively by Tarrentus Paternus (*Digest* 50,6,7):

> Certain soldiers are granted by their conditions of service some exemption from the heavier fatigues. These are men such as surveyors, the medical sergeant, medical orderlies and dressers, ditchers, farriers, the architects, pilots, shipwrights, artillerymen, glassfitters, smiths, arrowsmiths, coppersmiths, helmet-makers, wagon-makers, roof-tile-makers, swordcutlers, water engineers, trumpet-makers, horn-makers, bow-makers, plumbers, blacksmiths, stone-cutters, lime-burners, woodcutters and charcoal-burners. In the same category there are usually included butchers, huntsmen, keepers of sacrificial animals, the workshop sergeant, sick-bay attendants (?), clerks who can give instruction, granary clerks, clerks responsible for monies left on deposit, clerks responsible for monies left without heirs, orderly-room staffs, grooms, horse-trainers (?), armoury sergeants, the herald and the trumpeter. These are all then classed as *immunes*.

Many, if not all, of these categories of tradesmen would have travelled in one of the divisions of the Task Force and would have been found either at Base Headquarters or between there and the combat zone. In addition to these numbers one may be assured that regiments were tapped by their senior formation to provide men for duties at that level. An interesting document, dated about AD 87, shows the peace-time strength of a century, stationed in Egypt, to have been so reduced by demands upon its manpower for other duties, as to number only 40 men.[6] Some had been sent to granaries at Neapolis, near Alexandria, and others had been posted to other centuries for temporary duty. The parade state reveals that amongst these reduced numbers remaining in barracks, there were still those exempt from duty, including a supernumerary, weapon storeman, wagon-repairer, batman, three clerks, a housekeeper (one presumes the caterer) and, on guard, the unfortunate Domitius.

Taking all these specialists and duty men to account it is likely that the total effective strength of the units embarked for the invasion would have been about 40,000 men (all soldiers, tradesmen or otherwise in the combat zone are fighting soldiers); and the overall operational strength, including the specialists and others at Force Headquarters and at Base, would probably have been nearer 45,000.

SIEGE AND ARTILLERY WEAPONS

Britain had few strongholds which could withstand a concerted attack by the highly trained and well equipped Roman Army. It must be doubtful whether they employed against the British the sort of sophisticated, heavy weaponry which they used in their wars against the Jews. Nevertheless, we cannot be sure of this and there is some evidence (not related to the invasion years), provided by the discovery of stones at High Rochester and Risingham, weighing about one hundredweight each, that they resorted to the use of heavy artillery

68. Artillery in action: *carroballistae* when mounted were drawn by mules and served by a team of eight men, a *contubernium*. From a relief on Trajan's Column.

weapons upon occasion.[7] The full range of siege engines, and other weapons upon which they could call in assault, comprised a formidable list. It is necessary here to mention only a few in order to illustrate the magnitude of the task undertaken when shipping these to Britain from the continent as part of a balanced task force. If they were required for use in the later stages of their campaign, as opposed to its opening phases, then doubtless thought could have been given to constructing them on these shores.

The use of artillery, introduced into the West by the Greeks and Carthaginians about 400 BC, became an increasingly important factor in siege warfare and on the battlefield, when fired from the flanks in support of infantry. One Lacedaemonian general, rather in the manner of World War 1 cavalry commanders when they beheld the tank, remarked sadly: 'So that is what war has become?'[8] The design of the machines, all of which varied considerably in size, was based upon two principles: one, constructed like a giant cross-bow, fired metal shafts or huge bolts of wood, dependent upon the dimensions of the machine, and the other was built like an enormous slingshot, operated by the torsion of ropes and capable of hurling rocks over great distances. In broad terms, the first of these was categorised as a *ballista* and the second as an *onager*, a word meaning ass and implying that the weapon had the kick of a mule. The word *catapult* is of Greek origin and may be interpreted as 'pike-hurler'. Each legion was given[9] ten *onagri* on a scale of one per cohort, wheeled and towed by oxen, and sixty *carroballistae* or ten per cohort (one per century). The total of these weapons travelling with the task force would therefore have been 240 *carroballistae* and 60 *onagri*, with an equivalent number of carts to carry the *ballistae* and ammunition. It is easy to imagine that a legion commander would have wished, on occasion, to brigade these weapons (the attack on Hod Hill would have been a suitable moment) but whether or not they would have come ashore with the first wave of the assault troops must be left open to question. There may have been a role for the *ballistae*, firing over the heads of the troops going ashore and aimed at enemy concentrations awaiting their arrival.

The heaviest siege machine could launch stones weighing more than 175 pounds over a distance of some 800 yards[10] but normally a smaller projectile of about 28 pounds was fired over half of this distance and with greater accuracy. It should be emphasised that accurate records of their performance are unavailable and data that has been collated from various sources varies considerably. The range of the *carroballista*, firing an iron bolt with reasonable accuracy, sometimes much in the manner of a light mortar, has been estimated at about 300 metres.[11]

ARMOUR AND PERSONAL WEAPONS

Russell Robinson in his excellent work on the Armour of Imperial
Rome has clearly defined the military equipment worn by legionaries in
the period covering the late first century BC until early second century
AD. He has separated the total period into three divisions of time, the
first of which terminates, in his words, at the end of the first half of the
first century AD: in the second quarter of the same century, beginnings
of the next phase are seen to emerge and it would appear that there was
a period of overlap. From a logistical viewpoint, however, it is possible
we are concerned with the equipment of the first period rather than the
second.[12]

At the beginning of the first century AD the legionary wore a bronze
'jockey cap' style helmet, with a protective neck-piece, and a Gallic mail
shirt: he carried an early form of rectangular shield, which was in effect
the oval shield with its top and bottom cut off. His long pointed sword
and his dagger, each covered with silvered bronze plates, hung from
separate waist belts. He carried two javelins, each about seven feet long,
with a killing range of about thirty yards. Each javelin, or *pilum*, was
fitted with a long iron shank, the pointed head of which was tempered
metal and barbed: the shaft was soft metal and bent on impact. When it
was lodged in a shield the latter became an encumbrance to its owner
and had to be flung away, leaving him unprotected. These metal shafts
were fitted to the wooden head of the javelin by rivets and the weapon
called for a competent system of repair and resupply, with reserves held
close to the battlefield. It would equally have been important for the
Romans to be alert to salvage from the battle area any material which
could be recycled for further use. Their enemies, on the other hand,
could have gained some benefit by making it difficult for them to do this
and could have added to their troubles by subjecting their supply depots
and workshops to guerilla attack.

In Russell Robinson's second phase, the legionary was provided with
a strengthened helmet and a laminated cuirass of which an important
hoard was excavated at Corbridge in recent years. The earliest pattern
of this armour consisted of forty plates, twenty four in the collar and
shoulder units and sixteen in the girdle plates. His sword was now
suspended from the shoulder and was a lighter weapon, with a shorter
point. The javelin was given added penetrative power by the addition of
a lead weight below the placement where the metal blade was rivetted
to the wooden shaft.

Auxiliary soldiers were issued with two types of armour, scale or
mail. The scale armour consisted of overlapping metal scales fastened
either to fabric or leather to make a shirt of armour reaching down to

the thighs. The manufacture of mail was very much a task for specialist craftsmen, since it comprised a collection of metal rings, each one passing through four others: once again, the result provided its owner with a protective shirt reaching down to the upper thigh. The basic weapons issued to both infantry and cavalry were similar in type but varied in style or quantity: they consisted of sword and throwing spear, the latter being short, with an iron head fixed on a wooden shaft. Two were issued to each infantrymen and three to each cavalryman, who could also use theirs in close combat as a form of lance. The sword was short: in each case the length being dictated by the form of combat for which they were trained. The flat auxiliary shield was either oval or hexagonal.

When one is considering the logistical burden imposed by the provision of all this equipment, the cavalry requirement for saddlery must not be overlooked. In some cases horse armour was worn but there is little evidence that it was used by auxiliary cavalry. On the other hand, numerous pierced globular bronze eyeguards from horse chamfrons have been found on sites known to have been occupied by cavalry units, adding to the wide range of equipment employed by the Roman soldier and requiring administration.[13]

The craftsmen attached to a legion would almost certainly have been capable of making armour but it must be doubtful if they could have found the time, certainly in an operational area, to undertake major tasks of this nature more fitted for established workshops. Their task is more likely to have been a maintenance task for material and equipment, and the production of javelin heads, arrows and wooden shafts for both these types of weapon. It is clear that the commander of the invasion force would not have wished to experience a shortage of these items and ample reserves would have been shipped ashore behind the disembarking legions.

ROADBUILDING

We have already examined Plautius' logistical problems in keeping his troops fed, until he could set up secure internal supply sources. The construction of a highway, following the course of his advance from Richborough to the Medway and thence to London, must have ranked high with him as a priority, if only to free barges and shipping for use elsewhere in his riverine operations as the war moved forward. The first stage of his task would have been to construct an assault road to support immediate operations: later he would have wished to upgrade this tactical route to a strategic route, running near, but not necessarily along, the tactical road. The provision of the strategic road would have been a much longer term project, would have reduced the need for continuing maintenance on the tactical road and would thus have economised in labour.

The Commandant of the Royal School of Military Engineering at Chatham, whose headquarters lies close to the stretch of Watling Street between London and Dover, kindly authorised for me a study of the length of time required to build both these stages.

The tactical road would have been a simple construction following closely behind the vanguard of the task force; the road head might have been one or two days behind the leading Roman troops, its work force being protected by the main guard. In the early stage of its construction, presuming (none too confidently) that Plautius was seeking a road to bolster his river supply route, the work force was probably drawn from military sources (in this case possibly IX Legion) and, in the estimate of the Royal Engineers, would have numbered not much more than 1,000 men, each working 10 hours a day. They visualised that the road was constructed to the following standards:

a.   a cleared width of 8.6m with all trees and scrub cut to ground level.
b.   a levelled carriageway of 2.6m marked by timber kerbs.
c.   minimal or non-existent drainage.
d.   a corduroy surface over swamps.

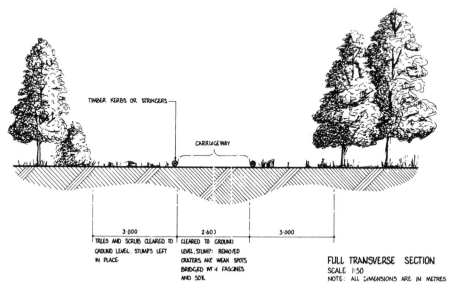

69.   A Roman tactical road of dry construction, from a drawing compiled by the Commandant, Royal Engineers, Chatham.

When considering the labour constants to be embodied in their calculations they allowed 100% for skill, for the evidence speaks for itself: 100% for military morale and 90% for slave[14] morale, whilst admitting that much of their output might stem from an intimidation factor. Output naturally would have depended to some considerable degree on physical fitness. In reaching their results they assumed, whilst granting a yardstick of 100% for a twentieth century Royal Engineer tradesman, that a Roman legionary was 95% efficient, an auxiliary 85% and slave labour only 75%. The auxiliary grading may be debatable but it provides a basis for comparison.

The Royal Engineers calculated the following norms for the construction of a tactical road over four types of ground:

    d. Grassland – 40 man hours per 100 metres
    e. Forest   – 600 man hours per 100 metres
    f. Heathland – 450 man hours per 100 metres
    g. Swamp   – 625 man hours per 100 metres

These figures enabled them to prepare the following suggested timetable for the construction of the road:

TABLE VI

Serial	From	To	Length	Man hours	Total Working Strength	Time	Remarks
			Km		Men	Days	
(a)	(b)	(c)	(d)	(e)	(f)	(g)	(h)
1	Richborough	Canterbury	27.5	48,841	495	10	consolidation west of Canterbury
2	Canterbury	Faversham	18.4	110,029	763	15	
3	Faversham	Medway	28.2	169,200	850	20	1. In two bounds of 14 Kms 2. Battle fought west of the R Medway
4	River Medway	River Cray	23.65	142,137	1056	14	
5	River Cray	River Thames at Westminster	21.70	99,575	1008	10	Ford across Thames at Westminster
6	Totals		119.45	569,782	1056	69	

Thus, using less than three per cent of the invasion force for road construction and allowing two weeks for bridgehead consolidation at Richborough and Thanet, one week for reorganisation at Canterbury and two weeks for redeployment and consolidation after the Medway battle, Roman troops could have completed a tactical road through to Westminster within a 15 week period. It would have been particularly useful for the movement of troops and reinforcements and perhaps for medical evacuation; but, as noted in Chapter VIII, the use of wagons for bulk transport was uneconomic when compared to river or coastal transport.

BRIDGE-BUILDING

Caesar has provided us with the most perfect description of Roman military bridge building. The occasion was his counter-attack across the Rhine, when repelling the German tribes who had invaded Gaul. It was 55 BC and only a few months before his first invasion of Britain (Gallic Wars, iv):

> Such, then, were my reasons for crossing the Rhine; but to do so in boats appeared too risky and was certainly below the dignity of a Roman general. To build a bridge would be a difficult operation because of the river's width, depth and swift current. Nevertheless I came to the conclusion that the difficulty must be overcome or the whole idea of crossing abandoned. Construction was therefore begun on the following plan. Two piles, 18 inches thick, slightly pointed at the lower ends, and varying in length according to the river's depth, were fastened together two feet apart to form a truss. They were then lowered into the water from rafts and driven firmly into the river-bed with pile-drivers. They were not set in the usual vertical position but inclining in the direction of the current. Opposite to them, and 40 feet downstream, a similar truss was fixed but this time leaning against the stream. The trusses were joined by a transom 2 feet wide, the ends of which fitted exactly into the spaces between the heads of the four piles. The two trusses were kept apart by iron 'dogs', which secured each pile to the end of the transom; and added strength was given by diagonal ties running from one pile to its opposite number on the same side. In this way the rigidity of the whole structure naturally increased in proportion to the current's force; additional piles were driven in obliquely on the downstream side to form a buttress supporting each truss and helping to take the weight of the water. A series of these trusses and transoms were connected by timbers laid at right angles so that if the natives attempted to destroy it by floating down tree trunks or boats, these fenders would lessen the shock and prevent damage to the bridge.

Within ten days after the collection of timber for the bridge had begun, the work was completed and the army had crossed over. The Germans were overawed. Caesar spent eighteen days beyond the Rhine and then recrossed into Gaul, destroying the bridge behind him. Despite the fact that this bridge was constructed in a remarkably quick time, the delay of ten days might have been unacceptable in the cut and thrust of a full-blooded battle. Vegetius relates how the Romans reduced this waiting time and it may be that the Batavians used either one of these methods to cross the Medway and later the Thames (see Chapters IV and V):

> Navigable rivers are passed ... in an emergency by fastening together a number of empty casks and covering them with boards. The cavalry, throwing off their accoutrements, make small floats of dry reeds or rushes on which they lay their arms and cuirasses to preserve them from being wet ... But the most commodious invention is that of the small boats hollowed out of one log and very light both by their make and the quality of the wood. *The army always has a number of these boats upon carriages*, together with a sufficient quantity of planks and iron nails. Thus with the help of cables to lash the boats together, a bridge is instantly constructed, which for the time has the solidity of a bridge of stone.

MEDICAL[15]

The purpose of the next few paragraphs is to examine the scale of the administrative effort required by the Romans to support their medical arrangements for troops on active service. These arrangements were provided at four, possibly five, levels:

1   all soldiers received instruction in first aid, and in the bandaging and dressing of wounds, as part of their military training.

2   each auxiliary unit, infantry battalion (cohort) and cavalry regiment was provided with its own medical team, headed by a doctor; this team will have included trained nursing orderlies, of whom individuals will have been seconded to centuries for operational reasons or when that sub-unit was on detachment.

3   the *praefectus castrorum*, or second-in-command of a legion, according to Vegetius, was 'responsible for the sick soldiers and the *medici*, by whom they were looked after, and also the expenses involved.' Hospital buildings were provided within permanent legionary fortresses: until these were built, or when a unit was on campaign, a field hospital was set up in tented accomodation.

70. A Roman Field Dressing Station from Trajan's Column: a legionary and cavalry trooper
receiving first aid.

4   a hospital would most certainly have been provided at Base headquarters to take care of wounded in transit and the health of local units.

5   considerable attention was directed to the welfare of convalescent soldiers, these being sent either to the coast or to curative spas (such as Bath, *Aquae Sulis*), where doubtless medical units were established.

Military medical officers were of high quality and were generally of Greek or Graeco-Asiatic nationality, for it was in these areas that the best medical schools were then to be found. Davies remarks that the most noteworthy point about the Roman army medical service was its efficiency at all times. Medical and surgical instruments were of a very respectable standard and some of their practices, such as for the emergency amputation of limbs, were still in use during the First World War. These standards of efficiency demanded plentiful stores, equipment, medicines and, necessarily, wagons to transport them. Additionally, carts and animals were provided to carry the wounded to hospital but at what level these were made available, from what source they derived or in what quantities they existed is obscure.

The battlefield conditions experienced by the British Army in the non-mechanised mid-19th century, apart from a serious increase in the severity of wounds caused by improved weaponry, are worthy of study for in some instances they bear comparison to those accustomed by the Romans. The British Soldier's Field Service Pocket Book (FSPB) of 1869, advises[16] that hospital accommodation should be provided for a constant average of daily sick, a sick reserve and wounded after an action, the number in each case being 5 per cent of the total strength of the operational force. It remarks, almost in the words of the Roman *medici*, that 'all the experience of late years proves that sick or wounded, particularly the latter, do much better under canvas than in buildings'.

The medical establishment with each British battalion, regiment of cavalry and battery of artillery was laid down as:

1   surgeon
1   pair of panniers on mule or horse
1   driver
1   orderly, Army Health Corps

Until the publication of this edition of the FSPB it had been the custom for regiments to be provided with their own transport for the conveyance of sick and wounded but this was now abolished so that a stop can in consequence be put to the nefarious and demoralising practice of permitting men to leave their ranks whilst in actual contact with the enemy for the purpose of removing or assisting wounded to the rear.

The ambulance establishment was in future to be based at divisional (the formation equivalent of legion but not necessarily comparable in size) headquarters. It was recommended that with each division there should be 76 ambulance wagons, 7 medical officers and a detachment of the Army Health Corps comprising 3 officers, 9 non-commissioned officers and 150 stretcher-bearers. These numbers were to include all persons required for tending wounded on the field, and for collecting them 'and ministering to their wants during journey to hospital'. The animals and manpower to look after the ambulance wagons were to be provided by the Army Service Corps.

The Divisional (Field) Hospital (again, comparable with the legion hospital) was to be sited as far forward as possible and the route to it from the front line was required to be signed so that 'wounded men able to walk or crawl could find their way without assistance'. The FSPB saw the need for as many as two or three Field Hospitals for each Division since its size should be restricted, to allow for mobility, to no more than 200 casualties. Severe medical cases were to be evacuated at the earliest moment to base General Hospital. A Field Hospital sited well forward was, especially in colonial style wars, vulnerable to attack. Davies writes

> In 53 BC p. Sextius Baculus, a former chief centurion of Caesar, had been left behind in camp with the other sick. Although he had been too ill to eat for five days, nevertheless he still managed to summon up the strength, when the German cavalry suddenly attacked to leave the hospital tent and supervise the defence of the camp, until he fainted from his wounds.

History is full of interesting parallels: in 1897, Lieutenant EW Costello, serving with the Malakand Field Force, went out from hospital with two sepoys to rescue a wounded havildar from ground overrun by enemy swordsmen. He was awarded the Victoria Cross.

To sum up, after taking to account the strength of auxiliary units working with their parent legions, the comparable strengths of the two formations may not have been significantly different. There must have been a considerable number of hospital wagons and ambulances held at each legion headquarters, adding to the shipping demands when the Roman General Staff were making their embarkation plans. Although Roman army soldiers were instructed in first aid it is unlikely, for the same reasons as mentioned in FSPB, that they were greatly involved in the rearward movement of wounded. If the task of collecting severely wounded was not performed by forward troops, as seems probable, then it must have happened that additional orderlies were attached to cohorts during battle especially for this purpose. This thought suggests that some loose grouping of orderlies, or even some organisation like the Army Health Corps mentioned above (which was recruited initially from the rank and file) was held at legion headquarters under the eye of the *praefectus castrorum*, who would have been responsible for their military welfare and for their detachment to units as operations required. Their medical training, when they were at legion headquarters, probably rested in the hands of the *optio valetudinarii* in charge of the fortress hospital.

On the basis of the sort of medical organisation discussed above, there would also have been an extra requirement for animals to work with the ambulances and wagons, and for allocation to the cohort medical teams, both auxiliary and legionary. This would have meant an extra 73 animals as pack transport (legionary cohorts 40, auxiliary cohorts 27, cavalry regiments 6), with, say an extra 30 carts per legion (the FSPB laid down a generous 76 ambulances per Division), or another 240 animals on the scale of 2 per ambulance for four legions, a grand total of an additional 313, say 300. There is a lifeline at which Aulus Plautius could have grasped! The FSPB advises

> When there is a choice between water and any other mode of conveyance, the former ought to be selected and large roomy boats should be especially prepared for moving the sick.

NOTES AND REFERENCES

Chapter I

1. Caesar, *Gallic Wars*, iii, 16.
2. L.V. Grinsell, *The Archaeology of Wessex* (1958), 157–8.
3. Sir R. Colt Hoare, *Ancient Wilts*, i (1812), 55, 66.
4. Caesar, *Gallic Wars*, iv, 20.
5. *ibid.*, iv, 23.
6. This is militarily interesting for, although the fleet with the main body of his army were trailing in until mid-afternoon, Caesar found it possible to call a conference of staff and commanding officers. He was therefore an early practitioner of the Orders Group battle drill evolved in World War II, whereby commanding officers travelled with the force commander to enable the quick passage of detailed orders.
7. Caesar, *Gallic Wars*, iv, 32.
8. *ibid.*, v, 1.
9. Bigbury Woods – GR 169/115577.
10. Caesar, *Gallic Wars*, v, 18.
11. *ibid.*, v, 22.
12. B. Cunliffe, 'Social and Economic Development in Kent in the pre-Roman Iron Age', *Archaeology in Kent to AD 1500*, CBA Research Report No 48, (ed. P.E. Leach, 1976), 46.
13. W. Rodwell, 'Coinage, oppida and the rise of Belgic power in south-east Britain', *Oppida in Barbarian Europe* (BAR Supplement, Ser 11, 1976), 210.
14. S.S. Frere, *Britannia, A History of Roman Britain* (1976, rev. 1978), 62.
15. Rodwell, *op. cit.*, 249.
16. C. Partridge, *Skeleton Green, a late Iron Age Romano-British site*, Britannia Monograph Ser., No 2 (1981), 353.
17. *ibid.*, 355.
18. Frere, *op. cit.*, 60.
19. *Roman Colchester* (Colchester Borough Council, 1980), 5.
20. Frere, *op. cit.*, 58.
21. Rodwell, *loc. sit.*
22. G.C. Boon, *Silchester, The Roman Town of Calleva* (1974), 38.
23. G. Webster, *Rome against Caratacus* (1981), 14.
24. M.W.C. Hassall, 'Batavians and the Roman Conquest of Britain, *Britannia*, i (1970), 133, note 21.

Chapter II

1. L.J.F. Keppie, 'Legio VIII Augusta and the Claudian Invasion', *Britannia*, ii (1971), 155.

2. Caesar, *Gallic Wars*, i, 3.
3. D.J. Breeze, *Bulletin of the Hadrianic Society*, No 1 (1983), 10–14.
4. These horses were probably descended from *Equus przewalskii*, possibly still to be found in Outer Mongolia, and were related to the Tarpan of South Russia, which was domesticated before 3000 BC. See T.G.E. Powell (ed.), *The Celts* (1980).
5. For greater detail see Graham Webster, *The Roman Imperial Army* (corrected edition, 1981).
6. I.A. Richmond, *Trajan's Army on Trajan's Column* (republ. Br Sch at Rome, 1982), 11.
7. Breeze, *loc. cit.*
8. *ibid.*
9. *ibid.*
10. R.W. Davies, 'The Roman Military Diet', *Britannia*, ii (1971), 122–42.
11. *ibid.*
12. *ibid.*, 124 Note 19.
13. Richmond, *loc. cit.*, 7–15.
14. *ibid.*, 13.
15. Davies, *op. cit.*, 123.
16. Caesar, *Gallic Wars*, v, 7.
17. Dio Cassius, lx, 19.
18. A.L.F. Rivet, *The Roman Villa in Britain* (1969), 195–7.
19. Calculated at the scale of 3lbs per capita.
20. C.G. Starr, Jr. *The Roman Imperial Navy* (1941), 152.
21. Tacitus, *Annals*, ii, 6.
22. Starr, *op. cit.*, 203, note 69.
23. J. Morris, *Londinium: London in the Roman Empire* (1982), 268.
24. Caesar, *Gallic Wars*, iv, 22.
25. *ibid.*, iv, 26.
26. Webster, *op. cit.*, 142.
27. Herodian (ed. C.R. Whittaker, 1969), iii, 14, 359.
28. Tacitus, *Annals*, xii, 12.1.
30. Caesar, *Gallic Wars*, vii, 75.
31. It is strange that this force of chariots, many of which may be expected to have been destroyed during the invasion battles with the Romans and most of which would have been destroyed or confiscated after the conquest, appear somehow to have been recreated undetected for use in Boudicca's rebellion in AD 60.
32. Tacitus, *Agricola*, 14.

Chapter III

1. Dio Cassius, lx, 19.
2. Tacitus, *Annals*, i, 3.
3. Suetonius, *Augustus*, 23.
4. Tacitus, *Annals*, ii, 22.
5. *ibid.*, 23–4.
6. Suetonius, *Claudius*, 17.
8. B. Cunliffe (ed.), *Richborough* v (1968), 37–40.
9. J.P. Bushe-Fox (ed.), *Fourth Report on the excavations of the Roman Fort at Richborough, Kent* (1949).
10. B. Philp, *The Roman Fort at Reculver*, 3.

11. George Dowker, FGS, 'On the landing place of St Augustine', *Arch. Cant.*, xxii, 122–42.
12. Caesar, *Gallic Wars*, v, 12–14.
13. Cunliffe, *op. cit.*
14. Dio Cassius, *loc. cit.*, describing how Plautius had great trouble in making contact with the Britons, who took refuge in the swamps and forests, hoping to wear the Romans down so that they would sail away, as Caesar had done. In short the Britons were employing sensible guerilla tactics.
15. *ibid.*
16. J. Wacher, *Roman Britain* (1978), 29.
17. I. Richmond, *Roman Britain* (1955, reprinted 1981), 20.
18. G. Webster and D. Dudley, *The Roman Conquest of Britain* (1965), 58.
19. S.S. Frere, *Britannia, A History of Roman Britain* (1967, rev. 1978).
20. Caesar, *Gallic Wars*, v, 22.
21. *ibid.*, v, 11.
22. *ibid.*, ii, 4.
23. G. Webster, *Rome against Caratacus* (1981), 30.

Chapter IV

1. Dio Cassius, lx, 19–20.
2. Generally identified with the Dobunni of the Cotswolds.
3. Caesar, *Gallic Wars*, iv, 24.
4. A.K. and B.T. Thould, 'Arthritis in Roman Britain', *British Medical Assn. Journal*, 287, 1909. The authors conducted a study of the height of the population by examining 148 male and 98 female skeletons stored at the British Museum. They found the mean height of the males to be 169 cm (5'6½") and females 157 cm (5'2"), about 2 inches shorter in each case than the twentieth century mean. The largest male skeleton measured 182 cm (6'). The life expectancy seems to have been 34.6 years for men and 27.8 for women.
5. Tacitus, *Agricola*, 35.
6. S.S. Frere, *Britannia: A History of Roman Britain* (1967, rev. 1978), 80.
7. G. Webster, *op. cit.*, 67.
8. I.D. Margary, *Roman Roads in Britain* (1955, rev. 1967), 2, 43.
9. S.S. Frere, *op. cit.*, v, 81.
10. C.J. Wright, *A Guide to the Pilgrim's Way and North Downs Way* (1971, 3rd ed. 1981), 210.
11. Patrick Thornhill, 'The Medway Crossings of the Pilgrim's Way', *Arch. Cant.*, xic (1974), 91–100.
12. B. Cunliffe, 'Social and Economic Development in Kent in the pre-Roman Iron Age', *Archaeology in Kent to AD 1500*, CBA Research Report No 48 (ed. P.E. Leach, 1982), 46.
13. *ibid.*, 47.
14. J.F. Ward Perkins, 'Excavations on Oldbury Hill, Ightam', *Arch. Cant.* li (1938), 137–81.
15. B. Cunliffe, *op. cit.*, 48.
16. B. Cunliffe, *op. cit.*, 43.
17. P. Thornhill, 'A Lower Thames Ford and the Campaigns of 54 BC and AD 43', *Arch. Cant.* xcii (1976), 119–28.
18. *ibid.*, 122.

19. *ibid.*, 123.
20. Tacitus, *Annals*, xii, 33.
21. M.W.C. Hassall, 'Batavians and the Roman Conquest of Britain', *Britannia*, i (1970).
22. G. Webster, *op. cit.*, 102: but the likelihood that the Romans crossed by some form of pontoon bridge should not be discounted (see Appendix C, p. 191). This would have had the advantage that a section of it could have been swung wide to permit the passage of heavy craft up and down the river.
23. Dio Cassius, lx, 21.
24. M.W.C. Hassall, *op. cit*, 131.
25. Tacitus, *Agricola*, 25.

Chapter V

 1. Dio Cassius, lx, 21.
 2. Tacitus, *Annals*, i, 1.
 3. Tacitus, *Agricola*, A, 13.
 4. Suetonius, *Claudius*, 17.
 5. K. Rodwell, 'Rome and the Trinovantes', *Invasion and Response*, BAR Series 73 (ed. B.C. Burnham and H.B. Johnson, 1979), 327.
 6. *Roman Colchester* (Colchester Borough Council), 11.
 7. Tacitus, *Annals*, xiv, 1.
 8. P.J. Drury, 'Roman Chelmsford – Caesaromagus', *Small Towns of Roman Britain*, BAR Series 15 (ed. W. Rodwell and T. Rowley, 1975), 163.
 9. *Survey of Bedfordshire: The Roman Period* (Bedfordshire County Council), 3, 18.
10. S.S. Frere, 'Verulamium: Urban Development and the Local Region', *Invasion and Response*, BAR Series 73 (ed. Burnham & Johnson, 1979).
11. Dio Cassius, lx, 20.
12. Caesar, *Gallic War*, v.
13. Oliver Rackham, *Trees and Woodland in the British Landscape* (1976), ix.
14. I.D. Margary, *Roman Roads in Britain* (1955, rev. 1967), 246.
15. C.R. Partridge, 'Braughing', in Rodwell and Rowley (1975), 145.
16. *ibid.*, note 17, 140.
17. K. Rodwell *loc. cit.*, 334.
18. P.J. Drury, 'Preliminary Report of the Romano-British Settlement at Chelmsford, Essex', *Essex Archaeology and History*, iv, 28, note 26.
19. A.K. Astbury, *Estuary: Land and Water in the Lower Thames Basin* (1980–5), 71.
20. *ibid.*, 5, note 5.
21. P.J. Drury, *loc. cit.*, iv, 5.
22. R. Bingley, 'The Coal Road – A Highway in Decline', *Thurrock Local History Society Journal, Panorama* (1982), 25. Mr. Bingley traces the course of this old road from East Tilbury Bluff, through Low Street, West Tilbury and Chadwell, to Stifford. Its width varies from a maximum of 30 feet to a minimum of 12 feet. It is not improbable, but not proven, that it has Iron Age origin.
23. W. Rodwell, 'Orsett "Cock" Cropmark Site', *Essex Archaeology and History*, vi, 34.
24. A. Babbidge, 'Sub-Rectangular Enclosures in Thurrock', *Panorama*, 16, 30.
25. G. Webster, *The Roman Imperial Army* (1969, reprinted 1981), 168.
26. Tacitus, *Annals*, xii, 33.

27. Hugh Chapman and Tony Johnson, 'Excavations at Aldgate in the City of London, 1972', *Transactions of London & Middlesex Arch. Soc.* (1973), 24.
28. Dio Cassius, lx, 22.
29. R. Merrifield, *The Roman City of London* (1965), 33–35.
30. Chapman and Johnson, *op. cit.*

Chapter VI

1. John Masefield, 'Tomorrow', *Other Men's Flowers, An Anthology of Poetry*, Field Marshal Lord Wavell.
2. Field Marshal Sir William Slim, *Defeat into Victory*, xxii, 513.
3. G. Webster, *The Roman Invasion of Britain* (1980), 6.
4. S.S. Frere, *Britannia, A Roman History of Britain* (1967, rev. 1978), 5, 91.
5. G. Webster, *op. cit.*, 6, 115.
6. Tacitus, *Agricola*, A 16, 66.
7. S.S. Frere, *op. cit.*, 5, 84–86.
8. Tacitus, *Annals*, xii, 29.
9. S.S. Frere, *op. cit.*, 84–86.
10. Anthony Barrett, 'The Career of Tiberius Claudius Cogidubnus', *Britannia*, 10, 227–42.
11. C.C. Hawkes, 'The Western Third C Culture and the Belgic Dobunni', *Bagendon: A Belgic Oppidum*, Elsie M. Clifford (1961), 65.
12. David Hill, *An Atlas of Anglo-Saxon England* (1981), 11.
13. S.S. Frere, *op. cit.*, 5, 85.
14. G. Webster, *op. cit.*, 6, 158.
15. *Map of Roman Britain*, Ordnance Survey (4th ed. 1978), 9.
16. S.S. Frere, *op. cit.*, 5, 94.
17. Tacitus, *Annals*, xii, 33.
18. S.S. Frere, *op. cit.*, 5, 93.
19. *ibid.*, note 17.
20. Tacitus, *Annals*, xii, 36.
21. Elsie M. Clifford, 'The Belgic Dobunni at Bagendon', *op. cit.*, vi, 160–63.
22. B. Cunliffe, 'Gloucestershire and the Iron Age of Southern Britain', *Bristol and Gloucestershire Archaeological Society*, Vol. 102 (1984), 11.
23. Elsie M. Clifford, *op. cit.*, (1961), vi.
24. I.D. Margary, *Roman Roads in Britain* (1955, rev. 1967), Appendix, Antonine Itinerary.

Chapter VII

1. Field Marshal Sir William Slim, *Defeat into Victory*, xvii, 398.
2. Suetonius, *Vespasian*.
3. J.K. St. Joseph, 'Air Reconnaissance in Southern Britain', p. 82.
4. R.D.H. Elkington, 'The Roman Period', *The Roman Lead Industry* (ed. Branigan & Fowler, 1976).
5. *Wiltshire Archaeological Magazine*, lxvi, 177 and lxvii, 96.
6. Sean McGrail, 'Cross Channel Seamanship and Navigation in the Late First Millenium BC', *Oxford Journal of Archaeology*, ii, 3 (1983).
7. Derek Allen, 'The Belgic Dynasties of Britain and their Coinage', *Archaeologia*, xc (1964).

8. I am grateful for this information to Mr. G.C. Boon, Keeper of Numismatics and Archaeology at the National Museum of Wales, Cardiff.

9. *Victoria County History*, i, ii.

10. B. Cunliffe, *Anatomy of an Iron Age Hillfort* (1983), 182.

11. L.V. Grinsell, *The Archaeology of Wessex* (1958), 109.

12. G.C. Boon, 'Belgic and Roman Silchester: Excavation of 1954–8', *Archaeologia*, ch. 39 (1976).

13. S.S. Frere, *Britannia: A History of Roman Britain* (1967, rev. 1978), 68.

14. *ibid.*, 311.

15. P.T. Bidwell, 'The Roman Army in South-West England', *Roman Exeter: Fortress and Town* (Exeter City Council, 1980).

16. Malcolm Todd, 'Hembury Hillfort', *The Antiquaries Journal* (1984), lxiv, 294.

17. S.S. Frere, 'Roman Britain in 1984', *Britannia*, xvi (1985), 305.

18. Dr. B. Bagshawe, 'Minerals at Nanstallon Fort', *Britannia*, iii (1972), 109: the garrison is estimated to have been a force of some six centuries, supported by four *turmae* of cavalry. An interesting Report by Consolidated Gold Fields Limited lists the precious metals to be found locally.

19. P.T. Bidwell, *The Legionary Bath House and Basilica and Forum at Exeter* (Exeter City Council and the University of Exeter, 1979), 16–17.

20. B. Cunliffe, *Hengistbury Head* (1978).

21. *ibid.*

22. C.A. Gresham, *Archaeological Journal*, xcvi (1939), 114 f.

23. N.H. Field & N.M. Lock, *Badbury Rings, Dorset* (1977).

24. Sir Ian Richmond, *Hod Hill Excavations* (The Trustees of the British Museum, 1968), ii.

25. Leslie Alcock, *By South Cadbury is that Camelot* (1972), 170.

26. Sir Mortimer Wheeler, *Maiden Castle, Dorset* (Her Majesty's Stationery Office, London, 1972).

27. Mortimer Wheeler, *Maiden Castle, Dorset*, 1943.

28. Professor Malcolm Todd, 'The Early Roman Phase at Maiden Castle', *Britannia*, xv (1984), 254.

29. S.S. Frere, *op. cit.*, 90.

30. S. McGrail, *op. cit.*, 322 and 325.

31. N.A.F. Smith, 'Roman Canals', *Transactions of the Newcomen Society* (1977–8), 75–80.

32. Caesar, *The Civil War*, I, 149 BC.

33. T. Severin, *The Brendan Voyage* (1978), Appendix III.

34. T.C. Lethbridge, 'Shipbuilding', *A History of Technology*, iii, 577.

35. Tacitus, *Annals*, xiv, 26.

36. P.A. Rahtz, 'Cannington Hillfort, 1963', *Proc. Somerset Arch. and Nat. Hist. Society*, 113, 56–58.

37. M. Langdon and P.J. Fowler, 'Excavations near Crandon Bridge', *Proc. Somerset Arch. and Nat. Hist. Society* (1971), 53.

38. H. Cleere, *Archaeological Journal*, 131 (1975), 171–99.

39. G. Webster, *Rome against Caratacus* (1981), 25.

Chapter VIII

1. Tacitus, *Annals*, xii, 32.

2. *ibid.*, xii, 33.

3. J.K. St. Joseph, 'Aerial Reconnaissance in Wales', *Antiquity*, xxxv (1961), 270–71.
4. Tacitus, *Annals*, xii, 40.

Chapter IX

1. Tacitus, *Annals*, xiii, 30.
2. Suetonius, *The Twelve Caesars*, Nero, 35.
3. Tacitus, *Annals*, xi, 36.
4. *ibid.*, xiii, 16.
5. *ibid.*, xvi, 14.
6. Tacitus, *Agricola, A*, 14.
7. *Tacitus, Annals, xii, 37.*

Appendix C

1. L. Keppie, *The Making of the Roman Army, from Republic to Empire* (1984).
2. P.A. Holder, *The Roman Army in Britain* (1982).
3. L. Keppie, *op. cit.*, Appendix 2, 'The Origin and Early History of the Imperial Legions', 208.
4. P.A. Holder, *op. cit.*.
5. *ibid.*
6. G.R. Watson, *The Roman Soldier* (1969), iii, 73.
7. Jacques Boudet, *The Ancient Art of Warfare* (1966), i.
8. *ibid.*, Chart 8, 128.
9. H. von Petrikovitz, 'Innenbauten' (1975), 54, from *Bonner Jahrbucher* 166, 966. 194 f.
10. Jacques Boudet, *op. cit.*, vii, 121.
11. *ibid.*, vii, 121.
12. H. Russell Robinson, *The Armour of Imperial Rome* (1975), Introduction, 9.
13. *ibid.*, 7, 192.
14. *The Roman Road from Richborough to London, and Estimation of the Construction Times for a Tactical and Strategic Road* (Royal School of Military Engineering, 1984).
15. R.W. Davies, *The Roman Military Medical Service* (1970).
16. Colonel Garnet Wolseley, *Soldier's Pocket Book for Field Service* (1869), i, 66–71.

BIBLIOGRAPHY

Alcock (1972)	Leslie Alock, *By South Cadbury is that Camelot* (Thames & Hudson, 1972).
Allen (1944)	Derek Allen, 'The Belgic Dynasties of Britain and their Coinage', *Archaeologia*, xc (1944), *Society of Antiquaries*.
Arnold (1993)	H.J.P. Arnold, *De Legione Augusta*, Hants Field Club, Archaeological Society, 19 (1993), 19–20.
Aston and Burrow (1982)	M. Aston and I. Burrow, *The Archaeology of Somerset* (Somerset County Council, 1982).
Astbury (1980)	A.K. Astbury, *Estuary: Land and Water in the Lower Thames Basin* (Carnforth Press & A.K. Astbury, 1980).
Bagshawe (1972)	Dr. B. Bagshawe, 'Minerals at Nanstallon Port', *Britannia*, iii (1972).
Barrett (1979)	A. Barrett, 'The Career of Tiberius Claudius Cogidubnus', *Britannia*, x (1979).
Bidwell (1979)	Paul Bidwell, *The Legionary Bath House and Basilica and Forum at Exeter* (Exeter City Council and the University of Exeter, 1979).
Bidwell (1980)	Paul Bidwell, *The Legionary Bath House and Basilica and Roman Exeter: Fortress and Town* (Exeter City Council, 1980).
Bingley (1982)	R. Bingley, 'The Coal Road, A Highway in Decline', *Thurrock Local History Society Journal, Panorama* 1982.
Bird (1994)	David Bird, 'The Origins of Roman London', *London Archaeology*, 7, (9) (1994), 268–70.
Boon (1974)	G.C. Boon, *Silchester: The Roman Town of Calleva* (David & Charles, 1974).
Boon (1977)	G.C. Boon, 'Greco-Roman Anchor-stock from North Wales', *The Antiquaries Journal*, lvii (1977).
Boudet (1966)	*The Ancient Art of Warfare*, ed. Jacques Boudet (Barrie & Rockliff, London, 1966).
Breeze (1983)	D.J. Breeze, 'The logistics of Agricola's Final Campaign', *Bulletin of the Hadrianic Society*, No. 1 (1983), 10–14.
Branigan and Fowler (1976)	K. Branigan and P.J. Fowler, 'The Roman Lead Industry', *The Roman West Country* (David & Charles, 1976).
Bushe-Fox (1949)	J.P. Bushe-Fox, *Fourth Report on the Excavations of the Roman Fort at Richborough*, Society of Antiquaries (1949).
Burnham and Johnson (1974)	B.C. Burnham and H.B. Johnson (eds.), *Invasion and Response*, BAR Series 73 (1979).
Campbell (1994)	Brian Campbell, *The Roman Army, 31 BC–AD 337*, (Routledge, London, 1994).
Casson (1971)	L. Casson, *Ships and Seamanship in the Ancient World*, (Princetown University Press, 1971).

Chadwick (1970)   N. Chadwick, *The Celts* (A Penguin Original, 1970).

Chapman and Johnson   H. Chapman and A. Johnson, 'Excavations at Aldgate in the
(1972)   City of London', *London & Middlesex Transactions* (1972).

Clausewitz (1968)   General Carl von Clausewitz, *On War*, Anatol Rapoport
                         (ed.), (A Penguin Classic, 1968).

Clifford (1961)   Elsie M. Clifford, *Bagendon: A Belgic Oppidum* (W. Heffer
                         & Sons Ltd, 1961).

Colchester (1980)   Colchester Borough Council, *Roman Colchester* (1980).

Cunliffe (1968)   B. Cunliffe (ed.), *Richborough* v (Soc. of Antiquaries, 1968).

Cunliffe (1974)   B. Cunliffe, *Iron Age Communities in Britain* (Routledge &
                         Kegan Paul, 1974).

Cunliffe (1978)   B. Cunliffe, *Hengistbury Head* (Paul Elek, London, 1978).

Cunliffe (1982)   B. Cunliffe, 'Social and Economic Development in Kent in
                         the pre-Roman Iron Age', CBA Research Report, No. 48,
                         Archaeology in Kent to AD 1500 (1982).

Cunliffe (1983)   B. Cunliffe, *Anatomy of an Iron Age Hillfort* (B.T. Batsford,
                         London, 1983).

Cunliffe (1984)   B. Cunliffe, 'Gloucestershire and the Iron Age of Southern
                         Britain' *Bristol & Gloucestershire Archaeological Society*,
                         Vol. 102 (1984), 11.

Cunliffe (1991)   B. Cunliffe, 'Fishbourne revisited: the site in its context',
                         Journal of Roman Archaeology, 4 (1991).

Davies (1970)   R.W. Davies, 'The Roman Military Medical Service',
                         Sonderdruck aus dem Saalburg-Jahrbuch, xxvii (1970).

Davies (1971)   R.W. Davies, 'The Roman Military Diet', *Britannia*, ii
                         (1971), 123–41.

Drury (1975)   P.J. Drury, 'Roman Chelmsford-Caesaromagus', BAR Series
                         15, *Small Towns of Roman Britain* (1975).

Dowker (1897)   G. Dowker, 'On the landing place of St Augustine',
                         Archaeologia Cantiana, xxii (1897), 122–42.

Eichholz (1972)   D.E. Eichholz, 'How long did Vespasian serve in Britain?',
                         Britannia, iii (1972).

Ellis (1994)   P.B. Ellis, *Caesar's Invasion of Britain*, (Constable & Co.,
                         London, 1994).

Field and Lock (1977)   N.H. Field and N.M. Lock, *Badbury Rings, Dorset* (1977).

Frere (1967)   S.S. Frere, *Britannia, A History of Roman Britain*
                         (Routledge & Kegan Paul, 1967, rev. 1978).

Frere (1979)   S.S. Frere, 'Verulamium: Urban Development and the Local
                         Region', BAR Series 73, *Invasion and Response* (1979).

Grinsell (1958)   L.V. Grinsell, *The Archaeology of Wessex* (Methuen & Co.,
                         1958).

Harden (1962)   D.B. Harden, *The Phoenicians* (A Penguin Classic, 1962).

Hassall (1970)   M.W.C. Hassall, 'Batavians and the Roman Conquest of
                         Britain', *Britannia*, i (1972).

Hill (1981)   D. Hill, *An Atlas of Anglo-Saxon England* (Basil Blackwell,
                         Oxford, 1981).

Hind (1989)   J.G.F. Hind, 'The Invasion of Britain, AD 43', *Britannia*, 20
                         (1989), 1–2.

Hoare (1812)   Sir R. Colt Hoare, *Ancient Wiltshire* (London, 1812), ii.

Holder (1982)   P.A. Holder, *The Roman Army in Britain* (B.T. Batsford Ltd, 1982).

Keppie (1971)   L.F.J. Keppie, 'Legio VIII and the Claudian Invasion',
                         Britannia, ii (1972).

Keppie (1984)	L.F.J. Keppie, *The Making of the Roman Army* (B.T. Batsford Ltd, 1984).
Keppie (1993)	L.F.J. Keppie, *The Origins and early history of the Second Legion Augusta, Caerleon*, Roman Museum, (1993).
Langdon and Fowler (1971)	M. Langdon and P.J. Fowler, 'Excavations near Crandon Bridge, Puriton', *Proceedings of Archaeological & Natural History Society of Somerset* (1971).
Lethbridge (1957)	T.C. Lethbridge, 'Shipbuilding', *History of Technology*, iii.
Margary (1981)	I.D. Margary, *Roman Roads in Britain* (Constable & Co. Ltd, 1971, 3rd ed. 1981).
McGrail (1983)	S. McGrail, 'Cross-Channel Seamanship and Navigation in the late First Millenium BC', *Oxford Journal of Archaeology*, ii (1983).
Merrifield (1965)	R. Merrifield, *The Roman City of London* (E. Benn Ltd, 1965).
Morris (1982)	J. Morris, *Londinium: London in the Roman Empire* (Wiedenfeld & Nicholson, 1982).
Partridge (1981)	Clive Partridge, *Skeleton Green, A Late Iron Age and Romano-British site*, Britannia Monograph Series 2 (1981), Society for the Promotion of Roman Studies.
Peddie (1994)	J. Peddie, *The Roman War Machine*, (Sutton Publishing, Stroud, 1994).
Philp (1970)	B. Philp, *The Roman Fort at Reculver* (Kent Archaeological Rescue Unit, 1970, 7th ed.).
Powell (1980)	T.G.E. Powell (ed.) *The Celts* (1980).
Rackham (1971)	O. Rackham, *Trees and Woodland in the British Landscape* (J.M. Dent & Sons Ltd, 1971).
Rahtz (1969)	P.A. Rahtz, 'Cannington Hillfort, 1963', *Proceedings of Archaeological and Natural History Society of Somerset* (1969).
Richmond (1955)	Sir Ian Richmond, *Roman Britain*, Vol. I (Penguin Books, 1951, reprinted 1981).
Richmond (1968)	Sir Ian Richmond, *Hod Hill*, Vol. II (The Trustees of the British Museum, 1968).
Richmond (1982)	Sir Ian Richmond, *Trajan's Army on Trajan's Column* (British School at Rome, 1982).
Rivet (1969)	A.L.F. Rivet, *The Roman Villa in Britain* (Routledge & Kegan Paul, 1969).
Russell Robinson (1975)	H. Russell Robinson, *The Armour of Imperial Rome* (Arms and Armour Press, 1975).
Rodwell (1976)	W. Rodwell, 'Coinage, oppida and the rise of Belgic Power in south-east Britain', *Oppida in Barbarian Europe*, BAR Supplement Series 11 (1976).
Rodwell (1979)	K. Rodwell, 'Rome and the Trinovantes', *Invasion and Response*, BAR Series 73 (1979).
Rodwell and Rowley (1975)	W. Rodwell and T. Rowley (eds.), *Small Towns in Roman Britain*, BAR Series 15 (1975).
Scott (1975)	J.M. Scott, *Boadicea* (Constable & Co. Ltd, 1975).
Sharples (1991)	Niall M. Sharples, *Maiden Castle: Excavation and Field Survey*, Historic Buildings and Monuments Commission (1991).
Slim (1956)	Field Marshal Sir William Slim, *Defeat into Victory* (Cassell & Co. Ltd, 1956).

Smith (1977–8)	N.A.F. Smith, 'Roman Canals', *Transactions of the Newcomen Society* (1977–8).
Soddington (1990)	D.B. Soddington, 'The origin and nature of the German and British fleets', *Britannia*, 21 (1990), 223–32.
St. Joseph (1961)	J.K. St. Joseph, 'Aerial Reconnaissance in Wales,' *Antiquity*, xxxv (1961).
Starr (1941)	C.G. Starr Jnr., *The Roman Imperial Navy, 31 BC to AD 324* (Greenwood Press, Connecticut, 1941).
Thornhill (1974)	P. Thornhill, 'The Medway Crossings of the Pilgrims Way', *Archaeologia Cantiana*, xic (1974).
Thornhill (1976)	P. Thornhill, 'A Lower Thames Ford and the Campaigns of 54 BC and AD 43', *Archaeologia Cantiana*, xcii (1976).
Thould (1909)	A.K. and B.T. Thould, 'Arthritis in Roman Britain', *British Medical Assoc. Journal* 287 (1909).
Todd (1984)	M. Todd, 'The Early Roman Phase at Maiden Castle', *Britannia* (1984), 15.
Todd (1984)	M. Todd, 'The Hembury Hillfort', *The Antiquaries Journal* lxiv, (1984), 294.
Wacher (1978)	J. Wacher, *Roman Britain* (J.M. Dent & Sons Ltd, 1978).
Ward-Perkins (1938)	J.F. Ward-Perkins, 'Excavations on Oldbury Hill, Ightam', *Archaeologia Cantiana*, 51, (1938).
Watson (1969)	G.R. Watson, *The Roman Soldier* (Thames & Hudson, 1969).
Webster and Dudley (1965)	G. Webster and D. Dudley, *The Roman Conquest of Britain* (B.T. Batsford, 1965).
Webster (1969)	G. Webster, *The Roman Imperial Army* (Adam & Charles Black, London, 1969, rev. 1981).
Webster (1981)	G. Webster, *Rome against Caratacus* (B.T. Batsford, 1981).
Webster (1993)	G. Webster, *The Roman Invasion of Britain*, (B.T. Batsford, 1993).
Wheeler (1943)	Mortimer Wheeler, *Maiden Castle, Dorset* (Oxford University Press, 1943).
Wheeler (1972)	Sir Mortimer Wheeler, *Maiden Castle, Dorset* (Her Majesty's Stationery Office, London, 1972).
Whitlock (1975)	R. Whitlock, *Somerset* (B.T. Batsford, 1975).
Wickenden (1990)	Nick Wickenden, 'Caesaromagus', *Essex Journal*, (1990), 58–63.
Wolseley (1869)	Colonel Garnet Wolseley, *The Soldier's Pocket Book for Field Service* (The War Office, 1869).
Wright (1971)	C.J. Wright, *A Guide to the Pilgrims Way and North Downs Way* (Constable & Co. Ltd, 1971, 3rd ed.).

Ancient Historical Sources

Caesar	*Gallic Wars (de Bello Gallico)**
Dio Cassius	*Narrative*
Diocletian	*Edict on Prices*
Polybius	*The Rise of the Roman Empire**
Suetonius	*The Twelve Caesars**
Tacitus	*Agricola**
	*Annals**
	*Histories**

*   Published by Penguin Books Ltd (Penguin Classics Series).

INDEX OF PLACES

Map References given against place names relate to the
National Grid System

GENERAL INDEX